When We Turned Within

edited by

Rabbi Menachem Creditor
& Sarah Tuttle-Singer

When We Turned Within

2020 Paperback Edition, *First Printing*
© 2020 by Menachem Creditor & Sarah Tuttle-Singer
Cover: "Out of the Fog" © 2020 by Karen Byer Silberman

ISBN: 9798650180951

This volume is dedicated to all those
who have given and continue to give
of themselves to save lives during
the COVID-19 pandemic.

WHEN WE TURNED WITHIN

CONTENTS

TORAH

TERUMAH

VAYAKHEL-PEKUDEI

SHMINI

TAZRIA-METZORA

BEMIDBAR

HOLY DAYS

SHABBAT

PURIM

PESACH/PASSOVER

YOM HA'ATZMA'UT/ ISRAEL'S INDEPENDENCE DAY

COUNTING THE OMER

PRAYERS

FOREWORD

JEWISH WISDOM FOR A TIME OF PANDEMIC
Rabbi Dr. Bradley Shavit Artson

The Coronavirus is now officially a world-wide pandemic. As of the time of this book's publication, there are more than 6,420,000 confirmed cases, of whom more than 383,000 have died. By the time you read these words, it is inevitable that the numbers will have risen.

Some people are responding with a level of panic rarely encountered, while others brush off this pandemic as if already under control. Both responses fail because they see our duty as isolated and individual: as if it's all about keeping me safe and distracted, regardless of its human cost or global impact. This isolated individual is a biological lie and a cultural dead end. We are ourselves only in relationship to each other and to all creation.

We are taught (Exodus 19:2 and Rashi) that the reason the Torah was given at the foot of Sinai is that at that particular moment, in that particular spot, the Children of Israel came together as one. Transcending their fragmentation and disputes, they circled that mountain united in hope and possibility. It was precisely because we were, for that instant, one united camp, that the One God would be heard.

This moment also calls us to form a united camp: not only the Jewish people, but all humanity coming together in the only kind of cosmopolitan universalism that counts: an affirmation of life, of caring, and of hope.

Bein Adam Le-Havero: Our Responsibility to Sustain Each Other

Finding the *Derekh ha-Beinoni*, the Middle Path to steer us between the crashing waves of hysteria and panic on the one hand, and the battering

1

rocks of denial and avoidance on the other will require determination and resolve. "We will hear and we will do (Exodus 24:3)" must become the mantra of this season. While it may be tempting to do nothing and to pretend that nothing has changed, we must mobilize the courage to first listen to the health experts and to then transform their guidance into government policy and personal practice.

Each of us must find the inner strength to be Nachshon, the brave Israelite willing to plunge into the Sea so it could part and allow the Children of Israel to pass to freedom. By daring to change our ways, we can take on a life of service for the sake of human health.

In that spirit, we must curtail our exposure to large crowds and to the possibility of infection. The Coronavirus is the new reality, and it won't go away. But limiting the range of its contagion and slowing its spread will literally create the difference between life and death for many of our vulnerable beloveds (older people, immunologically compromised people, and others). Jewish tradition teaches that love (hesed) is not merely an inner emotion, it is a way of behaving to others that makes the love manifest. We owe these dear ones our compassionate acts of self-restraint and responsibility: repeated hand washing with soap, avoiding touching our faces, greeting others with a wave or smile instead of handshaking or hugging, heightened levels of sanitation at work and in public places, alternatives to public assemblies, staying home when sick or exposed. Our choices can literally redeem the world.

Bein Adam Le-Atzmo: Responsibility to Self-Care

It is not enough to change behavior and to enact policies to care for each other if we don't also find better ways to care for ourselves. Humans begin to shrivel without contact with each other and without access to the joys of life. In excessive isolation we risk pandemics of the soul.

We must find ways to reach out to each other, to give and receive love and care so that we are nourished for the task ahead. The Biblical image of receiving manna each and every day, and of having to move our bodies to harvest this physical manifestation of love can inspire us through this wilderness as well. Let's use this time to strengthen whatever daily practice inspires and sustains us: daily prayer, psalms, meditation, exercise, a stroll, good fiction, poetry. Making time for inner renewal and physical vitality will be crucial in the stressful days and weeks to come.

That self-care itself has to keep the limits of our increased isolation permeable and flexible. Connecting to those we love through calls, texts, shared meals (Shabbat, anyone?), streamed movies with family or friends, will keep us alive. These occasions of relating strengthen us for the tasks we face and remind us that this, too, is life. Judaism's most beloved prayer, the *Shehechiyanu*, locates God as the one who enlivens us, sustains us, and brings us to this moment. Life is precious and invites celebration.

Judaism creates a calendar filled with opportunities for mindful joy, communal gathering, and celebration. Being more attentive doesn't require that we stop relating to each other and connecting. We just need to be more creative in making sure that we get what we need.

This pandemic will pass, creating a new normal in its wake. How we respond, supporting the scientists and their research to develop a vaccine, how we modify our behavior to limit the spread of the virus and to dampen its consequences, and how we find ways to feed our souls and to care for each other, these are the challenges and possibilities of this moment.

We do not venture into this fray alone. We walk with each other, carrying a Torah of wisdom and bearing the Divine image that allowed our ancestors to proceed forward to Promise. That Promise beckons us as well.

Let us journey together.

INTRODUCTION

Sarah Tuttle-Singer

"So who needs this book?"

Good question.

And I can tell you:

I need this book.

I'm a worrier.

I've been this way for as long as I can remember.

And ever since the news about a new virus began to eke into the news early this year, I could feel that sense of dread begin in a ripple down my spine. My hands shook. My teeth ached. My heart began to beat faster and faster.

Then, the numbers began to rise - the sick, the dead. People I love, the parents of close friends... I live in Israel with my two kids, but the rest of my immediate family is far away in Los Angeles - and as we careen through this new abnormal, this strange new world of face masks, of social distancing, where the world is at our fingertips, but flights to America are all but grounded, I felt a palpable sense of grief wrap its arms around me and pull me under crashing waves of this terrible storm.

It's been a rough time for me turning within, wrestling with myself in a room that felt like it had no windows and no doors, no light at the end of the tunnel, all the way down at the bottom of the sea.

I felt alone, and I felt useless.

But then, Rabbi Menachem Creditor reached out to ask me to be part of this special project reading the stories written by so many people from all over the world - people weathering the same storm, riding the same waves in their different ways, all of us as individuals and as a community.

I began to read each story.

And each story was exquisite -- some were poignant, others uplifting. A few even made me laugh out loud. But each one moved me. And suddenly, I was above water - the waves calmed enough for me to catch my breath. There was sunlight.

These stories BROUGHT the sunlight. These stories brought me back to the surface once again.

Because I realized something powerful while I was reading through each one:

While each of us is a universe unto ourselves, we are not alone.

We are all here, sharing the same wild storm together - rough waters, high waves, dark clouds. Maybe we are mourning someone we love dearly, and looking for a minyan to say Kaddish somehow. Maybe we are struggling with unfathomable loneliness. Maybe we are feeling trapped in a house with young kids and no community support. Maybe we are risking our lives to heal the sick in a COVID-19 ward. Maybe we are out of work and afraid we will never recover financially. Maybe we have to go to work where we make minimum wage as a checkout clerk. Maybe we need to offer solace to a member of our community when we, too, are seeking solace and don't know how to ask.

And while we each experience this period in profoundly different ways, all of our individual experiences are true, and holy, and speak to a greater shared human experience: We are all in this together.

And as I realized this while reading through these stories, I felt less alone. I felt my feet back on the shore again, my toes in the sand.

So who needs this book?

I need this book.

And maybe you do, too.

And I'm so glad that we are able to share it with you.

INTRODUCTION
Rabbi Menachem Creditor

During the past months, our world has truly turned upside-down. We've lost so very much. What was casual just yesterday has become priceless today: smiles are covered beneath masks, generations divided by invisible boundaries, and physical togetherness deemed a danger.

And yet. Harmonies have been sung from balcony and bedrooms spanning the globe. Applause regularly erupts for cashiers and sanitation workers and nurses and those everyday heroes who keep the world balanced.

And yet. Synagogue buildings are empty and the comfort of a minyan has become digital. Funerals are hug-less, as are intergenerational family moments. And the number of souls we've buried… There simply aren't words.

And yet. The skies are clearer and birdsong has returned. More people have convened for many a Zoom meal or online class than ever could have in person. We have come to know our neighbors just a bit more.

And yet. Amidst all this, protests erupted in reaction to the horrific killings of George Floyd, Breonna Taylor, Ahmaud Arbery, unarmed black people whose deaths have sparked an international response, shining light on the systemic racism and injustice that have cast a long, harsh shadow on the United States since its earliest days. The pandemic exacerbated already-present inequalities, and the murders in 2020 America of three human beings for the colors of their skin gave this injustice a face.

And yet. The responses to racism and isolation are growing in volume, and the voices of common citizens of all colors and orientations and faiths are calling out for justice, for an honest reckoning with the way things have been, for the end of all that keeps us apart, for a world in which no virus nor societal illness can deny a person their breath.

Friends, this book is much more than a record of loss. It is a collection of reflections, prayers, and poems of many, many individual souls who collectively tell the story of right now with depth and heart and startling brilliance. On these pages you will find honest testimony of a very difficult time on our planet.

It has been truly humbling work to assemble these voices and see patterns emerge, to feel the pain and longing and hope and faith and frustration and loneliness and transcendence of each contribution. I am more convinced than ever that all people share a common humanity, that our souls bind us together, that a better day is possible.

The arc of history will only bend toward justice under enough pressure, and the glorious weight of us all will be enough.

A few acknowledgements:

To the serious, reflective, luminous, and lyrical authors who shared their hearts on these pages, thank you. You represent a true diversity of voices from within the Jewish community, grounded in reality and intentionally vulnerable, and allowed us to include you here to amplify each other's vision of good in the world. Thank you.

To my co-editor, Sarah Tuttle-Singer, whose brilliant and intuitive writing style has made her a widely-read and accessible touchstone for our time, thank you for joining me in this project. Your careful eye and sensitive soul are the reason so many authors lent their words to this undertaking. Working with you has been nothing short of sacred sharing. Thank you.

To my colleagues and friends at UJA-Federation NY, where I am privileged to serve as the Pearl and Ira Meyer Scholar in Residence, my deepest gratitude. For allocating more than $46 million to date to meet needs across the New York region and Israel for the most vulnerable people, for embodying the heart and soul of our community, thank you. Proceeds from the sale of this book will support UJA-Federation NY's work to make this world a better, safer, more just place.

To my precious family, (especially you, Neshama,) for inspiring me to build this world from Love, for being my holiest, safest, funnest place in the universe, thank you.

And finally, to the Source of Life, for being the invisible string that connects us all, thank You.

May the days ahead be better – for all people – than those we've left behind.

Sivan 5780
June 2020

TILLIE AND ME, IN THE PLAGUE SEASON
Rabbi Avram Mlotek

We weren't on a date. It was more intimate than that. I was to be her rabbi and she, nearing 100, wanted clergy to perform her funeral.

"At my funeral, I want the rabbi to know me," Tillie (not her real name) said defiantly. "I don't want a stranger rabbi."

Tillie is secular — she doesn't belong to a synagogue — and I was up for the task, or so I thought. I met her through DOROT, an agency on the Upper West Side committed to alleviating social isolation among seniors.

"That's rude," was one of the first things Tillie said to me, with a glare that cut deep. I had glanced at my phone periodically to check the time. Her bluntness caught me off guard, refreshingly.

"You're not my typical clientele," I teased Tillie as we were first getting to know each other over two years ago. Tillie was 96 then, six decades between us, and I was very much used to working with millennials in Manhattan, young adults seeking meaning, love and purpose. Here was Tillie on the other side of life, ever mindful of her mortality, defiantly independent, eager to live.

But, of course, death is everywhere these days, these Covid days and nights, the sirens screaming past my apartment on the Upper West Side. Tillie and I don't meet face-to-face anymore, but we're still in touch, each in our own way trying to beat back the isolation blues. We talk on the phone and regularly shoot each other emails and links to news stories.

9

Tillie shared she had first reached out to an Upper East Side synagogue in search of a rabbi, but they told her to call Plaza Memorial Chapel, a funeral home, which would oversee her arrangements. Perturbed, she explained she wasn't looking for funeral details at the time rather for a community. The rabbi then invited her to a "ladies luncheon," but she was seeking a rabbinic counselor, not a mah-jongg club.

When we first met, Tillie kept to the facts and offered a review of her life.

Raised in the Lower East Side to immigrant parents, her father spoke to her in Yiddish, calling her a *"vilde khaye,"* a wild animal. A former ballerina turned real estate agent, a college graduate, Tillie liked to claim she was a feminist long before women's liberation hit in the 1960s.

Before the pandemic, and these days too, we talk politics; her disdain for our president gets a constant airing. We talk about books and films and museums, though she professed that she'd never before opened a Bible.

And so we learned the Book of Ecclesiastes together for months. Little did we know that it would provide such a rich backdrop for today's cruel calculus of life and death.

"Everything is futile," the text read, and Tillie was surprised by the book's subversive nature, its contradictions and raw passions. The charge to enjoy the physical pleasures of the world appealed to her as she looked back in her life, thirsty for more. *To every thing, there is a season... a time to dance...*

Tillie shared how her husband had come home one day and sifted through her closet. He found a box of letters from Tillie's lovers and affairs over the years. Tillie left their home that night bloodied and bruised and stayed at a friend's house. She called herself stupid as she remembered the pain.

"And it wasn't the first time," she told me crying. She returned to her husband and stayed with him until he died. *A time to break down, and a time to build up...*

In Jewish tradition, one might recite a *vidui*, or confessional, on the death bed. Taken from the High Holiday liturgy of Yom Kippur, this is a prescribed text penitents read. Tillie, though, taught me how her own words, her personal confession, were the required liturgy.

10

She sees my rainbow *kipa* (she's called me "an unorthodox Orthodox rabbi") and tells me how hard it was for her to come to terms with her son's sexuality and what it was like raising a little boy who couldn't see. She called herself biased and bigoted, and explained how she came to love her son despite his blindness, and how proud she was of his career. And mostly, how much she adores her son's husband, whom she refused to meet at first. *A time to rend, and a time to sew…*

Before COVID-19, they would visit her regularly in the city, and they would spend weekends together at their farm upstate. For the time being, she's living with them, far from the city and its eerie emptiness.

With New York being the epicenter of the pandemic, Tillie says she's mostly grateful to be away from the city. She's reveling in the natural world upstate, and she talks about the beautiful trees and flowers around her. She misses the city, especially the opera, and doesn't feel she can come back anytime soon. She refuses to use FaceTime because, as she says, "I look horrible on it."

Sitting with Tillie, week after week, month after month, thoughts of my own bubby, who passed when she was 91, come to mind. She was a brilliant woman who recited Shakespeare's plays in alphabetical order to soothe her encyclopedic mind. But Bubby never talked about death with me the way Tillie does.

Tillie asks me what happens in the afterlife, and I tell her if anyone tries to answer that question definitively you should run away as fast as you can.

"I don't run anymore, Avram," she quips.

We talk about what it means to live on through each other, through our children. Tillie has no grandchildren. She knows the clock is running out, and she craves answers. *A time to every purpose under heaven…*

Tillie and I have talked many times about the assignment that first brought us together. We've reviewed her funeral service, and she's reminded me how she wants me to sing Yiddish songs. She's concerned no one will come to the funeral. I've asked her if she would want to read what I write before she dies, but she refuses. She said she'd only read this piece if it were published. I think she trusts me now, even if every now and then I glance at my iPhone.

(This essay originally appeared in the New York Jewish Week
May 19, 2020)

DREAMING FROM RAIN TO DEW
Rivka Hecht

It is in early October 2019 when I dream of the first rains.

In Jewish Tradition, we pray for the first rains in the Land of Israel on the 8th day of the Festival of Booths - the Atzeret Festival.

I have dreamed of the first rains in previous years. My head turned towards the heavens, celebrating with dance as those big first raindrops of the water of life cascade down in showers of blessing. Usually my mouth is opened to catch the first drops. And I turn in circles, alive, in sync with the universe, my palms turned upwards as earthenware vessels. Often these dreams have prophetic qualities as a pre-empting of the first rains to fall.

But this dream was different.

On the Sabbath prior to the Holiest day of the Jewish Calendar - Yom Kippur, on the Sabbath of Repentance, just over two weeks before our communal prayer for rain *"Mashiv HaRuach U'Morid HaGeshem"* - I dream. In this dream I see a downpour of rain, continuous torrents, causing huge ripples and puddles. I see myself walking along with some family members on the wet cobblestone alleyways of Jerusalem, but simultaneously in tandem parallel, walking through the streets of London in the rainstorm, and then too, along the wide avenues of Manhattan, NY and the grand boulevards of Berlin.

Instantaneously, we are everywhere, in the downpour of first rains, throughout the world.

I awake on Sabbath morning and tell my sister that I dreamed of the first rains, and that they were global. Shortly after relating my dream, I hear the pitter patter of the first Jerusalem rains on my skylight, and the heavens open up, raining on our Jerusalem stone alleyway.

12

And indeed, the winter of 2019-2020 is a very wet one in Israel with more rainfall than we had seen in many years, and the Lake Kinneret in the Galilee overflows for the first time in a long time. So my dream was kind of prophetic and visionary. Yet, what I didn't understand then was the global element; how the first rains of Jerusalem were connected to the rains of other Metropolitan cities, such as London, Berlin and New York, which had all specifically featured in my dream.

Only months later, could I begin to understand and connect that a global pandemic and its ripple effects would unite our entire world in a way that humanity had not yet experienced in this century or perhaps ever. That the rains of blessing that I had seen in my dream in early October were maybe a vision of the rains of the reign of COVID-19 affecting the entire world in 2020. COVID-19: the great leveller, non-discriminatory and indeed a huge downpour - grounding flights, bringing politicians to their knees, overturning our global economy, healing animals and nature, locking down humans… - that would forever change the lives, mentality and outlook of our generation.

But the dream doesn't end there. There is a sequel.

During pandemic lockdown, in late April 2020, on a Sabbath just over two weeks after Passover, when we communally pray for dew (as opposed to full rainfall) - "*Morid Hatal*", I dream another dream of rain. In this dream I am having an academic discussion with a farmer. And I philosophize, "*Surely the rains now are not a blessing because the winter has passed. We have stopped praying for rain as this season only requires dew.*" And the farmer responds, "*No. Rain is always a blessing, even now*". And I look at him quizzically and I persist, "*What? Always a blessing? Even when it floods? How can a farmer harvest during flooding?*" (Imagining the wheat harvest of Shavuot in flooding rains and wild windstorms) And he calmly looks at me and says, "*Yes even flooding is a blessing…*"

I awake that Sabbath morning and it is raining. The final rains of the season. I have forgotten my dream. Our Sages say that the last rains are healing too. But we have already prayed for dew on Passover, so why is rain *after* the dew prayer still healing, and still considered a blessing?

I discuss this with my sister and as we philosophize, I remember my dream and the deja vu is powerful. Yes, these rains too are a blessing. Even flooding for a farmer is a blessing.

I don't really know how this is possible in a farmer's world and if it even makes any sense. But once again, I see the dream as a prophetic vision for our current times. In the deep dream / nightmare state of this pandemic chaos, with the myriads of challenges, the waters of the unknown, the flooding of emotions swinging like a pendulum on a cuckoo clock for everyone on every level, both personally & collectively, these global rains reigning for all of us now, flooding our harvest, soaking us to all extremes, are a blessing too.

How?

Perhaps COVID-19 is a wake-up call on the macro level for humanity to arise from our slumber and take a good look at other types of viral diseases that are systemic, endemic and rampant on the social, cultural, metaphysical, emotional and spiritual scales.

Maybe today is the day we reset, upgrade, or simply tweak a little closer to the state of a healed world. Where more often than not, our new world is privy to examples of inspired leadership; impact investments; business models with integrity; celebrations of unity as well as diversity; robust discussions stimulating healthy progression, compassion, loving kindness and a giving mindset. A world that celebrates good news. A world that cooperates in partnership and rejoices in the rising voice of a better today and an even better tomorrow.

I'd like to believe that we are paying attention. That we are woke. That COVID-19 and the trials and devastation that come along with this physical virus can be a learning curve for humanity to apply more broadly to all of those metaphysical, emotional, spiritual, cultural and social viral diseases that have had more than their fair share of half-lives and lifetimes of infection to grow and fester. That today, the healing antibodies of lessons learned, tried and tested, are well on their way to bringing humanity back to a healthy and strong state of balance, where both the flooding rains as well as the dew of our dreams can finally become a true blessing in reality.

CHESED SHEL EMES: A TRUE KINDNESS
Rabbi Benjy Spiro

It's 2:23am. The phone vibrates. I open up my Whatapp. The notification reads:

> *"Head over in the truck to 1354 13th Avenue.*
> *Chaim, Yitzchok and Yoely will join you."*

As I drive across the quiet streets of Boro Park, New York, I begin to think about the work that I am about to undertake. I wonder: Was he a father? Was he a grandfather? Did he have brothers? Was he a business owner who has employees that were counting on him for their paychecks? Another precious soul has departed this world; a victim of this horrible tragedy that has afflicted this planet so quickly named coronavirus.

As I get out of my truck, and grab a Tyvek suit, goggles, mask, gloves, and a face shield, I join my colleagues and enter the home. The thoughts hurdle through my head. When was the last time he saw his family, had he been alone, will we be encountering some crying children who don't understand why their father is sleeping so deeply? We quickly and carefully do our holy work and take this beloved departed soul to the local funeral home, where he will be prepared for his funeral in just a few hours. We wonder about who he was as a person, and what he will be remembered for, what legacy he has left for his family and those closest to him. They will likely be no semblance of a typical funeral, no opportunity to honor this person, to share the experiences that this person gave to everyone around him.

As my colleagues and I begin to figure out his identification, we immediately start notifying the family and painfully share the sorrow news that they too have lost someone to this virus. It never gets easier; it might even get harder.

As different volunteers head over to the funeral home to complete the *Tahara* (ritual preparation for burial), suiting up head-to-toe with

15

protective safety equipment sometimes in 90° heat, inspired, motivated and driven to help close the chapter of another soul's life. As we expeditiously handle yet another case of the day, the intensity and the level of detail does not waver. This is how we define *Chesed Shel Emes*; a true kindness - one that can never be repaid.

We have rapidly shifted from doing one or two of these, and now today we are handling 35 or even 40, in just one 24-hour period.

Lives have been put on hold. Passover Seders have been interrupted from an important phone call regarding a deceased. Rabbinical scions have been consulted on what to do during these unprecedented times, and how to manage the mounting caseload. The emotions remain the same from the first case to the hundredth case; we are here to serve our fellow Jew who deserves respect in every moment of his or her life, even in their final moments.

While there are many people who jump at the opportunity to do a kindness to a fellow person, there are small but mighty group who do the work of the last responder. The volunteers of *Chesed Shel Emes* are there at all times, for any Jew in need, to help give the final respect to the deceased no matter what the situation may be; complicated or simple, rich or poor, observant or non-observant, day or night. We jump on a moment's notice, we come in and complete our holy and emotionally draining work and return home with little fanfare or acknowledgment of the work that we have just completed. We silently know that we have helped a family, community, or just an individual be buried in a time when so many people need to be buried, without wavering on Jewish tradition or law. We are grateful to God who has enabled us to continue to perform this *mitzvah*; this quiet and behind-the-scenes *mitzvah*, this important mitzvah that has helped close to hundreds if not thousands of people over the last two months.

As I crawl back into bed, and close my eyes for just a moment, my phone rings again. The notification reads: head over to 15th Ave and 53rd Street, as someone else is in need of our services. I jump down the stairs, with a large coffee in my hand, and head over to perform yet another mitzvah, and get another opportunity to help a family get closure, yet another victim of this horrible plague.

עד מתי ,ה' ,עד מתי!
Until when, God?! Until when?

GOD HAS A LOT TO ANSWER FOR

Dr. Arnold M. Eisen

My father, a good and pious man who thanked God every morning for the gift of another day, would have said -- were he alive right now -- that God has a lot to answer for.

So much death and suffering! So many hopes for a better life, destroyed by pandemic. Such an incalculable amount of trust -- in government, in the future, and in God -- undermined or irreparably lost.

People of faith often wonder aloud at moments of personal and collective tragedy how a good God could permit "bad things to happen to good people." They also tend to turn (or return) to religion for help in bearing the unbearable. In coming months, Americans will more strongly feel the hunger for community and meaning as we come back together (at least to some extent) and seek to find purpose in our suffering.

The nation's ability to heal its body and soul will heavily rely on whether or not religious institutions can find new ways to bring people together and find meaning in what we've experienced.

One of the cruelest aspects of the coronavirus pandemic is that it forces so many people to die or grieve the dead alone. The Hasidic Jews who congregated, without social distancing, on Brooklyn's streets for a public funeral recently gave vivid expression to the frustration and anger that many Americans feel at not being able to accompany their family and community members to the grave.

Funerals and shivah visits conducted through a computer cannot offer the comfort of tearful hugs, outstretched hands and physical presence. Nor can we celebrate high points of our lives together in this "virtual" way.

Religion thrives in normal times, and helps its adherents thrive, through in-person rituals: these are regular experiences of communal solidarity, taking form as baptisms and weddings, breaking a Ramadan or Yom Kippur fast, or raising voices together in prayer.

17

In time, we may see evidence of theological revival. Rabbi Abraham Joshua Heschel liked to point out that experiences of justice and compassion often unlock the door to faith far more effectively than doctrinal argument.

Confidence in God's healing power grows when one witnesses doctors, nurses and first responders selflessly risking their lives to heal others. By the same token, evidence of injustice -- such as the unequal access to health care and so to life itself -- mocks and undermines the claim that God's loving shelter encompasses everyone.

God is not alone in having a lot to answer for these days. The burden falls on all of us, and especially on members of religious communities (in the words of Jewish morning prayers) "to give strength to the weary and raise up those who are bowed down."

(This essay originally appeared on CNN.com
May 18, 2020)

DIGNITY AND DISTANCE
Rabbi Rachel Putterman

I'm just wrapping up a year-long chaplaincy internship at Brigham and Women's Hospital in Boston. Early in the pandemic, the governor banned all students from entering the hospital. When asked if I was willing to be retrained as an administrative support person for the Covid units, I vacillated. Though I longed to be in the hospital and help out, I was also deeply anxious about becoming infected and bringing it home to my family. But after a colleague said it was less stressful in the hospital than in a grocery store, I decided to give it a try. I was tired of reading all the horror stories about hospitals and wanted to see for myself. I also wanted to be of service, and had been feeling frustrated at being isolated in my house with plenty of food and no immediate worries other than the abstract fear that me or my loved ones might get sick.

So, over the last couple of months, I've covered several shifts as a unit coordinator on a Covid Intensive Care Unit. It was as chaotic and stressful as one would imagine. But what was simultaneously both most impressive and most heartbreaking were the complex procedures in place to protect staff and other patients from the patients who were infected with Covid. An entire additional shift of nurses is now present whose sole job is to assist the front line nurses with putting on and then taking off all of the personal protective equipment they must wear to go into the Covid patients' rooms. I describe this as heartbreaking because the patients are so extremely isolated. They're frequently spending several weeks in the hospital, during which time they are not allowed to have any visitors, and every doctor or nurse they come in contact with is swathed in so much protective gear as to be practically unrecognizable.

I became acutely aware of the hospital's single-minded focus on preventing spread when I was asked to bring the belongings of a patient who had died to the Patient Relations Department so they could be sent to the patient's family. I was assured - *and could see* - that the belongings

19

had been triple-bagged, so I picked up the bag with bare hands and brought it where it needed to go. When I arrived, the woman behind the desk looked at me, looked at the bag, and before I could get a word out - she barked at me, "drop the bag on the floor!" She then put on gloves, whisked out disinfecting wipes and approached the bag as if it were a bomb.

I totally understand the very valid fear that we're all living with, especially those who work in hospitals, but I was still saddened by the woman's response to a bag of belongings of someone who had died of Covid. Of course, I recognize the need for protocols involving PPE but what about the real human consequences of their use? I worry about Covid patients and their belongings becoming mere signifiers of that which we fear. In the midst of all the measures we're taking right now for the sake of *pikuach nefesh*, saving a life, it can be easy to forget that each of us, including those infected with Covid, are made *b'tzelem Elohim*, in the image of God. Despite our high anxiety levels, my hope is that we accord Covid patients the highest dignity both in life and death, even if we have to do so from a safe distance.

THE HEARTBREAKING LONELINESS
OF MOURNING DURING A PANDEMIC
Jordana Horn

On Friday morning, my father-in-law died. He was a lucky man in general: He lived to 92, he got to meet his nine grandchildren, and he lived a full and happy life until the very end.

But it's that "very end" that I want to write about now. Because this ending is not just my story — it will, in all likelihood and all too soon, become yours, too.

Because chances are very good that you, too, will soon have to bury someone you know and/or love in these strange times. Whether they die from the disease that is currently plaguing our world, or from some other more mundane cause, like old age or a car accident, you need to know that no matter what, any death during this pandemic is… something else.

My father-in-law was a smart and determined person, living with an aide in the home where my husband and his brother grew up. He went into the hospital for a fever the week before his death and tested negative for COVID-19. Still, once he went through those hospital doors, he could no longer have visitors due to the virus' deadly spread.

He was too weak to communicate by phone. Instead, we got updates from hospital staff — they did their best, but it was clear they were thinly stretched. They finally told us that his kidneys were doing poorly, that he was a poor candidate for starting dialysis, and that he would be "sent home." (The words "to die" were not added to that sentence; rather, we were simply asked to fill out the hospice care forms).

And so, he came home from the hospital Thursday night. By the time my husband arrived at the house in which he grew up on Friday morning, it was too late to say goodbye. He had died in his bed, in the house he had never wanted to leave.

At that point, in more normal times, Jewish mourning rituals would commence. We would prepare a funeral, write eulogies, arrange who would be in what car from the funeral to the cemetery. The body would be cared for by a holy society that would guard it, clean it, and prepare it for burial.

But with all gatherings prohibited, since New Jersey (the site of the burial) and New York (the site of the death) are both under stay-at-home orders, none of these rituals could take place. Instead, my husband spent the afternoon of his father's death on the phone, negotiating with the cemetery and funeral personnel for four, rather than three, mourners to be allowed at the graveside, in order to allow both my husband and his brother to bring their spouses.

On Sunday morning, my husband and I drove down empty highways to the cemetery, some 30 miles away. It was my longest trip out of the house in weeks. The funeral director approached our car, standing at a distance of six feet from our window. She told us that, due to restrictions on the numbers of people at the cemetery, the hearse and casket would have to go to the gravesite before we did. Once the casket had been lowered into the grave and the gravediggers left, only then could we proceed to the grave.

We waited in the cold rain, a triangle of six feet of distance on each side — my husband and I at one point, our rabbi at the second, and my husband's brother and his wife at the third. The two brothers couldn't even embrace. We stood in the cold, hands only warmed by rubber gloves, waiting for the gravediggers to finish their work.

The gravedigger foreman, mask over half his face, came over and told us brusquely that only three people total would be allowed at the grave due to the prohibition against gatherings. Apparently all my husband's prior discussions were for nothing. And those three people, the gravedigger said, would be the funeral director, the rabbi, and one mourner.

The not-so-pleasant "discussion" with the foreman over this point took 20 minutes, at the end of which he stated that he would take only three people to the grave — and then he would take his leave, "and what you do then is up to you."

"That guy needs to work on his bedside manner," I muttered to my husband in spite of myself as we headed to the grave once we saw the foreman beating his retreat.

"I think you mean 'dead side manner,'" my husband offered.

Any comfort provided by humor, however, was gone by the time we got to the grave, keenly feeling the absence of all those who would otherwise have been there — the grandchildren, my siblings and parents, my father-in-law's long-term caregivers, my husband's friends and those of his brother. The wooden coffin lay at the bottom, separated from us. It was not lost on me that we were also separated by six feet.

In Jewish tradition, the mourners shovel the first dirt into the grave, covering the coffin. Not only would we not share embraces with each other in these strange times, we were also told before arriving that we could not even share a shovel: We were instructed to either bring our own shovels or simply throw handfuls of earth into the grave.

The thumps made by the sound of earth hitting the coffin were excruciating. I have always felt shaken by that sound at funerals past: each "thump" sounds like an emphatic period at the end of a life. But the sound brought tears to my eyes this time as I realized that, in a "socially distanced" funeral, this was the only small bit of contact permitted us: only the casket and the earth were allowed to touch.

There was no traditional meal of consolation awaiting us when we got back to our house, and no mourners pulling up to the curb to spend time with us as my husband sat shiva. During the seven days of shiva, mourners are supposed to have every physical and emotional need met by their community. Friends and family sit with you, feed you, and share your stories or your silence. Mourners are never supposed to be in isolation — they are always supposed to be surrounded by community.

Instead, we sat in front of a computer screen as "visitors" dialed into a Zoom shiva room. Like some sad version of The Brady Bunch on a monitor, people from all points in my husband's life dropped in and out to pay their respects.

But perhaps the saddest part of all of this is that so, so many of you reading this are going to have to mourn the same way over these next days, weeks, and months.

And those of you fortunate enough to somehow remain unscathed by death during this time will have to think: How can I possibly offer the comfort of my arms to a mourner through a text? When someone in your life experiences loss, how will you approximate that moment when you first see each other and you fall into each other's arms and sob? How will you create an ersatz togetherness, a jerry-rigged approximation of what it once used to be to love and to mourn?

In short, how can we be present when we are not allowed to be present?

Long before COVID-19, we created a world in which we regularly spend hours on our phones, "liking" each other's happiness, flicking through slideshows of others' lives. But now we can plainly see the bottomless inadequacy of these screens as we stare into them, hoping to connect with others but only seeing the reflection of ourselves. Bereft of our rituals and of one another, we are doubly bereft.

But my husband and I, I realize now, were the lucky ones. We could at least hold each other's hand. We stood at the grave, and heard and said prayers said by our people for thousands of years. Thousands of mourners to come may not have those chances.

Despite this new serrated edge of mourning and loss in the time of COVID-19, we are not alone. But that is only because so, so many more people are about to be alone, just like us.

(This essay originally appeared on Kveller.com
Mar 31, 2020)

I'M NOT A DOCTOR, BUT I AM A RABBI. HERE'S MY SPIRITUAL PRESCRIPTION FOR THE CORONAVIRUS.

Rabbi Shmuly Yanklowitz

I am not a medical professional, an epidemiologist or an expert on pandemics. I leave the serious information in those important fields for the professionals who have the appropriate training to help us get through the coronavirus epidemic.

Even though I do not possess medical knowledge, as a rabbi and social activist, I believe I can try to humbly prescribe ethical vaccines that can remedy jilted nerves and worried minds. My words are not meant to heal physically but to inspire spiritually.

At this challenging time, it seems appropriate that those in the positions to (re)build confidence should do so. In that spirit, I am sharing thoughts on how we might be able to spiritually cope with the uncertain reality that has rapidly spread throughout the world. The coronavirus is not only a disease of the body, but also presents an existential crisis that has put governments, businesses and, most important, communities and individuals on edge.

I pray that we can get through it all. People are scared — and rightly so. We are truly living in an era of plague; we are largely unprepared. Communities throughout the world have been caught off-guard by the virus' potent potential for wanton havoc and daily disruption.

But hope can't be lost. At this moment, we want to protect ourselves and our families; this is human nature. From a Jewish perspective, from a social justice perspective, from a human perspective, we cannot descend into pointed tribalism at a time when we must come together as a collective of mind and soul. The coronavirus is a huge burden placed on humanity, but one that can be handled through shared action, compassion and a desire to see this disease contained before more lives are needlessly lost.

As I reflected inward about how the coronavirus is affecting the world, I thought about soul remedies that could help guide us — in the Jewish community and beyond — through this arduous ordeal and into a brighter tomorrow. Here's my six-part prescription for getting through this crisis with our souls intact.

1. There is no value in placing blame.

We are already seeing our worst impulses play out in this crisis. Because the present strain of coronavirus originated in China, some are blaming "the Chinese" or even all Asians for the outbreak, which is absurd and hateful. And then there are community leaders such as an ultra-Orthodox rabbi who bizarrely blamed the LGBTQ community for spreading the disease. These are the wrong reactions: Whatever we do, we cannot fall into the trap of blame. Blame harms more than it helps; it is myopic and never leads to practical solutions. Of course, we must hold reckless public officials accountable if they neglect public welfare, but this is different from directing baseless blame at large populations. Rather than join the blaming team, we should join the helping team.

There are times where we cannot help as much as we'd like, but we can still do as much as we can from a distance. We must simply adjust our mindset to think about how we can all effectively work together with the help of experts to deal with the task at hand.

2. Be afraid.

Yes, this must sound like unusual advice in a time of pandemic. But we must be skeptical of those in office who say "Everything is fine. Stop panicking and live your life!" It is a natural human emotion to be afraid of the unknown and the uncertain. We live in times where every day's events constitute a reminder that we cannot control the world as much as we might want. Politically, culturally and spiritually, the world is experiencing levels of disequilibrium that are difficult to endure. It would seem then that, rationally, we should live in fear of what tomorrow may bring. Rather than denying that human impulse to have fear in the face of serious risks, we can channel that fear productively.

26

Hold the fear. Hold your loved ones close. But don't be held motionless — physically, emotionally or spiritually — by this disease. Feel it but own it, refine it, control it. Use it. We need to react boldly to situations such as the one that challenges us right now and with the clarity of mind that tells us that fear should inspire us to be courageous; troubling times calls for passionate and resolute leadership. Our fear can inspire us to hold one another even closer and with deeper resolve.

3. Wipe out evil.

In the Jewish tradition, the nation of Amalek is synonymous with the worst evil imaginable. The Amalekites saw the most vulnerable among the Israelites and instead of helping them, pursued and killed them, targeting in particular the weakest among the weak. The Torah records the deeds of the Amalekites and their actions, juxtaposing the meekness of the Jewish people with the pure cruelty of the nation of Amalek. We are commanded to vanquish Amalek and eliminate its memory from this world. The coronavirus — the disease itself! — is Amalek-like since it appears to have the most serious consequences for some of the most vulnerable among us, the elderly and the immunocompromised. By protecting and supporting the most vulnerable people around the world, we have the ability to live up to the commandment to wipe out Amalek once more.

As tensions among communities may run high, we must learn again the lessons of interdependence: The coronavirus demonstrates the profound ignorance of the belief that we keep ourselves "safe" by building walls to separate us from our neighbors and by locking up immigrants at the border. In a world as interconnected as ours, we keep ourselves safe by respecting the truths revealed by science, by cooperating and working together within and among nations, by caring for the most vulnerable among us, and by creating a society that keeps as many of us as possible healthy and financially secure. In a world so focused on "us vs. them," the coronavirus reminds us that in a profound sense, there is only us.

The only sane path forward is more compassion, more justice, and more humility about the degree to which we need each other.

4. Embrace a sabbatical.

One of Judaism's great gifts to the world is the idea of the Sabbath, the sacred break from the labors of the week. But the Sabbath is more than lounging around with nothing to do. It's about renewal and the need to nourish the soul through extra time to study. One of the side effects of the coronavirus might be the ability for those who need to stay home to use that time away from the workplace or the outside world productively. Some folks need to show up at work, travel and go about business as usual. But to the extent that one can, it will be vital to care of yourself and those that you love. Through the gift of physical and spiritual rest, we may experience breakthroughs that will allow our society to manage this disease more effectively.

5. Be gentle.

Always be gentle with others. Everyone is doing the best they can. Human beings are fundamentally frail. To compensate for uncertainty and imperfection in this moment, some people will act out with pure hubris. But this hubris hides vulnerability and pain. We do not know what others go through on a daily basis.

The coronavirus may give us the ability to realize that humility in the face of great challenge can be a factor leading us toward communal healing. To be under quarantine, as whole countries are essentially imposing at this point, cannot be a pleasant feeling. It's isolating and humiliating. To be gentle also means to be empathetic to those who find themselves cut off from society. This disease has upended routines all over the world. We can be understanding of how it has ruined the daily lives of people who only want to support themselves and their families. This universal reality brings us together rather than tearing us apart. Let us have the strength to be understanding and kind in this time of great tumult.

6. Love is contagious, too.

The coronavirus is highly contagious, but so are the actions we can take inspired by love and joy. We are reminded yet again of the total interconnectedness of all life on this planet. The amazing phenomenon of life and its parallel humbling frailty can inspire wonder and deeper empathy. While, of course, we must heed medical experts to undertake precautionary measures to avoid the spread of the virus, we can also do our best to spread happiness and positivity, international cooperation and a positive attitude to help quell this virus.

To give up on the better angels of our nature is akin to defeat. At the least, to acknowledge people's good intentions and engage others out of love

28

rather than fear are ways to help defeat the trials put before us by the coronavirus. Spread love, spread warmth, spread optimism. The times may seem bleak, but we can all do our part to ensure that a brighter tomorrow is around the corner.

Friends, this is a difficult time for all. No one has been spared from the effects of the coronavirus. Not all of us will be infected by the virus, but we are already affected. There is no denying that the global attention to this ailment has radically shifted the world's power landscape indefinitely. But, for a moment, looking past these macro-effects can offer an opportunity to consider how each of us, at an individual level, can be spiritually renewed in our collective efforts to halt this disease and get through this moment.

(This essay originally appeared on JTA.org
MARCH 11, 2020)

A REFLECTION ON COVID-19
Ruth Messinger

None of us knows when this crisis will recede or even what recede means. A horrendous consequence of the pandemic would be for people to "go back to normal", to put their lives and their organizations and the broader community back as they were. Instead, we need to look at what we are learning as this crisis unfolds and prepare to put ourselves together in some new ways. Let me mention four things I hope will be different.

First, that there is much more attention to global problems and global needs. We cannot continue as a healthy society if we tolerate growing inequities worldwide, if we ignore poverty, hunger, oppression, land theft, denial of human rights around the world. in country after country where American Jewish World Service works the virus is spreading, and it is likely that the impact will be worse and last longer than in the rest of the world because these are countries with limited health infrastructure, often literally no water and soap, and beleaguered governments that cannot handle even "ordinary" problems. And where there are not more deaths from the virus there will be deaths from hunger because markets are not functioning and deaths from other diseases because vaccination rates are slowing.

Second, that the Jewish community take a lead in looking at all the structural and systemic inequities that are being laid bare by the pandemic and be a voice for creating a health care system that works for all Americans, for exposing the limitations of our education systems and the ways in which poorer people and people of color are the losers and for adopting immigration policies that make it possible for others to come into our country. If we take seriously the Jewish mandate to pursue justice, then there is much for us to do in the 21st century. Our funders should be supporting the range of newer progressive initiatives directed against racism, for gender equity, for refugees and asylum seekers.

Third, that funders, foundations and federations in the Jewish community should be willing to dip into endowments to accept more of the challenges I have just mentioned. We were, many of us, raised to "save for a rainy day", and we are desperately in need of leadership in our community, some of which is already evident, to say that it is raining — no, pouring — now and wise use of additional funds to bail out this group or that effort will make a huge difference in moving us toward a more just world.

And, finally, the changes I am talking about — a commitment to helping the most marginalized people locally and globally, the reentry of the US into shaping environmental policies and practices that will protect the planet, a massive effort to end hunger and hatred where these destroy the quality of people's lives and lead to unnecessary deaths — require organized policy advocacy. It is long past time for funders, faith leaders and opinion makers in our community to not only invest wisely in the groups delivering critical services and fighting for change on the ground but to support advocacy efforts. Non-partisan work to develop or reinstate policies that advance equity are core to who we must be to make substantial and substantive change going forward.

ONLINE JUDAISM IS AN ECHO CHAMBER. WILL WE EVER SEE THOSE WE DISAGREE WITH AGAIN?

Dahlia Lithwick

I'm hardly the first to observe that the speed with which so much Jewish communal life leaped online in the first weeks of shutdown was head-snapping. I've been to more Zoom classes, Zoom Shabbat services, Zoom concerts and ceremonies, more Zoom funerals and shivahs and bar mitzvahs in six weeks than I ever could have managed in real-time.

My kids Zoom to day school and my son baked a cake in Hebrew for Shabbat. Perhaps because Jewish ritual and observance is so communal, by definition it migrated online almost seamlessly. Long after we first panicked about the demise of brick and mortar Jewish institutions, it's clear that Judaism can and will thrive so long as there's a moderator, a camera, a dial-in number and a microphone.

But I worry now more than ever about bubbles; about the ways we are self-selecting our communities in ways that only amplify our own views and preferences. Jewish communal life in reality-based-times was one of the last bastions of diversity of ideas; of the chance encounter with someone whose politics and ideology diverged from yours. Shabbat mornings forced you to rub along beside people who voted differently, thought differently, observed differently, and we made space for each other – reluctantly sometimes, uncomfortably sometimes – because as long as there have been Jewish spaces, there have been profound differences to transcend.

But as I move online, I notice that I'm studying with people who think as I do; I'm worshipping with people who share my exact values; my Zoom calendar is a massive array of pick-your-own-ending experiences that often end precisely where I began.

Who knew that someone in Madison, Wisconsin might share my precise taste in melodies, books, and values? And now that I have met them, why would I ever again sing with, learn from, or give tzedakah to, anyone with whom I have profound disagreements? Behold how good and how pleasing it is for all of us to sit together in perfect unity.

But maybe not every single day.

I'll admit it: I need to hear things I dislike; I need to pray next to people who make me crazy; I need my children to hear from people whose ideas diverge radically from my own. And long after the world split apart into its ideological bubbles, and we all succumbed to whatever epistemic closure most suited us, Jewish communal life forced us to listen to, get along with and even honor a great many people we didn't encounter in other places and spaces.

And while I can't yet contemplate how this crisis will end, and I am deeply grateful every single day for the rabbis and teachers and camp counselors who have lit the path through the darkness, I fear that we will never again return to some of the Jewish buildings, spaces, and experiences that forced us to confront the fact that as Jews our job sometimes is to fight, to shake our fists, to insist that we will never again darken the door of someplace or other again, and then show up sheepishly the next time.

I hope that after COVID, we realize that we do best when we make space for Judaism that is different and uneasy, even though we have learned that we need never grapple with it again.

(This essay first appeared in The Forward
May 24, 2020)

TWENTY SECONDS TO SAFETY
Rachel Sharansky Danziger

I'm standing by the sink, rubbing my hands around my toddler's smaller ones. I'm singing "Happy birthday," and my voice sounds foreign to my ears. Its cheerfulness belongs to someone else — someone I heard once. Was it a puppet in a children's show? Was it a kindergarten teacher? It can't belong to me. Not now, at any rate. Not while the latest obituary in my newsfeed is still twisting my insides.

My son giggles, and I startle. How long have I been staring at the mirror? How long have I been singing for? Was it enough? Or am I still one stanza away from security, one note away from beating death?

"Let's sing the ABC song as well," says the stranger's voice upon my lips, and I restart the process. But this time, I am counting seconds in my mind. One. "A, B." Two. "C, D." Three.

My mind is a metronome, a stopwatch, a shield.

* * *

My son's hands are so small in my own, and so unmarked by life. And yet, despite my learning and my scars and all my grand adventures, I feel so very small right now, as small as he is. What good are all my thoughts and words and past achievements, when here I am, with naught but hands and song and soap to fend off death?

And numbers, of course.

I go on counting.

When I was little and unmarked myself (or do I only think so now? I never felt brand-new when I was younger), my teachers said that we should

34

always imagine ourselves as if we are hanging in the balance between God's Book of Life and Book of Death. Every little act might be the one to tip the scale, they urged us. So don't grow complacent! Make every act count!

And here I am now, working hard to stay on the literal side of the living, never knowing what act will be the one to tip the scale. Does the line between the Books of Life and Death lie in this droplet, or the next? Four. Five.

* * *

Numbers don't come naturally to me. Passwords and dates slip through my mind and leave no traces. Even now, when numbers carry weights I cannot ignore, they come and go and fail to change me. Two-Hundred-and-Nineteen dead in Israel, total. Two-Hundred-and-Fifty-Two dead in Massachusetts, in one day. I hear the words — I know that they should horrify me — and then they pass again, and I'm unmoved.

But then I catch a name. Or see a picture. Or a detail jumps at me as I scroll down, ever down, on my screen and through obituaries. A woman I do not know sang to her father on the phone as he lay dying. A man I never met woke up from intubation and learned that his own father died of COVID-19 while he slept. A friend visited three Zoom shivas, and found no words to share there. Another lost a cousin whom he loved but rarely saw.

Each detail, each name is like a nail that wasn't tightened properly, waiting to snag my attention and pull threads of grief and worry from what used to be well-woven peace of mind. Each of them sends me down a rabbit hole of "what ifs" and escalating sorrow. Each of them unravels me, and leaves me breathless and undone.

Stop, I tell myself.

(Six, seven.)

Stop. Focus on what is within your power to control.

(Eight, nine.)

Don't think of the deaths (my God, to die alone like this, so far from your

35

loved ones, and what if we get sick, who'll watch our children…), don't think of the mourners (my beloved sister-in-law is a nurse in NY, what if she gets it? My parents aren't young, what if, dear God…), don't think of the future (will we ever meet our friends again, and lean against each other with careless, casual affection?).

(Ten, eleven.)

Stop.

Think only of what is within your ability to do, right here, right now.

Twelve.

Ask yourself: What's in your hands?

Focus on that.

I rub my toddler's hands in mine.

Thirteen. Fourteen.

* * *

Years ago, there was a time when I felt unhappy with some circumstances. "Let me tell you what worked for me when I was a prisoner in the Soviet gulag," my father told me (instantly – and unintentionally – putting my ennui in comical perspective). "You can't control your circumstances. So think, instead, about what you can, and wish, to achieve within them. And then ask yourself: what can I do today to make it happen? What can I do right now?"

The fate of humanity doesn't lie in my hands right now.

My loved ones' tomorrows don't lie in my hands right now.

But right now, right here, my toddler is mine to protect.

Right now, right here, his joie de vivre is mine to uphold.

Right now, right here, my attitude is mine to shape.

And so: I sing. And this time, I own the cheerful voice upon my lips.

I smile.

My son is laughing, and my love for him burns painful in my chest.

Fifteen. Sixteen.

* * *

The priests in the Temple used to count too: one, one and one, one and two. Each number was part of the Yom Kippur service, their way to beg God to grant us more life. Did their hands ever tremble, did their voices ever falter? Did they ever feel fear, did they ever lose count?

And how did they feel when they handled the offerings, when they held, in their hands, so much more than mere flesh? Each offering is an expression of someone's regrets, hopes, or gratitude. Did the priests ever balk in the face of this intimacy? Did it make them feel powerful, unworthy, afraid?

There's flesh in my hands. Flesh — and some bubbles. Transient, mortal. Here today, later — gone.

But for now — there is life. For now — we are here, still.

Yes, we can die. But for now, we can live.

Seventeen. Eighteen.

* * *

"Once I saw a violinist playing and I thought: Between his right hand and his left — only the violin," Yehuda Amichai wrote once. "But what a between, what music!"

I am no more a musician than I am a priest in the Temple. Yet right here, right now, with my son's hands in my own and a song upon our lips, the distance between my hands contains its own sort of hopeful symphony, its own way of transcending the limits of mere space.

I know that I can't protect my son forever. God's Books of Life and Death can't fit within my grasp.

But as I imbue my actions with choice and with intention, I write myself, for this one moment, into the book of those who are truly, fully, irrefutably alive.

Nineteen. Twenty.

* * *

I dry my son's hands, and turn away from the sink and the soap and the mirror. New chores await, new trials, new sad news to undo my peace of mind. I walk on, and pray for everything that lies beyond my powers. And as I walk, I ask myself: in this new moment, what is in my hands?

(This essay first appeared in The Times of Israel
May 1, 2020)

JAZZ AND JUDAISM
IN THE DAYS OF CORONA
Akiva Gersh

I've been thinking that Judaism looks a lot like Jazz music these days.

In Jazz, you have all these different pieces and parts, instruments and sounds combining together to create a multi-layered auditory experience. Once you get to the solos, however, some of those pieces and parts start fading into the background, if not sitting out entirely.

Then you get to the bass solo, and usually it's just the drummer who's still hanging on with a light, soft rhythm as backup.

But when it comes to the drum solo, it's only the drums, no one and nothing else. The drums stand on their own and show the listener that they are the driving force behind the music, and have been the whole time. The drums need no support from anyone or anything else.

Right now, we're seeing something similar with Judaism.

Those who are familiar with it know that, while beautiful and inspiring and incredibly meaningful, Jewish practice is also super complex and complicated and filled with a seemingly infinite amount of detailed laws that could be dizzying at times.

But right now, as a result of the dangerous and deadly spread of the Coronavirus, so many of those laws and customs that in normal times seem like "God's word from Sinai" are losing their usual place at center stage of Jewish life and are being moved to the side, if not completely disappearing for the time being.

Going to synagogue, davening in a minyan, public Torah reading, public celebrations of weddings and other life-cycle events, visiting those in mourning, and even, in some places, burying the dead in the traditional Jewish manner are just some of the Jewish practices that have not only been put on hold, but have been banned by governmental and communal leaders.

And what's left standing, for the grand solo that needs no backup or accompaniment, is the everlasting and indestructible Jewish value of…*Life.*

It is able to stand on its own because, since time immemorial, it has been the eternal and essential teaching of Judaism. To value life, to love life and to live life to the fullest. And to do all we can to allow others to be able to do the same.

The rest of Judaism is just commentary.

Blessings of Life to all in these challenging and unprecedented times.

L'chaim to all on the deepest level.

(This essay originally appeared in Times of Israel
March 30, 2020)

GETTING OVER BY GETTING THROUGH
Rabbi Danielle Upbin

How many times have I told myself, "let's just get this over with already…" whether it was a board meeting, community event, family visit… you can fill in the blanks. My husband jokes that I would ask "what time are we leaving?" *before we even arrived.* But when the COVID-19 pandemic settled in, I quickly realized that we are not getting over this anytime soon. While there is no graceful way out (or at least not one that I would choose), there are a myriad of ways *through it* that don't require suffering. I found my own way by tapping into a well of resources that have always been available to me, but I never fully embraced. I discovered that the trio of meditation, yoga, and contemplative study, are grounding forces in what is otherwise a whirlwind. I would like to share some of these practices with you as a "gift of calm" within the storm.

Aligning the mind-body-spirt connection requires that we tune into our breath. In Hebrew, the soul-breath connection is made evident: *Neshimah* - breath, is tethered to *Neshamah* -soul. Attuning to our breath allows us to slow down as we tap into our inner guiding compass, our very own life force. The intentional act of "committing to our breath" even for just a few moments every day, can help anchor us into the highest experience of our inner-truth.

Try it for a moment. *Close your eyes and take a long deep breath. Follow the inhale as you fill your lungs, and then follow the exhale to the end.* Then begin again. Providing a mental break from the normally scheduled program of "As the World Turns: Pandemic Edition", can instill a feeling of calm and clarity. When combined with a curriculum of gentle movement, like yoga, and creative activities, such as writing or visual arts, we can begin to develop a scenic road through a challenging course.

The wisdom of our tradition has been my cherished partner, offering solace and spiritual direction. Through study, we join a chain of wisdom that has accompanied our people through it all. It is astounding how the

41

Psalms are jumping off the page as if *David Ha'Melech* wrote them specifically for today: "*Teach us to number our days so that we may attain a heart of wisdom....* (Psalm 90:12). The works of survivors are equally poignant. Consider the words of the prominent author, psychologist and Holocaust survivor, Victor Frankl:

> "*Between stimulus and response there is a space. In that space is our power to choose our response. In our response lies our growth and our freedom.*"

The Mussar teachers have a name for this required space necessary for that critical moment of response: "Choice Point" *Nekudat Behira*. We have hundreds of Choice Points each day, which become the "pavers" on our path through life - in a pandemic and beyond. We can choose compassion over critique, curiosity over judgement, stillness over chaos. When we don't create the space to choose, we risk flying into tantrums and tirades, furthering our pain instead of fostering seeds of healing.

This brings me to my final point. Often, anxiety and fear obscure our Choice Points. They drive us to respond before we have fully chosen. I have come to realize that these very forces were what prompted my "let's get this over with" attitude, pre-Pandemic. Instead of savoring the moments and cultivating curiosity, I allowed my "fear of the unknown" to take over my joy and the fullness of my life. During our current challenge, I have taken a cue from this uplifting Hassidic teaching on "overcoming fear":

Many of us are familiar with the song, "*Kol Ha'Olam Kulo/The Whole World is a Bridge*" with a catchy melody written by Rabbi Baruch Chait:

> *Kol Ha'Olam Kulo gesher tzar me'od v'ha'ikar lo l'fached klal. The whole world is a very narrow bridge, but the important thing is not to fear at all.*

While this song has been the spiritual battle cry throughout contemporary Jewish history. The original teaching of Rebbe Nachman of Bratzlov, upon which this song is based, adds a new dimension that speaks to our current moment:

> דַּע, שֶׁהָאָדָם צָרִיךְ לַעֲבֹר עַל גֶּשֶׁר צַר מְאֹד מְאֹד ,וְהַכְּלָל וְהָעִקָּר – שֶׁלֹּא יִתְפַּחֵד כְּלָל
> *Know, too! A person must cross a very, very narrow bridge. The main rule is: Do not make yourself afraid at all! - Likutei Moharan II #48.*

Rebbe Nachman reminds us that in times of uncertainty, we must not add to the *mishagas* fear-mongering and *what ifs*. While we can't control the situation, we are free to choose our response. Let's choose to learn how to grow in compassion. This is how we will see each other through to the other side - more wise, more centered, and perhaps more calm than we have ever been.

Now, let's begin with our breath.

SHALOM BAYIT
Rabbi Adrienne Rubin

Shalom Bayit, peace (or wholeness) in the home, guides us to make different choices for the sake of a higher purpose. Here are a few suggestions:

- **Realize what compromises we need to make**. Maybe it is asking your teenage son not to stream YouTube when you have a Zoom call. Maybe it is stopping your work to help your child manage the complexities of e-learning. Maybe it is eating at a different time than you otherwise would have. Instead of "either/or", like Gloria Steinem, you might discover a whole world of "and."
- **Temper our anger with laughter and good humor**. We are all frustrated by what we cannot do. We all share some apprehension about what is happening. And it is easy to lash out over small things when we are tense. When your spouse opens the dishwasher door while it is running, laugh (together). When your child eats the last of the Girl Scout Cookies, chuckle. Remember, a good, hearty laugh relieves physical tension and stress. So laugh whenever you can!
- **Practice gratitude**. Remember the saying, "Don't sweat the small stuff – and it's all small stuff." Be grateful for the small things. When the cats wake you up at 5:00 a.m. because they are hungry, be grateful that you have cats. When you have to walk your dog in the rain, be grateful that your dog ensures you get out of the house. When your children complain about e-learning, hear them. And also remind them to be grateful for the teachers who love them and are making that possible. When you find dishes in random places in the house, be grateful that you have enough.
- **Communicate.** Remember that we cannot read each other's minds. If you need quiet at a specific time, ask for it. If you would like to eat a certain meal – or support a local business by getting takeout, tell your family. If something is bothering you, say so (when you are not angry about it). Use mealtime as a time to connect and talk about what is working and not working and how

this situation is making all of you feel. Expressing your feelings to each other can help. Everyone wants to feel heard and understood.

As Lao-tse said,

"If there is to be peace in the world, there must be peace in the nations.
If there is to be peace in the nations, there must be peace in the cities.
If there is to be peace in the cities, there must be peace between neighbors.
If there is to be peace between neighbors, there must be peace in the home.
If there is to be peace in the home, there must be peace in the heart."

My best wishes to you all.

WORKING WITH FEAR
Rabbi Shefa Gold

The general consensus and our deep conditioning tell us that it is our fear that will keep us safe. … that if we know all the horrible things that might happen, we'll be better able to deal with them … that our fear will keep us vigilant against danger… that expecting the worst will help us guard against disaster.

What if this consensus is totally wrong? What if the truth is that all fear is ultimately toxic, and that it prevents us from truly accessing the deepest wisdom and the greatest love? Fear (that is sustained and not just a momentary startle) raises the level of stress hormones, lowers immunity, sends us to our reptile brain, shuts down our connection to the higher brain functions like empathy, understanding, intuition and love. Fear separates us and blinds us to the miracle of our interconnectivity. Fear shuts down the heart, keeping it from receiving the blessings of this precious moment. Fear is …

> **F**antasized
> **E**xperiences
> **A**ppearing as
> **R**eal

I like this acronym because it reminds me that fear is happening in the mind. If I can create just a bit of distance and perspective about my fearful thoughts, I can notice when they emerge, and release them with compassion. In a moment of fearlessness, I can choose wisdom, assessing the risk before me with clear-eyed deliberation, and act in alignment with the force of the Great Love.

Yes, fear happens in the mind. I get startled and that sense of alarm activates a cascade of fearful imaginings. "What will happen to this fragile world, to my health, my finances, to all my loved ones?!" These questions inevitably lead me towards anxiety and despair.

What the real and useful questions can be are, "How shall I live the gift of my each and every moment? Will this moment be fueled by that fear? How can I release the illusion of control, and surrender to the Divine Will that dwells within me? Will my worries cloud the possibilities of joy, right here, right now? How can I rise to the extraordinary challenge that this moment holds, with all my faculties at the ready?"

I believe that anything we do from fear is tainted or somehow distorted and might do as much harm as good. Doing that same action, sourced in love, can by its very essence, transform the doer. If anything might keep me safe, it will be my clear-headed, open-hearted presence… my ability to respond wisely to the gifts and challenges of this moment.

What an amazing opportunity for practice! Every time we have the presence of mind to release fear as it is arising, we strengthen that spiritual "muscle," and we build the capacity for unconditional joy, infusing every moment with an inner buoyancy and steady calm, no matter the weight of outer catastrophe or the disturbance of unexpected turbulence.

As I investigate each moment of fear or anxiety as it arises, I suspect that all these thoughts have their root in the Fear of Death. That root-fear holds me captive in its chains of limitation. When I am held hostage by that Fear of Death, I can't know the truth of my infinite Soul. And it is in knowing, really knowing myself as a Soul, that I am liberated.

As a Soul I experience Life, and Death, as a great adventure. I am open to learning from everything and everyone. I welcome joy and sorrow in equal measure. As a Soul I dive into this amazing story of loss and redemption, and yet I remember that forms and identities come and go. The small "I," (*mochin d'katnut*) will be swept away while the large "I," (*mochin d'gadlut*) will know itself more deeply and thoroughly because of this journey.

When I know myself as a Soul, my root-fear of Death fades and recedes and no longer fuels a life that is driven by fear. Those thoughts still happen, but they no longer compel.

This time of pandemic holds an extraordinary opportunity for facing our fears, turning towards love, awakening to the truth of our interconnectivity and knowing ourselves as radiant Souls that shine God's light. This is the light that heals and makes whole a world that feels so broken.

THE COURAGE TO LIVE
WITH UNCERTAINTY

Richard S. Moline

"Faith is not certainty. Faith is the courage to live with uncertainty."
-Rabbi Lord Jonathan Sacks

A colleague joked with me recently that since his kids will now be home for the summer, he was going to build his sukkah so he could have some privacy. It made me think of the fragility of the sukkah.

As sturdy as it may seem after you first build it, a sukkah is subject to the whims of nature. A strong wind can knock it over and a soaking rain can make it inhabitable.

Yet our liturgy asks God to spread a Sukkah of Peace over us. Strange. Why the precarious sukkah? Why not something strong and sturdy, something unmovable and impenetrable?

Maybe because like a sukkah, peace is fragile. To sit in a sukkah is itself an act of faith. And faith, as Rabbi Sacks says, is the courage to live with uncertainty.

During these uncertain times, may we strengthen our courage to confront uncertainty, so we can reinforce our faith and spread our own sukkot over those we love.

(This essay originally appeared in The Times of Israel
May 26, 2020.)

THE THINGS WE CAN'T CONTROL
Lela Casey

The anxiety had been building around us for weeks. It started as a whisper in my ear... *A virus? How many dead? Where are the cases... California, Washington, New York... my state, my town, my neighborhood.*

By March, the whisper had grown to a rumble so loud I had trouble hearing anything else.

I sat outside in our overgrown yard, staring at my phone reading article after article, *thousands sick, hundreds dead, school closings imminent, stay home, shut your doors, anyone could have it, EVERYONE could have it.*

My daughter danced around me, her hair filled with sticks and leaves, her freckles multiplying in the sun. She was saying something... she'd drawn a picture? Built a castle? Wrote a new story? The rumbling inside me was too loud to make out her words.

There was nothing I could do about the rumble... but her hair! Weeks of neglect and barely-brushes had turned her auburn waves into thick matted chunks.

Since she'd been born, people had been complimenting her on her hair. It grew long and wavy, well past her waist. It was the color of a sunset in the desert.

When she was tiny, she would dream of growing her hair so long it would wrap around the entire world. She'd tell me how she was going to have to spend her whole life wandering back and forth just to keep from tripping on it. But, she wouldn't mind one bit. It would be a grand lifelong adventure.

Her hair was her identity, a blazing symbol of her untamed nature. As one by one, her friends got cute little bobs and fashionable bangs that made their Snapchat selfies pop, she held onto that hair like a steady rope tying her to her childhood.

50

Now the long willowy waves that had defined her for so long were swallowed up by a tangled jungle.

How had I let things get so bad? I couldn't control the news, couldn't silence the rumble, but I could untangle those knots.

She cried when I made her come inside. Big fat droplets that seemed too dramatic for the occasion. She kept going on about whatever it is she wanted to show me. Whatever it was I had missed.

But, I had little patience for her tears.

Inside the house, she sulked on the couch as I ran the bathwater. I stayed in the bathroom alone, ignoring the way the thick air opened my skin to its kisses, ignoring the sweet smell of lilacs that drifted in from the open window, ignoring the chorus of birds that announced spring's arrival.

Instead, I slammed the window shut and went back to my phone, swiping through article after article. *Incompetent leaders, mounting cases, anger, division, hopelessness, bodies, bodies, bodies.* I was so lost in the news, I didn't even notice that the water had spilled out over the tub. It took me another 10 minutes to mop up the soapy water off the bathroom floor.

By the time I was ready to wash her hair, my daughter had run back outside, leaving a trail of dirty socks and shoes behind her.

My knees shook as I threw the backdoor open. How dare she defy me like that? I prowled around the backyard calling her name, alternating between bribes and punishments. I'd become Snow White's evil stepmother, The Little Mermaid's Seawitch, Rapunzel's captress.

When I finally found her, she was lying in a thick patch of brush in the neighbor's yard, her hair spread around her head like a crown of fire lilies. A fat beetle delicately wove its way in and out of her tangles.

On another day, I would have gasped at the beauty of the scene, counted my blessings that, at almost 11, adolescence still hadn't stolen away her fairy magic.

But this was *not* just another day. Death was creeping around the corners, preying on the weak and vulnerable. What could be more vulnerable than a changeling who didn't respect rules, wouldn't stay within the boundaries? How could I keep her safe if she wouldn't listen to me?

I grabbed her hand, pulled her back into the house and plunked her down into the bath. She screamed as I poured the water on her head. Maybe it was too hot? Maybe she just didn't want to be in the bath. It didn't matter. There was work to be done. Knots to be undone.

The heavy smell of late summer peaches filled the bathroom as I emptied an entire bottle of conditioner into her hair. She sobbed silently as I poked my fingers through the maze of knots, trying to feel my way out.

When the peach conditioner was gone, I dug around my closet for others. Half a bottle of green apple conditioner, a quarter bottle of coconut, the sticky bottom of papaya. A heavy smell of rotten fruit salad filled my lungs as I jerked her head from side to side, wiggling first my fingers, then a fork toothed comb through her hair.

I tried to be gentle. I did. But, as the minutes ticked by, I felt my grip get tighter, my hands move faster.

She sat very still as I worked. Sometimes she gasped, sometimes she whined, but mostly she was quiet, her salty tears turning the bathwater briny.

As my fingers wove in and out of her hair, my mind went on its own twisted journey. I saw our family locked up at home while the days turned into weeks and months and maybe years. I saw missed birthdays and lonely holidays. I saw my 80-year-old parents aging and dying alone. I saw coughs turning into alarms and fevers into death sentences. I saw long days of work and homeschooling leaking into each other without end. I saw mounting deaths and diminishing hope and this rumbling inside of me growing so loud I'd stop even trying to listen to anything else

After hours of poking and pulling, a scream pierced the silence. My daughter looked straight at me, her mouth open, her nostrils flared, her whole fiery fairy self-concentrated into a high-pitched wail that harmonized with the rumble inside of me. A chorus of pain.

My hands jerked away from her and a spray of conditioner flew at my face, stinging my eyes and filling my mouth with bitterness. I whirled around and caught a glimpse of myself in the mirror. Thick steam blurred my features, blotted out my eyes, smeared my mouth into something ugly and twisted. I was not myself. I was someone else. Someone who could let her sweet daughter spend a beautiful afternoon indoors, in pain, screaming. Someone ugly. Someone out of control.

I took a deep breath and turned back around. After over two hours of work, I'd only gotten a few sections of her hair done. Finishing it would take the rest of the day... maybe even the next day. I stayed with my back to her for a few more moments, trying to sort the whirl of emotions inside of me into something calm, something reasonable, something parental.

"OK. We have 2 options. One is that we can keep at this until we get all the knots out. The other is that I can cut it."

My hands swished around her cheeks as I spoke, my lips twisted into a playful smirk. I was bluffing and she knew it. I'd never cut hair. She loved it too much. *I* loved it too much.

And anyway, I was terribly bumbling, utterly uncrafty, and completely lacking in anything that required hand-eye coordination. Completely unqualified to even touch her lioness's mane. The only scissors I owned were the ones we used to cut paper dolls. Still, I had to give her some options. Give back some of the control I'd stolen from her.

She lifted her head. For the first time all afternoon she looked me straight in the eye. This time her words cut right through my rumble.

Cut it.

I swallowed hard and looked at her face again. Was she serious? Words began tumbling out of my mouth in quick succession.

"I don't have the right scissors, you know... it will be all uneven, maybe we could just put your hair back in a bun and try again tomorrow."

Cut it.

"Why don't we just wait until the salons open back up and have someone do it right?"

Cut it.

53

"You're sure?"

Cut it! Cut it! Cut it! Cut it!

My daughter who still slept with the stuffed squirrel she'd gotten at birth, my daughter who refused to part with her puke-stained bedroom carpet because she got it when she turned two, my daughter who wouldn't give the tooth fairy her baby teeth for all the money in the world, this strong stubborn daughter of mine who was more adverse to change than anyone I'd ever known in my whole life... my daughter wanted to cut her hair.

Now it was my turn to cry.

I turned away from her so she wouldn't see my tears. Had I gone too far? Pushed her into a corner? Was she going to blame me for taking away something that was tightly bound to her identity?

I wanted to give her some kind of out. Or maybe I wanted to give myself one.

Should I pretend I couldn't find the scissors? Try to hold her off until she'd calmed down a little and could make a more rational decision?

But then there she was, holding the scissors out to me with a gleam in her eyes.

Go ahead. Cut it.

My hands shook as I held the scissors. My heart crept so high into my throat I could barely breathe.

Just do it, Mama!

I made one cut, then another. A handful of tangles fell to the floor. Then two more. The paper scissors squeaked and strained as they worked their way through her thick waves. I stood back and looked at my work. The cuts were jagged and uneven, but not unfixable. If I stopped right now, a skilled stylist could probably turn it into layers.

Hurry up, please.

I kept on working my way across her head, cutting off 11 years of dreams. But... had it always really been *her* dreams? Had I been so caught up in my own worries that I hadn't noticed that she's changing? Had I stopped really listening long before this deep rumble of anxiety had taken me over?

Was it possible that somewhere along the way I'd allowed her hair to become part of *my* identity, to become one of the few things that I could control? With every piece of hair that fell to the floor, I allowed myself to let go of some of the weight I was carrying.

When I was finished, she turned around to face me. Yes, her hair was uneven, and no, the knots were still not all out. But, none of those things really mattered. What *did* matter was that she was dancing and twirling in front of the mirror, hopelessly in love with the new image that *she* had chosen.

After a long time of admiring herself in the mirror, she collapsed into my arms and gave me a big hug.

I squeezed her tightly

Thank you! Mama! I love it.

She skipped away from me towards the door and then suddenly whirled back around.

Oh... I almost forget! Here's the picture I wanted to show you earlier when we were outside.

She tossed a crumpled up piece of paper into my lap. Another wave of guilt crashed over me as I remembered how I'd ignored her earlier. How'd I'd been so caught up in my own worries that I'd missed what she was so excited to show me.

I held the crumpled paper in my hand and started smoothing it out. It was a picture of my daughter and me. We were standing outside in the grass. One of her hands was in mine, the other was clutching her stuffed squirrel. My hair hung long and dark as I looked down on her. She looked back up at me, her big round cartoon eyes smiling, her hair cut into a short little fiery bob.

ARE WE THERE YET?

Rabbi Craig Scheff

I don't recall much from my childhood, but I can clearly remember those moments when my sisters and I would climb into the back seats of the family car as we'd be setting out to visit relatives, and the cry would carry forward to my parents in the front, "Are we there yet?"

More accurately, I recall those occasions when I was old enough to appreciate the question as a recurring joke. After all, at that point of my life the signs along the way had become familiar: the Howard Johnson's off the Merritt Parkway; the Charter Oak Bridge bypassing Hartford; the entrance to the Mass. Pike; the ramp onto Route 128. Even as a child, I knew how long was the trip, and what time was the time of our estimated arrival. And I'd certainly recognize my grandparents' driveway on West Roxbury Parkway to know we had arrived.

In the second month of the second year of the Israelites' wandering, they do not yet know that they will be destined to wander forty years. I can imagine the children asking with each leg of the journey, "Are we there yet?" Even with the commandments as a guide, new rituals for drawing near to God, and the structure of a community that encamped as one, I imagine a lingering uncertainty that gnawed at even the most faithful. After all, so many of those commandments were given to be observed in the Promised Land; when would we get a chance to put them into practice?

In these days of confusion and uncertainty, I am reminded of that child in the backseat, before the question was posed for a laugh. Impatient, cooped up, unable to measure the passage of time, his anxiety is compounded by the fact that there seem to be no lanes on the road; that every driver is traveling at a speed of their own choosing, changing lanes at will; and that we are all supposedly heading towards the same destination with no one actually knowing its address.

As we approach the holiday of Shavuot and the celebration of receiving Torah, I appreciate more than ever the teaching of the Kli Yakar (Shlomo Ephraim Luntschitz of Prague, 1550-1619), who offered that the Torah avoids explicitly naming Shavuot as the occasion of the Torah's giving so that we may view every day as the day of revelation. Reflecting from the backseat of this journeying vessel, I question whether the destination does in fact lie somewhere ahead of us. What if this pandemic signifies a moment in time when we are asked to redefine the priorities of our lives, to reexamine the use of our resources, and to reconsider the distribution of our wealth? What if this is the moment of revelation to prepare us for future pandemics and crises that will confront humanity more than once each century? What if this is the time to which Torah speaks with more meaning and relevance than ever before?

Perhaps this is not a grim view of the future. Perhaps it is the opportunity to see Torah operate more fully in our lives. Perhaps it is our chance to shape a world of compassion and caution, of empathy and equality; a world that necessitates the constant navigation of risks and benefits, of conscious living; a world of respect for personal boundaries and concern for the boundaries set by others.

Perhaps we are already there.

57

NANNY'S KORONA KITCHEN

Sally Abrams

Our grandchildren, ages newborn to six, are part of the joyous fabric of everyday life. Two sets of kids live minutes away, enabling us to see them almost every day. Another set of precious grandkids live in Chicago. Too far for daily visits, but close enough for frequent and cherished long weekends together.

In early March, as the COVID-19 pandemic spread, we began hearing a steady beat of warnings advising grandparents to distance from the grandkids. Little kids can by asymptomatic carriers of infection, they cautioned, silently passing along a killer disease to the old folks.

At first, I brushed these warnings off. We are 'only' 63! Did they really mean us?? Who were they calling 'old" anyway?

Like the Baby Boomer that I am, this dose of reality landed hard. It took a few days for me to accept that while 63 is not 83, it is also not 43.

By late March we made the tough decision to temporarily isolate from the grandchildren.

The decision was driven primarily out of concern for our kids. Working from home while caring for young children, this is the Olympics of parenting. Their days are long and exhausting. I thought about how much stress we'd add to our kids' overflowing plates if either my husband or I got sick. That sealed it. We isolated from the grandkids to minimize our kids' worry for us.

We stayed at home, hothouse flowers in a carefully calibrated greenhouse. We saw the kids and grandkids via Facetime. Shabbat became Zoom Shabbat, a pale substitute for being together.

58

But isolating did nothing to address the real, every day needs of overextended, exhausted families at an uncertain, frightening time.

Then I had an idea.

A simple way I could help our local kids and grandkids, while maintaining a safe distance.

I could cook dinner. Every day except Saturday.

And that is how *Nanny's Korona Kitchen* began.

Sunday through Friday, dinner for two families, with three kids each, plus my husband and me, and our newlywed son and his wife, who were sheltering with us. Thirteen people.

I couldn't wait to get going!

Every morning I sent our kids a text of what would be on the menu for dinner that night. It was a tiny thing to look forward to at the end of the day.

Every afternoon I cooked a huge meal, packed it up in disposable containers, and our kids picked it up and took it home.

Every evening my phone pinged with grateful thank you texts.

You know who the Korona Kitchen helped most? Me.

Cooking for my crowd filled my afternoons with peace and purpose. By 3:30 or so, I'd be in the kitchen, chopping vegetables, stirring a sauce. Cooking's repetitive motions were calming. The steady progress from start to finish gave me a tangible sense of accomplishment. As one day blurred into the next, the dinner menu was often the only way I kept the days straight. Not Monday, not Tuesday, but the day I made shawarma, or the day I made salmon.

Pickup time gave me a brief daily interaction with our kids. At first, we were meticulous- dare I say, fanatic- regarding the distancing. I waved from the front door as the kids picked up the food containers on the front steps. Gradually, we eased up, they came inside, and we had a few minutes to chat before they hurried home.

And then, we all sat down to dinner, all thirteen of us, spread across three households.

But each table held the same meal.

A kind of togetherness.

After six very long weeks of isolation, we reasoned that our grandkids, also isolating, were as germ-free as they were ever going to be. This was the time to see them. Our distancing eased.

Nanny's Korona Kitchen has been churning out the meals for over two months. Winter gave way to spring, now summer is almost here. I'm going to a Monday-Wednesday-Friday schedule for these warm months, when picnics and patio restaurant dining are possible. But quit cooking? Not yet. My grandchildren are still home all the time. Their parents' days are still long and exhausting.

And that's why I will keep at it until things return to some form of normal. Cooking for them is still a big help. Helping them has helped me. Lightening their load has lightened mine.

Meanwhile, I pray that this terrible time of sickness, fear, and distancing will end, soon.

*(This is an updated version of an essay
that originally appeared on sallygabrams.com
March 27, 2020)*

HALLEL

Jaclyn Novatt

Sunday, December 20, 1992 I was called to the Torah as a bat mitzvah. My bat mitzvah was on the first day of Chanukah, so unlike my friends who all learned the Saturday morning Shabbat service, I learned and led Hallel. Hallel is a special service that we do on holidays, containing psalms 113-118. This is a very joyful service where we praise God and thank God for all of the wonderful things God has done. One of my favorite phrases translates to "This is the day the Lord has made – let us be glad and rejoice in it!"

Because I was unique among my friends in learning and leading the Hallel service, I felt a kind of ownership over it. In the years following my bat mitzvah, whether I was leading it or simply participating, whenever we did "my" special service, I felt a sense of pride and a connection to God that I never felt at any other time. I'm now 40 years old, and that feeling is still there. I began leading Hallel regularly at my shul several years ago, and it means so much to me. I love the joyful words and the happy melodies. I love the true sense of gratitude for and celebration of God's greatness that comes with Hallel.

This year I was to lead Hallel as usual for the four holy days of Pesach, and this turned virtual as my shul organized services over zoom. As I put on my tallit the first morning, my kids sprawled out on my bed next to the computer, I was concerned. Would it work to lead Hallel from my bedroom? Would it mean the same thing singing with faces on a computer as opposed to singing with my friends in person? And, most importantly, with so much tragedy and suffering happening both in my circle and in the whole world right now, how would I find the joy to sing these psalms? Does Hallel even make sense now?

Well... it turns out that Hallel not only makes sense, it was exactly what I needed. As I began to read the prayers, I found myself thinking about where we can find something to celebrate and be grateful for during this crisis. Where we can find God's presence?

I believe God's presence can be found in…

> •the compassion, knowledge, skills, and courage of every health care provider. For every patient fighting this horrible disease, there is a team of doctors, nurses, pharmacists, respiratory therapists, first responders, and countless other people fighting with them.

> •the hard work and bravery of the grocery and food service workers, sanitation engineers, postal employees, gas station attendants, bus and train drivers, police and security officers, fire fighters, hospital cleaning staff, and other essential workers who are helping us obtain the necessities and stay safe.

> •the journalists who are doing the best they can to keep us informed.

> •the daytime and nighttime television hosts and their crews doing shows from home to bring us some laughter and normalcy during this time.

> •the teachers and other school employees who are doing everything in their power to help our children transition to this new and temporary reality.

> •the parents who are doing their best to help their children navigate distance learning while doing their own jobs and trying to keep life as "normal" as possible.

> •everyone who is staying home and practicing social distancing.

> •the rainbows appearing in windows all over the world.

> •the nightly rounds of applause for healthcare workers in NYC and elsewhere.

• the musicians and artists sharing their work online to bring joy to others.

• the meals being provided to hospital employees and quarantined or otherwise homebound friends and neighbors.

• the clergy, social workers, and others who are working to help their community navigate this crisis.

• the creators of zoom and other technologies and the IT professionals that are helping us stay connected.

I can go on, but I'll stop here. As I sang the words of Hallel this Pesach, I found myself truly thankful. In this time of so much anxiety and worry, I find comfort in knowing that God's presence is truly found in so many ways amidst this crisis.

And I don't think I ever before sang these words of Hallel with such passion and urgency – "*Please God, save us now!*"

GROCERY STORE
Eden Wofsey

In the Talmud (Pesachim 50a) a story is told of Rav Yosef the son of Rabbi Yehoshua ben Levi who became ill and was on the verge of death. He recovered and his father asked him what he saw as he hovered between life and death. 'Olam hafuch Raiti,' he responded, "I saw an upside down world, father, those who are important and recognized in this world were low in that world and those who are unimportant in this world were important there and held high there." Rabbi Yehoshua told him "Olam Barur raitah', "The world of clarity you have seen."

"I'm not really anybody special, I'm just doing my job," said the dark-haired woman standing in a grocery store in Chicago. The store was beautiful and bright and there were yellow peppers piled just behind her on the left and tomatoes piled on her right a little further in the distance. The image of her standing there in a clean beautiful grocery store with an abundance of healthy lovely food was incredibly reassuring and so calming all in one brief moment.

I guess this was the point of the news clip, to show appreciation for people going out every day to keep things running for everyone. Her humility and good cheer were beautiful, and she was sincere. The news briefly highlighted this woman and some other people who they interviewed, and it felt like a real sign of our times during coronavirus.

One of the most intriguing and powerful parts of the coronavirus epidemic is that the importance of people who are sometimes invisible and taken for granted in our society has become steadily and inexorably more apparent. It has become abundantly clear that those who grow and harvest and pack and ship and stock and deliver, and clean and carry and then do it again and again and again are not only important but are the

64

foundation, the scaffolding, the beams, the walls the windows, the warp and woof of our society.

There are more famous people, more recognized, and certainly more remunerated people, but without the people who have to leave their houses to go to work none of that would matter.

Maybe it will always be thus, that those who serve and care for and clean and deliver will do so with graciousness and a smile, but it does not have to always be, that our society takes so many people for granted whom we so clearly depend on.

"I'm no one special," said the dark-haired, humble woman standing in the meticulously cleaned grocery store, next to the beautifully stacked piles of fruits and vegetables. My fervent hope as we move forward after our experience with the coronavirus is that in words and deeds and policy, as individuals and as a society we take actions to make it clear to this woman that she is wrong.

GOD WANTS US TO STAY INSIDE
Rabbi Joshua Hammerman

In the early days of the lockdown, I groped for ways to help my congregants grasp this ungraspable new reality. So I suggested that God wants us to stay inside, preferring constricted confines like those deep cleaned crevices of the Kotel, that birth canal from Egyptian slavery to freedom, or those narrow slits between our fingertips and nails, where both sanctity and viruses can grow.

Truth to tell, I don't have any idea what God prefers. But any God I invoke would want us to preserve human life at all costs.

The Talmud makes it clear that God wants us indoors during a pandemic, stating:

> *If there is plague in the city, gather your feet, i.e., limit the time you spend out of the house, as it is stated in the verse: "And none of you shall go out of the opening of his house until the morning."*
> *- (Bava Kamma 60b)*

But when morning turns to evening, and days to weeks and months, does God still want us to quarantine? To make that argument, I needed to bring in the heavy artillery: Kabbala.

Lurianic Kabbalists believe that God withdrew Godself into Godself, in effect creating space for the material/moral world to evolve. It is a complicated concept called Tzimtzum, but basically it means that God, like any good parent, backed away voluntarily so that the kids could mature on their own.

Okay, but what about tractate Avot, which says, *"Al tifrosh min ha'tzibur"* - "Do not separate yourself from the community"? I suggested that at this point in time, we need to amend that to, "Don't break from the community, but, like God, do create a modicum of personal space so that you and others may live."

There are times, such as these, when the act of separation from community is the most community-affirming thing we can do.

I backed up my claim with an array of supporting voices, ranging from Nachman of Bratzlav, who pleaded to God, "Grant me the ability to be alone," (although presumably meaning with nature and not crossword puzzles), to Greta Garbo, who "vanted" to be alone (the actual quote is, "I want to be left alone," though it's clear either way that she wasn't looking for the nearest minyan).

But in the end those prooftexts sounded hollow and no one was pining to make America Greta Again.

And then I heard the Voice of God in the form of this Twitter thread from a garbage collector, and I cried.

It made me understand that all this distancing ultimately is bringing us closer together. All over the world, we share the same destiny, the same fears, and the same desire to love our neighbor as ourselves.

Why does God want us to separate? Perhaps to help us understand that ultimately, the walls we hide behind, however necessary, are illusory, that we are all part of the same organism. There is no real place where "I" ends and "you" begin. The air we breathe is shared, not just with other humans but with all creatures, and we are engaged with vegetation in acts of mutual and reciprocal CPR as we barter oxygen for carbon dioxide. Every time I touch a doorknob, my body is welcoming in millions of your germs. Every time I sneeze, part of me is paying a visit to your immune system. Each hug is a potential dagger, not just for the person opposite you but for people on the other side of the world. Our fates are literally in the hands, washed or unwashed, of millions of people whom we will never meet. Our bodies – not just our souls - have become inseparable.

We've never been so lonely and fearful, sitting in our cold, quarantined rooms; but through our very separation, we've never been so inextricably interconnected.

Dr. Martin Luther King, Jr. wrote in his letter from the Birmingham jail,

> *"We are caught in an inescapable network of mutuality, tied in a single garment of destiny. Whatever affects one directly, affects all indirectly."*

I learned that from @JustMeTurtle, and that week when I took out my trash, I wrote "Thank You" on the lid, to hail an unseen, underappreciated hero.

CALLING ON OUR ANCESTORS FOR HEALING

Gila Silverman

The last few weeks have been difficult, as our entire world has changed in response to the coronavirus.

There have been times recently when I have been overwhelmed by fear and sadness and grief. At other times, I have savored the quiet of a slowed-down life and been awed by the generosity and compassion of people stepping up to take care of each other in so many different ways.

I am starting to understand that — like any grief — this one sometimes knocks me sideways when I least expect it, and that it is going to take a while to adjust to the "new normal" of a world turned upside-down.

At some point in the last few weeks, I started to think about Judaism's tools for times of illness and loss. Although I have spent years studying those very teachings and rituals, as both a student of our tradition and an anthropologist, I have had a very hard time seeing how these traditions could be useful. What we are facing felt too new, too big, too difficult to understand.

Yet when I revisited the Mi Shebeirach, the Jewish prayer for healing, I found much to guide me as I find my way through these strange and challenging times.

There are many variations of this prayer for healing. The most well-known may be by Debbie Friedman, which is sung in many Reform synagogues. This week, I found comfort in this version, from the Conservative movement's *Siddur Lev Shalem*:

> *May the one who blessed our ancestors,*
> *Abraham, Isaac, and Jacob,*
> *Sarah, Rebecca, Rachel, and Leah,*

69

Bring blessing and healing to all those who are ill.
May the Holy One full of compassion,
Restore them to health and vigor,
Granting them refuat ha'nefesh v'refuat ha'guf,
Spiritual and physical well-being,
Together with all others who are ill,
And may God grant strength to those who tend to them.
We hope and pray that healing is at hand.
And let us say, Amen.

By calling on our ancestors, we connect ourselves to all of those who came before us. We remember that — while they may never have faced anything exactly like what we face now — the generations before us did face tremendous challenges, and they prevailed and even thrived. As we invoke their names, we take strength from the examples of their lives and gain confidence that we too will be resilient and will prevail.

The Mi Shebeirach also reminds us that healing takes place in many ways — *Refuat ha'guf v'refuat ha'nefesh* — healing of body, healing of the soul. Illness, disease, and un-ease can affect us in many ways, sometimes in our bodies, sometimes in our minds and our spirits, sometimes in the places where all of these connect. Like many of us, I have experienced all of these in recent weeks. The Mi Shebeirach recognizes that healing, too, happens on many different levels, and it reminds us that, as we move through this strange time, we need to take care of our physical, emotional, and spiritual selves.

This prayer also teaches us that we are all in this together. The words of the Mi Shebeirach call for healing for all those who are ill everywhere. We have learned so clearly now that we are all interconnected, that our healing comes only when we work together as a community. Each of us has a role to play — for most of us, our role is to stay home. And, we can only succeed at the task at hand if every single one of us fulfills our role completely.

When we recite this Mi Shebeirach, we seek strength for all of those who are working for healing. In our world today, that includes medical personnel, and also grocery store workers, delivery drivers, sanitation crews, farmers and factory workers, those sewing masks,and 3D printing protective gear, policymakers, scientists and researchers, and — as I've already noted — all of us isolating in our homes.

Finally, the Mi Shebeirach also reminds us that it is up to us to watch out for one another. Traditionally, you do not say the Mi Shebeirach for yourself; you say it for someone else. It is one of the many ways that we can connect to each other, prompting us to reach out in whatever ways we can to ensure that we help each other to stay healthy, and, when needed, that we help each other continue moving toward healing — physically, emotionally, and spiritually.

As we make our way through these uncertain and challenging times, may we all be blessed with strength and resilience, courage and connection. May we be well, in our bodies and in our spirits, and may we continue to work together, to heal each other, our community, and our world.

(This essay originally appeared in the Arizona Jewish Post
April 17 2020)

A SIMPLE SMILE
Jake Epstein

I can't seem to remember what the smile of a stranger looks like.

The warm, unassuming look someone gives as they pass by. It didn't matter if it was on the street, boarding a flight or in line at my favorite ice cream store. From those we've never met before, a smile meant nothing more than a stranger's friendly acknowledgement of your existence.

Now, as the coronavirus pandemic sweeps across our world as we know it, masks cover any hint of a smile. Everywhere in public, people go about their daily lives with masks, thankfully, as a way to help curb the spread of the virus.

It's been so long since I've seen the genuine smile of a stranger.

Ordering food or walking past people in the park, conversation is muffled by the restrictive masks — all you truly have is the look in someone's eyes or the shape their eyebrows make in response to a remark.

But a smile — the most innocent measure of acknowledgement we, as humans, have — was stripped from the arsenal of our interactions or mannerisms that we can choose from when we come across people.

While masks do an excellent job of helping us combat this pandemic, they also take away from our ability to show emotion in public. The nature of the situation is almost dystopian, and people avoid each other in fear of spreading or contracting the virus.

Spending time in public, especially as the warm summer weather teeters on our horizon, can seem almost nightmarish, as I long for any sort of resemblance for normalcy. I miss the interactions I used to have with strangers. After all, a friend always starts as a stranger. Few things come close to the raw excitement of meeting new people.

But I know this won't happen soon, and it's a reality I've been forced to accept.

There are many themes that have been defined by this pandemic. One of them has been the nature of adaptation, and our ability to change the trajectory of our plans, both big and small, to be as flexible as possible.

The pandemic has proven to us that the only certainty is uncertainty.

I ACTUALLY SPRAYED MY CAT LULU WITH ALCOHOL!

Caren Singer

What do we do when life becomes so crazy that we can't do the things we usually do, and we can't do things the way we usually do? We adapt; we persevere—just as Jews have been doing for thousands of years since the destruction of the Temple.

I have always been the organic, natural cleaners and homeopathic-remedy-kind-of-girl. I had never bought any Lysol product in my life, but March 11th, when the Lysol Wipes appeared on the Gelson's shelf—for all of ten minutes—Robert and I each bought two.

That Sunday, we had planned to meet our friend Greg at the Hollywood Outdoor Farmers' Market where Robert and I have gone religiously since its opening twenty-nine years ago, but with COVID-19 cases growing in Los Angeles, Greg decided not to join us. "You are braver than I," he said.

Robert and I persevered. We would be careful even though we didn't even think of wearing masks then. Almost no one did. Early on, one of the vendors sneezed—right at me—from about two feet away. I ran to the parking lot and up the stairs to our car where I had those Lysol wipes, and I Lysoled my entire face— my eyes, my nose—even my nasal cavity. This was another first—resourceful—but terrible for my complexion. I would know in fourteen days whether I had contracted the virus.

Sadly, we haven't been to the Market since.

March 16 was the last day we had students in our home. It just wasn't safe anymore. We had to adapt. The following Monday, thanks to technical support from our nephew Adam, we started doing our teaching sessions on Zoom. Albeit fewer students than usual, we are fortunate that we can work at all and gratified to be able to support our students during these

74

trying times.

On March 30th, one of our neighbors called to say she and James were going to Gelson's and asked what we needed?

"That's so kind of you," I said, a bit surprised. "I have been going to the store, darting about, shopping for us and for my elderly neighbor. "It's scary though," I added.

"Well we're going tomorrow," she says. "Send me your list." That's the good news part of the story.

"Thank you so much," I said, deeply touched by this act of kindness. "And the next time we go to Gelson's, I will call you and see what you need," I offer.

"No," she says. "You and Robert shouldn't be going out now."

Really? Uh oh, I think. And this is the bad news part of the story. I have been pegged as older, even when I try so hard to be youthful — and even after I mentioned my elderly neighbor.

We took Vanessa's advice in earnest though, and she and James continue to shop for us, as do Giancarlo, Kate and Robert, and Cousin Joey. We are lucky to have their help because Vanessa was right.

So what do we do with the groceries when we get them? We disinfect everything.
We used to spend three and half-hours disinfecting three bags of groceries before we adapted and became more resourceful. I knew the alcohol wouldn't last, but Clorox made me sick. Mind over matter, I thought, I can use Clorox too, and sadly, now I do.

Even with a fan raging in the window, we locked the cats out of the kitchen because of the fumes and because we didn't want them to touch anything that might be infected, and as far as I was and still am concerned, everything might be.

During one of these disinfect-the-groceries-marathons, I stepped away for a minute, and when I returned, Lulu had somehow nosed her way through the wood-slatted door into the kitchen. She knows how to persevere too. And I saw her brush against one of the grocery bags. Oh

75

no!

Robert turned white.

"You can not avoid petting Lulu for nine days," I tell him—as we do with the mail, the grocery bags and the boxes. "She will be in our bed tonight. You have to forget about it. She didn't get COVID-19 from the grocery bag," I say with as much conviction as I can muster, but secretly, I thought, we will know in two weeks.

I put Lulu in the sink and washed her with Dr. Bronner's Hemp and Tea Tree Oil Soap. She was not happy about it.

I later put a lighter spin on this scary incident when I retell it to friends and family. "You will be proud of me," I laugh; "I didn't spray Lulu with alcohol or Clorox Bleach." That was April 6th.

Ten days later, we had another incident. Garbage day has become scary too, like getting the mail out of the mail slot or the newspapers out of the ivy with the kitchen tongs, one of the most valuable and versatile tools for these times. When I went outside to deposit the big bag of garbage, Little Lulu had pushed the back door open and much to my horror was standing on the possibly COVID-19 infested back porch. Oh no—my new mantra.

I put poor Lulu in the sink again and thoroughly washed her feet with Dr. Bronner's Soap. But then I was afraid that wasn't good enough. So what did I do? G-d help me; I sprayed Lulu with alcohol—just her feet— and after a minute, rinsed it off and thought, I will know in two weeks.

"And what about Passover?" my niece Sarah asked me. Sarah was supposed to be coming in from Israel and spending a week with us, sleeping on our couch, her Grandma Goldryn's couch. When the Jews fled from Egypt and had no leavened bread? They ate matzoh. So what would we do? We would have a Zoom Seder, and we did. I even decorated, not as elaborately as usual, but still, the Zoom view had lovely lights, and Jewish stars, and candles, and it was wonderful!

Now it's June 5th. Two of my friends have died—one just before Passover—Lori Golden of the Pet Press—friend to the animal humane community—and another on June 2nd, Ivette Silberman, my friend from Rose Gold's legendary modern dance class at Fairfax High School— neither from COVID-19. And in between, George Floyd was murdered, and the country is in a state of unrest, and the super-secret enemy of all people, the one that does not discriminate — COVID-19 — is yet afoot.

Still, I am hopeful as Robert, Lulu, Izzy, and I are about to make our circle of love and light the Shabbos candles. This will not go on forever, and we will persevere. It's in our DNA. What we do now matters. Through resourcefulness and acts of kindness, our resiliency will win out.

JERUSALEM, 19 APRIL 2020
Timna Seligman

It's Four f-cking thirty in the morning. I've been lying in bed since I turned the light out at 1 am, but haven't fallen asleep. I think I may have dozed for a while. My son joined me at some point. His preteen dreams sometimes turn dark and wake him, then he seeks comfort with me. He keeps stealing the duvet and trying to sleep on the diagonal, pushing me closer to the edge (literally and figuratively). At least he is asleep and calm now.

I'm sure I've never heard these Easter bells before. They started at Three, a doleful roll through the open window rather than a bright daytime chime. When they finished there was a mosquito. She bit on my knee. I only heard the buzz when it began to itch. I knew what would come next; I was waiting for it, yearning for the call. The Muezzin started long, low and mournful. I only ever hear it at this quietest hour that is four in the morning. I love it, gently washing across the predawn sky. First one sole voice, then a quiet, distant chorus. It soothes the soul, and usually, if it has been a bad night and I've been tossing and turning, it calms my mind and I finally manage to drift off for a few hours before the alarm goes off, But this is Corona time. We live by a different schedule, and no alarm has been set. But this is Corona time. And tonight I'm wired. And scared. Even as I search for the comfort in the sounds, I don't think it's going to do its magic tonight (this morning?). Soon the harmonious voices will be replaced by the craw of the crows who give a cacophonous undertone to the melodious dawn chorus. They in turn should be drowned out by the rumble of busses and garbage trucks as the city come to life. School and work brings people out of the houses and onto the streets, the sounds change. It is no longer the music of the night, but the noise of mundane day, and the enchantment of the eternal Jerusalem dawn will be lost. But this is Corona time. The garbage truck, that essential service so derided in normal times, comes by on schedule, a solo act. The first bus and then the second come later, piercing the early morning, occasional interruptions to the quiet rather than a continuum of disruption. And still, I do not sleep.

This is Corona time. It wasn't the bells or the Muezzin keeping me awake. Not even the crows. I love the gentle night sounds. Something else happened that night. Many friends commented that they could not sleep. That night, Corona time seemed to hang in the air like a thick, inescapable fog... It wasn't the bells or the Muezzin keeping me awake. Not even the crows. That night it was Corona time. And we all felt it in those quiet early hours when our defenses were down.

SQUEAKY THE MOUSE IS LIVING IN OUR HOUSE AS THE WORLD BURNS DOWN

Sarah Tuttle-Singer

We have a mouse in our house.

He moved in about a month into COVID-19.

And we've been Sheltering in Place together ever since.

There are a lot of things that are my fault, but this isn't one of them: I've been keeping the house super clean because I am an anxious germophobe on a good day, and then throw in a litttle COVID-19 for funsies, and I become That Woman who washes and scrubs and sanitizes the whole entire universe.

In other words, I become my mother Z"L.

But for real: I wash the floors every day, the counters too – with bleach. I clean all the tables, and the door knobs and even the light switches. Obvs the sinks and toilet, too.

Like, our house legit smells like a swimming pool.

So this *really* isn't my fault.

The first time I saw the mouse, he was just a streak of grey in the kitchen. I thought maybe I hallucinated. I googled "COVID-19" and "hallucinations" and "grey streaks."

Apparently, hallucinating grey streaks in the kitchen is not a symptom of COVID-19.

I kept telling myself there is no way we have a mouse. The house is so clean, we have a dog… the neighbors' cats all hang out on our porch… Then, I heard the squeaks.

(BTW "hearing squeaks" and "auditory hallucinations" are also not symptoms of COVID-19)

I managed to convince myself that I just had too much ear wax. You're welcome for the visual.

But then, one evening, I saw the first real legit signs in a kitchen drawer. I won't get into the details, but trust me: Mouse shit is very, very real and definitely not a hallucination and ALSO not a symptom of COVID-19 — although maybe it causes COVID-19.

I should probably google that.

I poured bleach over everything. All the surfaces.

Like, even the neighbor's front porch.

(PSA: Do not google "Hantavirus.")

My kids named the mouse Squeaky.

I fucking hate mice and I fucking hate Squeaky.

Rodents of any shape or size are my worst nightmare — like, I literally I have nightmares about them — I don't mind snakes — in fact, I like them. Spiders are rad. A big huge lion could come strolling into my front yard, but that wouldn't bother me.

But a mouse? A little grey house mouse? I cannot deal.

I fucking hate mice.

I called the landlord.

He brought over a bottle of this thing you spray into the cracks in the house.

Our house was built in 1949. It is one year younger than the State of Israel. In other words, our house is charming and quaint and has good bone structure, but there are literally cracks everywhere. I found some of them, and sprayed the foam — but then it backfired and got into my hair.

The landlord brought over another bottle.

I got more in my hair.

Have you ever seen the TV show "I Love Lucy"? I am living an episode of I Love Lucy. A two-month episode of I Love Lucy. With wall sealant in my hair. And a mouse in the house.We got a humane trap at ACE hardware — the kind where you put a little thing of whatever on a hook, and theoretically when Squeaky takes the bait, the trap shuts, and Squeaky stays safe until we release him in the fields.

Or flush him down the toilet.

I didn't write that. I would *never* flush Squeaky down the toilet.

Anyway: Squeaky took the bait, had himself a grand old time, and then somehow strolled out of the trap.

I fucking hate mice.

Also, I changed my mind. I *will* flush Squeaky down the toilet.

And during all of this, the numbers of folks sick with COVID-19 climbed throughout Israel and the world, the dead right along with them.

Several close friends were incapacitated for weeks — some still are.

Three of my friends lost their parents.

My family in LA — way too far away.

And it feels like there are no more grownups close by to make the mouse go away.

My GOD I miss grownups.

I stopped sleeping at night.

Then we got a kitten.

Not because we want her to kill Squeaky, but maybe a little because we want her to kill Squeaky.

We got her when she was 6 weeks old, and only marginally larger than Squeaky.

We named her Tzippy.

I think Tzippy and Squeaky met in the teeny tiny space between the oven and the kitchen counter and became best of friends, so *that* didn't help. So then we called an exterminator.

TRIGGER WARNING: If you have issues with killing rodents, stop reading. For real.

The exterminator set poison bait outside. He also set glue traps where theoretically Squeaky takes the bait and gets stuck and then dies.

Squeaky found the glue traps. And ate the bait. And then got out of the glue traps. I know this because the glue traps all have mouse shit in them, and no mouse.

And Squeaky is still alive.

I know this because I continue to see him and hear him -- and not just in my nightmares, but when I'm awake, too.

I fucking hate mice.

He's been hiding out in the kitchen. He even played dead at one point, only to scurry away when we got closer to try to get him.

The kitten is now 8 weeks old and she's totally adorable and totally useless.

I think she's even protecting him, which is what I guess friends are *supposed* to do, but still: Not cool. She should be on MY side.

And yesterday was the worst. I spent over two hours looking for his nest, spraying bleach in random places, trying to figure out where he goes when he goes…

It doesn't take Sigmund Freud to figure out why yesterday was so bad. Yesterday WAS bad.

Yesterday was REALLY bad.

I'm seeing the COVID-19 numbers rise again as people get sick here in Israel because the virus never went away to begin with, and so the little forays we've been making out into the world are going to end for us until it feels safer, and honestly? I don't know if it will ever feel safer.

The kids won't be going back to school anytime soon, and the house feels like it's shrinking, plus I keep seeing that streak of grey everywhere now, and hearing the scratches in the walls, and the place I should feel safest now feels invaded and violated.

And outside is even worse: George Floyd was murdered on camera in America, and many of my friends have Black sons and daughters and have had to have "the talk" with them about what to do if they're arrested so that they can survive the police.

Read that sentence again:

And George Floyd was murdered on camera in America, and many of my friends have Black sons and daughters and have had to have "the talk" with them about what to do if they're arrested so that they can survive the police.

And cities across America are seething — people are in so much pain, and my hometown of Los Angeles is burning. We've ignored the pox of racism upon our house for far too long, and now it is fire.

And then Iyad Halak was gunned down in the Old City — shot at least seven times in the back — because he's an Arab and the police thought the cell phone in his hand that he used to stay in contact with his mom and dad was a weapon, when he really was just an Autistic 32-year-old, who was scared and didn't know he was supposed to stop when the men with guns yelled at him.

It's like nothing is safe, and everything is infected and infested and stomach churning, and the world is falling apart and out of the cracks come this viscous liquid that is poisoning our lungs and our intestines and our thoughts and our hopes and the future and I FUCKING HATE MICE.

84

And the whole world as I know it is burning down — the illusions of safety, the cushions of basic human decency.... engulfed in noxious flames. A pox upon our house.

My eyes sting.

Every noise sets my teeth on edge.

Even the kids.

The world feels very, very dark – and I just want some sign – anything! – that there is light somewhere, but I can't see it. All I see is the darkness dropping, and the mouse in the corner, and the world burning outside the window — it's all just too much and I lost it after dinner.

I dropped the pan on the floor, and my ears rang with the sound of metal on tile and I screamed.

"What's wrong?" my son asked when I screamed through my teeth from the bowels of my soul.

"I FUCKING HATE MICE. THEY DISGUST ME! THEY TERRIFY ME! THEY MAKE ME WANT TO RIP MY SKIN OFF. I FUCKING HATE MICE!" I screamed, just like the responsible adult I am.

My son patted my hand.

"I understand Mom. I feel the same way about Moshiko." (Moshiko is a boy in my son's class. Moshiko is also not his real name.)

I love my son.

Anyway. We went to Home Center to try a different kind of humane trap – It looks like a tube. I couldn't figure out how it works, so we asked one of the guys at the store, and he didn't know, so he asked someone else, who didn't know, and finally they asked Abu Elias who was sitting on one of the lounge chairs in the gardening section.

Abu Elias is very senior and very respected.

But I'm not actually sure if he works at Home Center.

He showed us how to put in some peanut butter, balance it carefully and when Squeaky comes in, the trap shuts, and Squeaky gets to have his peanut butter and we get to take Squeaky out to the fields.

(Or the toilet depending on my mood.)

We set the trap.

We used Skippy.

Tzippy kept jumping on the trap to close it and protect her friend.

I locked her out of the kitchen.

We waited.

Suddenly, the trap snapped. I was thrilled. I went to see if it was for real – and I opened the top just a crack and saw something grey fluttering inside. I screamed — like a beautiful, operatic scream. Like, I think missed my calling and I should be in the Magic Flute and sing The Queen of the Night.

Aaaaah…

Meine Tochter nimmermehr.

Aaaaah…

So bist du meine Tochter nimmermehrrrrrrrrrrrrrrrrrrrr

My kids came running.

"We got him!" We all high-fived.

We put on our shoes and went outside.

I held the tube out from me as far away as I could.

The stars shone bright in the big black sky.

I could hear the nightbirds calling.

I felt peace descend for the first time in months — we got him. The Mouse in our House was now in the tube, and I could sort things out, and compartmentalize, and solve everything one step at a time.

We got to the fields and I could feel the wind on my face.

"Shall we let him go here?" I asked.

"Yes," they answered.

I put down the tube.

I recoiled in horror and disgust as I lifted the door....

And out flew a moth.

Not a mouse. A moth.

A tiny grey moth.

A tiny grey moth that fluttered gently toward the stars.

So fuck my life, Squeaky is still in the house.

And George Floyd couldn't breathe and he was murdered.

And America is burning along with the last vestiges of the safety I once felt in the world.

And Iyad Halak was shot in the back at least seven times on his way to his school for people with special needs.

And there are cracks in the walls, and in the world, and in my heart and everywhere, and nothing feels safe anymore, not even my house.

And I fucking hate mice.

But… the stars were out as we walked back from the fields, back home, to a house full of cracks… and in all this darkness, the stars shine more brightly than I've ever seen.

(Originally published on Times of Israel May 31, 2020)

A CRUEL AND UNUSUAL THEOLOGY
David S. Zinberg

It must have been very hard to pay Job a shiva call. What can you say to someone who has just lost everything? All ten children killed in a single day. A prodigious estate decimated by bandits and fire. Then, to deepen his sorrow, indignity, and loneliness, Job's entire body is wracked with a painful and deforming skin disease.

Yet, three friends found the courage to visit him.

As we all know, however, these were friends with an agenda. They were less interested in consoling Job than in convincing him — and no doubt themselves — in chapter after chapter of pompous sermonizing, that he deserved to suffer because God could not have punished him in vain. Despite your claims of piety and model citizenship, they said while wagging their fingers, you, Job, must have done something wrong. Think hard enough and it will come to you.

Our current experience includes, on some level, elements of mourning. For many of us, the anguish of social isolation is real. Those who are not sick themselves may suffer from the fear that they or a loved one will soon contract our modern global plague. Many have already lost income and some will lose their entire livelihood. Families have been separated. Our lives have been upended by privations large and small, not necessarily comparable to the sufferings of Job, but in ways that are just as tangible, physically, emotionally, and financially.

For millennia since the Book of Job was written, and likely millennia before, religious thinkers and philosophers have struggled with the problem of evil. How could an all-powerful and all-knowing God inflict (or allow) suffering on human beings, especially children, who have never sinned? Like Abraham, people of faith expect God to act justly, and every religion has one or more solutions to this problem. Following major catastrophes in our own history, especially the Holocaust, the problem took on a new urgency, forcing Jewish thinkers to revisit traditional responses.

The temptation to provide a theological exegesis of our current trials may be too great to overcome. Some religious people will always see divine messages in human suffering. And there are multiple variations on the theme: Perhaps the pandemic should be taken as a spur to introspection, a sort of global psychic reset. A more extreme version interprets coronavirus as divine punishment for a whole host of moral and religious sins; a Noah's flood for our times. Someone even suggested recently that antisemities who blame the Jews for all the world's ills — including, of course, coronavirus — are actually correct because the Jewish people, as the metaphysical firstborn among the nations, have not modeled ethical behavior to their younger siblings and, therefore, the entire world must suffer on their account.

The problem with some of these ideas is not so much that they are speculative and untestable, but that they are offensive, especially when spoken in front of a world in semi-mourning, seeking comfort instead of rationalization. Yes, you will find theology of this kind in rabbinic literature. But after Auschwitz, the Talmudic rabbis themselves would consider it obsolete. Some ideas do come with an expiration date.

There are many things to say at a shiva visit, but thoughtful and sensitive people will hesitate to serve up theology, even in small portions. As intellectually satisfying as any particular explanation may or may not be, to tell someone in mourning that you have determined the cosmic reason for their loss and suffering is quite literally cold comfort. It is also, of course, supremely arrogant to think that you have discovered the reason.

The rabbinic establishment deserves the highest credit for their wisdom and courage in shutting down our shuls and yeshivot. We appreciate such practical life-saving measures and encourage more of the same.

We should also expect high profile rabbis to exercise humility, empathy, tact, and common sense — the latter known as "sechel" in the vernacular — before pronouncing grandiose solutions to intractable problems, solutions that will satisfy few modern people, and alienate many.

In the final chapter of Job (42:7), God says to Eliphaz the Temanite: "I am incensed at you and your two friends, for you have not spoken the truth about Me as did My servant Job." What, then, was the truth behind Job's pain? Because we are not God, we are not supposed to know — that is the book's message. We can be certain, though, especially now, of this: It is better to offer a hand in true friendship, though it leaves an ultimate problem unresolved, than to speak an ugly untruth.

(Originally published on Times of Israel
March 23, 2020)

ON DEREKH ERETZ AND RUAH HAKODESH: THE WAY OF THE WORLD AND THE HOLY SPIRIT

Lawrence Kaplan

Two days ago was Shabbat Hol ha-Moed Passover, when traditionally the Song of Songs [=SoS] is read in the Synagogue. SoS, together with Proverbs and Kohelet (Ecclesiastes), are all attributed by the Bible to King Solomon.

There are two rabbinic views regarding the order in which King Solomon authored these three books. R. Yonatan's view is that he wrote these three works at three different stages in his life. He first authored SoS, then Proverbs, then Kohelet. And R. Yonatan brings support for his view from *Derekh Eretz*, the customary way of the world, or, perhaps here, people's ordinary life trajectory. "In one's youth one sings love songs, when one grows up one recites sententious proverbs, when one gets old one reflects on life's vanity." A second, widely-held view is that "the holy spirit," *Ruah HaKodesh*, "rested on him and he recited these three books: Proverbs, Kohelet, and SoS." What is striking is the order: first Proverbs, then Kohelet, then SoS. Here we have a different chronological order from that suggested by R. Yonatan. According to this view, the Holy Spirit devolved on Solomon in his mature years. It would make sense, then, taking R. Yonatan's paradigm, that he first recited Proverbs, and then, when old and disillusioned, Kohelet. How, though, are we to account for the anomalous place of SoS in this view as the *last* book Solomon wrote, *after* Proverbs and Kohelet?

But this is precisely the difference between *Derekh Eretz*, the customary way of the world, and *Ruah HaKodesh*, divine inspiration. According to the first view, as we saw, Solomon's authorship of these three books followed the path of *Derekh Eretz*, one's normal life trajectory, which leads from the exuberance of youth to the maturity and sententiousness of adulthood to the melancholy of old age — and that is the end of the matter. But according to the second view, while Solomon in his maturity first followed the path of *Derekh Eretz*, teaching the practical wisdom of Proverbs in his adulthood and engaging in the melancholy, disillusioned reflections of Kohelet in his old age, that was not the end of the matter. Kohelet was NOT Solomon's last word. For drawing upon *Ruah HaKodesh*, the inspiration of the Holy Spirit, Solomon was able to transcend, to overcome his melancholy and depression and find within himself the strength to begin anew and sing, with youth's rapturous exuberance, SoS, that great song of the individual's and community's love of God.

When the corona virus first struck, we were in a Proverbs mode. We searched for practical wisdom, perhaps reflected on those proverbs calling for preparation and cooperation. We contemplated the unpredictability of life, and many of us cited the verse "Many are the designs in the heart of a man, but it's the Lord's counsel that is fulfilled" (Prov. 19:21). But with the virus' inexorable spread and exponential growth, with the ever growing number of sick, dying, and dead, with the hospitals and health care professionals being overwhelmed, with the need to practice social isolation, with the devastation of the economy, we sank into a Kohelet mood, and together with the melancholy King recited "Vanity of vanities. All is vanity" (Eccles. 1:2). The verse which seems best to reflect our current condition is: "Like fish caught in a evil net, and like birds held in a trap, so men are ensnared by an evil time, when it suddenly falls upon them" (Eccles. 9:12).

This year, with schools and synagogues closed down, we did not recite SoS two days ago. The question is: Once this plague is over, once synagogues reopen, will we be able to recite SoS again, recite it, that is, in the spirit of rapturous exuberance it demands? We are no longer privy to divine inspiration. But though we cannot draw direct inspiration from God, we can draw wisdom and inspiration from our families, our communities, our people, our Torah and tradition. May we, individually and collectively, find within ourselves the strength and hope to overcome and transcend our anxieties and depression, to not allow Kohelet to be the last word, but to move on, to once again hope, build, rejoice, and sing.

MY TWEEN IS FROZEN IN PLACE, & I AM MOMENTARILY ABLE TO RELAX

Estelle Erasmus

Before COVID, anxiety lay on my chest like an elephant as I worried who my daughter was friends with, whether anyone was being a mean girl, whether her friends' moms were safe drivers, whether sick kids were showing up in school, whether boys were being too physical during gym, and on. Sheltering in place has moved all these worries offstage.

Instead, there is an invisible, silent enemy beyond the walls of our home, and the hardships are about the absence of those relationships, a coming adolescence put on pause.

While in quarantine, I'm missing my aging parents (who are also in lockdown), while my 11-year-old daughter is forgoing rites of passage like her fifth grade graduation ceremony, spring concert, and April birthday party.

Though a million memes and PSAs have joked about how frustrating it is for parents to have kids underfoot all the time, I have discovered a silver lining: a reprieve from my hypervigilance as parent of a blossoming tween.

Now, as we shelter in place, our family is making the best of our new normal. As a writing professor at New York University, I'm doing Zoom classes with my students, and my husband is situated in the dining room on daylong conference calls as my daughter does remote learning. As her changing friends group transforms from real time to FaceTime, I know exactly what she is doing (mainly Roblox) and whom she is doing it with.

93

To keep her safe online, I've locked down her privacy and I've installed the app Bark, which monitors texts, email, apps, and social media so I can be notified of potential cyberbullying, violent or sexually inappropriate chat the minute it happens. Plus while ensconced in our home, she isn't meeting anyone new, and nobody is offering her drugs or the chance to vape (nobody did before, but now they really can't).

If there were a perfect age to be home during a pandemic, from this mom's point of view, it would be during the tweenage years. For now at least my daughter isn't too old to favor her friends over her parents (though I know that day is coming). During the week, in between classes, we bake together and she explores science for free via NASA. On weekends, we play fun family games like Kids Against Maturity, Never Have I Ever, Dance Charades, and Spontaneous. I bought her a mini trampoline for our balcony and we do Zoom workouts. We did a virtual scavenger hunt for her birthday and she is building a "Life in the Time of Corona" time capsule. In between school and FaceTime, she tries on makeup using my makeup mirror and plays tug of war with our pre-pandemic puppy whom we had the prescience to bring home in October (like us, she desperately needs a trip to the salon).

I will let go once again when I need to return her to the world.

During moments of boredom and when she is most upset at being stuck inside, I remind my daughter to look at the big picture: like generations before us who survived the Spanish Flu, the world wars, and 9/11, our mantra is "this too shall pass." In the meantime, I want her to get through this time unscathed, so I parse what I say, and keep her away from images of sick people on ventilators and makeshift morgues.

While bereft about what's happening globally, it gives me solace that even if I can't protect anyone else, I can still protect her.

Our sheltering in place is working. The curve appears to be flattening, although our state's governor says there is a caveat: until we get a vaccine, he believes students will need to wear masks if they go back to school this year. Those images conjure up a horror scene out of a dystopian novel that I can't let my mind rest on too long.

Like all parents, I can't control what is happening around me and I'm struggling to adjust. I know that we will be going back and it is unrealistic to think that I can surround my daughter with a force field of love that will permanently keep her safe. I will let go once again when I need to return her to the world. I think I understand better than before what is truly worth worrying about and what isn't all that important. But just for now, before life reforms into the next new normal, I've found a safe place at home surrounded by my family where despite being mom 24/7 I can relax.

While the world pays rapt attention to its breathing, I will exhale.

Even if it's just at home and just for the moment.

(This essay originally appeared on Romper
May 4, 2020.)

I FOUND MY FIRST GRAY HAIR
THE OTHER DAY

Rivka Hellendall

I found my first gray hair the other day.

I was doing my make-up and standing in super-close proximity to the mirror, and there it was, growing out of my side parting. At first, I thought it was bleached from the sun, although I haven't spent that much time in the sun lately. My never-been-dyed hair color is a fairly dark brown, with some dark blonde sunlit strands in between. In the summer, the hair around my forehead and temples lights up further to a golden yellow color, like a strange little halo. When I saw this particular hair, I thought, for a hot second, that this hair further marked the beginning of spring. But it didn't. I held it between my thumb and index finger. This hair was, upon close examination, silver-colored, and a little too curly-wiry in comparison to the surrounding ones. This baby hair was undoubtedly my first gray hair.

It would be easy to make a bunch of seemingly profound yet at the same time incredibly mundane observations about this one gray hair: that it didn't mark spring and new sunlight, but rather my own emerging aging process, the passing of the "seasons" in my own life and whatnot. Those statements sound too grandiose for me, too much like a parody of the earthy hippie lady type that I love but happen not to be at all. Still, I turned 24 years old last month, and maybe I would have been annoyed at this gray hair under normal, non-Corona circumstances. I can imagine my old self, an old self that I didn't realize had renewed until about two weeks ago, thinking: wasn't I too young for gray hair? Didn't I have better genes? My mom didn't sprout any gray hairs until a few years ago, and she is at an age where so many women have been coloring their hair for decades. (She still hasn't, by the way, and it looks great.) Her grandmother's hair was close to jet black until she was seventy years old. Of course, we never know what we'll look like in the future, and this gray hair was my first tiny confrontation with that reality, flowing around in an imaginary breeze.

Still, what I really felt when I pinched that hair between my thumb and index finger was a sense of real, joyous wonder, a feeling close to relief. I almost giggled to myself, and completely by myself. I had not gone insane, not yet.

My father went to the local clinic the day before I saw the hair. He was rushed to the hospital with COVID-19 on the same night. He likely got the virus from one of my brothers and me, who went to a number of Purim parties two days before social distancing was enforced in the Jewish community as well as country-wide. We'd spent Purim celebrating Haman's evil decree to kill the Jews. Haman had chosen the date for the genocide to happen on the 14th of Adar by casting lots, that is, he left the day of the decision up to chance. I did not believe that it was chance at play when my father got COVID-19, but the misfortune of him being one out of roughly four members of the community who became deathly ill still hurt: why him? He is not yet sixty and in good health overall. We didn't know.

Testing materials were and are very scarce in The Netherlands. He had been really ill and breathing shallowly for days before his hospitalization, but he reached a low on March 25th. When the ambulance came, the EMTs told my mom and me that we could follow them in our car to the hospital. I remember trying to put together an emergency WhatsApp video call with my siblings through the haze of anxiety. When we got to the hospital, the receptionist stopped us at the entrance. Why would the EMTs tell you to follow them? He asked. Surely you couldn't see or visit him anyway in the isolated ward. The see-through sliding doors remained shut, so we left, scared and completely dumbfounded by his realistic yet surreal response. We had no idea when we would see him again, even though he was a ten-minute drive away.

We cleaned the house from top to bottom the next day, when my brother, of whom we weren't sure whether he had had the virus yet, came home from his student apartment to be with us. My dad was on a ventilator for the foreseeable future, closer to Death than to Life. I remember cleaning the bathroom while my eyes stung from tears and bleach that Friday morning.

My dad contracted the virus two weeks before Pesach. My mom, my three

97

siblings, and I did not know whether he would live through Pesach, let alone be home for it. We held two Seders without him. Though we wanted the ordeal to be over, though the word "enough" did not even begin to cut how we felt about the stress and the anxiety about my dad, we omitted Dayenu on both nights. It would not be the same without my dad, by far the most enthusiastic singer of Dayenu, pounding his fist rhythmically on the table. Our local Jewish community delivered frozen meals shortly before, during, and after Pesach. My sister and I made extensive meal plans with them, noting who wanted to eat what dish and when. Our moods shifted from panicked and worried to numb and from grateful to hopeful and back. I stayed in touch with my friends and family online mostly, whether they lived five minutes from me or more than 5,000 miles. I taught my 90-year-old grandparents how to use Zoom to video chat with their children and grandchildren in the US. God knows when we are all going to see each other again.

My dad was discharged from the hospital on the eighth day of Pesach after spending more than two weeks in the ICU, on a ventilator, and another week on an isolated COVID-19 ward. The hospital staff had arranged iPads on the ward so he could video chat with us. When he asked what the plan was for Pesach, we had to tell him over Skype that he had completely missed Seder that year. Thank God there will be a next year for him: here, in Jerusalem, it doesn't matter to me. At least he's alive and recovering well.

I had no idea how much my first gray hair would ultimately mean to me so soon after I found it; how much more it would shake up my ideas about fate, mortality, and death so dramatically when I almost lost my father to COVID-19. I am proud of the old me, the me before my father nearly died and the mirror confronted me with my own mortality in the middle of a global crisis, because I was able to laugh about it from a genuine place. I am proud of the new me, who lived through this grueling time and has come out with so much more appreciation for the preciousness of life and good health. That is a cause for celebration.

(This essay originally appeared in The Times of Israel
March 26, 2020.)

A SMALLER, SIMPLER CIRCLE OF LIFE
Rabbi Hannah Estrin

Before the COVID -19 pandemic I had a favorite walking train which I would frequent several times a week. This little piece of heaven on earth is filled with 700-year-old oak trees and beautiful citrus trees. On one of my last visits before the stay-at-home order was given, I was greeted not only by the sounds of nature and the shade of the magnificent trees but by a yearly delight - the smell of citrus blossoms.

As I drank in the scent of the blossoms I concurrently reached up and picked an orange. Citrus trees are the only trees I know where fruit remains on the tree while it is preparing for the next crop by producing flowers. And it struck me how huge this is…. Because this is what we do. We prepare the next generation while still existing in this one. Instantly I was reminded of one of my favorite Talmudic stories. Honi. He was a circle maker (which is a different story for a different time). He was also a planter and preparer for the future. The Talmud relates:

> One day, [Honi the Circle Maker] was going along the road. He saw a man planting a carob tree. [Honi] said to him, "How many years does it take to bear fruit?" [The man] said to him, "Seventy years." [Honi] asked, "Is it clear to you that you will live [another] seventy years?" [The man] said, "I found a world full of carob trees. Just as my ancestors planted for me, so I plant for my children." [Honi] sat down and ate. Drowsiness overcame him and he fell asleep. A rock formation rose around him, he became hidden, and he slept for seventy years. When he rose, he saw a man picking [fruit] from [the tree]. [Honi] said to him, "Are you the one who planted [this tree]?" [The man] said to him, "I am his grandson." [Honi] said to him, "Therefore, I must have slept for seventy years." (Babylonian Talmud, Tractate Ta'anit 23a)

Honi witnessed the passing of physical sustenance from one generation to the next. But, sustenance comes in all forms, education being one of them. Judaism is replete with commands to teach our children (children by blood, by choice, by profession). As we continue to struggle with the realities of COVID-19, many of us have the 'opportunity' to take on this commandment in an unforeseen way.

The story of Honi is actually a Talmudic answer to the question which precedes it. The Talmud relates:

> Rabbi Yoḥanan said: All the days of that righteous man, [Ḥoni], he was distressed over this verse: "A song of Ascents: When the Lord brought back those who returned to Zion (from the Babylonian Exile), we were like those who dream" (Psalms 126:1). He said: Is there [a person] who can sleep and dream for seventy years?

This story of Honi sleeping for 70 years is the rabbi's response to the seventy years of exile in Babylonia following the destruction of the First Temple. They equate the sleep of Psalm 126 with the exile. The carob tree is the connection from one generation to the next, the gift given that ensures the continuation.

So much has been said this spring of the results of the stay-at-home order. Technology has taken over dining rooms and bedrooms around the world as we attempt to maintain the education of our children, our own employment and connections. It has not been easy. Parents have become teachers, teachers have become technology wizzes, front line workers have become the heroes and unemployment has skyrocketed. As sickness and death filled the news, we have awoken from the routine of our lives and returned from the exile of the outside world to our homes.

We have been forced to let go of some of our dreams as we concentrate on a smaller, simpler circle of life. In some cases, intellectual learning has been supplemented by discussions of values and morals. We have had opportunities to actively remember the basics of family and community; helping others, responsibilities at home, being together. Neighbors have come out of their homes to recreate neighborhood communities and families have dusted off the games and puzzles.

Honi awoke and understood that the fruit of tomorrow is planted today. The exiles returned to the parched land of Jerusalem because the heart and soul were more important than the riches of Babylonia. Perhaps we too have been granted a reprieve to wake up and return. A chance to find the fruit we had forgotten.

We harvest from trees planted before we were born; we plant trees so that our children will have something to harvest after we are gone. This is a literal and spiritual truth. Honi's legacy is the carob tree, what do we want ours to be?

Questions for Reflection:

> 1. How can we keep the world in good condition for our future generations?
> 2. How do we help ensure that those future generations will do the same?
> 3. What do you want your legacy to be?

THE SPIRITUALITY OF ZOOM

Rabbi Jeremy Gordon

I've always loved the Priestly Blessing. As a child, I would run through the crowds of Rosh Hashanah and dive under my dad's Tallis so I could peek out at the hooded figures on the Bimah. As a Rabbinic student I learnt the reason – so we would not be distracted by facial imperfection of those we gazed at. That reasoning made sense to me. Back in those 'usual' times. Before all this.

Nowadays, of course, we daven on Zoom, and the only thing to see is ... faces. "I love it like this," one regular shared, "I love seeing people's faces when we daven together."

The great French philosopher-Talmudist, Emmanuel Levinas (d. 1995) devoted his career to the significance of encountering the face. He would have loved Zoom. For Levinas, the face of the other is the root of all ethics. Seeing another face, wrote Levinas, makes us doubt our own supremacy over the world. We see, in other faces fragility and mortality and we are moved.

On Zoom I can see the face of a member who wasn't allowed to attend the funeral of their father. He's been coming every day to say Kaddish. There's another member who is at home alone, for whom we've provided a tablet and WiFi connection. She's here for a sense of community. Was that a yawn I saw on the third screen in from the right, fourth row down? On Zoom we are all imperfect together, sharing and staring at the perfection of imperfection human creation.

The Chassidic master, Naftali Tzvi Horowitz (d. 1827), prefigured Levinas in a teaching on revelation (Zera Kodesh, Shavuot p.40). He begins with a tradition of his teacher, Menachem Mendel of Rimanov – that the sound of revelation on Sinai was the sound of the first letter of the first of the Ten Commandments. That's so good it's funny – the first letter of the Ten Commandments is an Aleph, a silent letter. Horowitz goes on to suggest that Moses, therefore, experienced revelation not as a sound at all, but a vision; the vision of God's face. After all God does speak to Moses, 'face to face.' And that the Divine face is that Aleph, with the constituent strokes of the Hebrew letter making up a nose and two eyes. Indeed, all be-faced humanity, carries an imprimatur of God in our face. This is the meaning of our creation in the image of the Divine. We carry godliness in our face, in our beauty, in our imperfection, and most of all in the beauty of our imperfection.

Sometimes, when I'm davening on Zoom, I gaze out at these faces, gazing at me, each of us in our little Zoom boxes. And it does feel I'm gazing at the image of God. It's bloody awful, this lockdown existence. But it's not all bad.

Dedicated to the New London Synagogue
Zoom Shacharit Minyanaires

103

SEEKING, INSIDE AND OUT
Kelly Hartog

The jasmine in my front yard is starting to bloom; soft, white buds straining to kiss the sunlight drenching my front porch. Its intoxicating scent, coupled with the unfettered blue skies, herald the arrival of spring here in Los Angeles, laden with the promise of a sweet, blissful future.

But the jasmine also needs to cling fast to my porch railing if it is to thrive. It wraps itself ever tighter with its earthen cords, once, twice, three times around the weather-beaten wooden slats, seeking further purchase on the mottled, stucco grey walls.

And this, I realize, is how I am living my life during the never-ending quarantine, now entering its third month: seeking the sweet nectar of life on the outside but needing to hold fast to the safety of my four walls within.

And just as the jasmine finds comfort from its own small but vibrant community — the tiny hummingbirds who pop by every single day to feast on its nectar, their precious wings fluttering in tandem with their heartbeat, I too seek sustenance within my community, to stave off the fear, the isolation, the loneliness, and the knowledge that this virus, should it seek me out, will indeed kill me. I do not have the luxury of scoffing at its power or challenging its singular mission.

Out in the streets where I, with my deeply immune-compromised body can only venture to walk my dog twice a day, it is my synagogue community that calls to ask if I need someone to shop for me. It is my friend who every Friday heads to the kosher supermarkets and bakeries to buy challah and other goods for her elderly neighbor and always picks up anything I need. It is another friend from my synagogue community who bakes me a cake and then comes by to "chat." She sits at the tiny wrought-iron table on my patio, which I cover with a bright floral tablecloth, like a spiritual goddess, and I throw open the window

104

overlooking the porch that faces my living room and we bask in the simple pleasure of connection. Me inside on the couch, her on the other side of the screen, framed by the jasmine.

And then there is the spiritual sustenance that comes from my synagogue community. It comes these days via Zoom and Facebook Live. Via heartfelt shiva services. Via Havdallah. Via Torah study and via Shabbat services with hundreds tuning in to soulful, spiritual tunes, stirring words from our rabbi, joyous shouts of "Shabbat Shalom," typed furiously into the comments box followed by a million heart and smiley emjois.

It is the deep, resonant words of Torah by smart, erudite, passionate young men and women celebrating their bar and bat mitzvahs. They dig deep, somehow, intrinsically knowing that the words they share today will be the foundation of a better world they can and will carve out. A world where they can tell their children and grandchildren that truly, a party is not what this rite of passage is about. That they lived through COVID-19 and trust them, they know what's important. And I listen in awe to these beautiful young adults and I weep, openly, onto the keyboard along with their parents and siblings and the rest of the congregation at the knowledge that these b'nai mitzvah have so much to teach us in these pandemic times about faith, hope, love, resilience and the true essence of Torah.

And then I venture "out" into the world to my day job, where I have the privilege to write and edit and collate stories of our Jewish brothers and sisters and how they are living their lives; sharing their Torah and finding ways to keep moving forward every single day.

Even as I sit at my computer in my home office every day, I can still throw open my front door, smell the jasmine, see the hummingbirds and continue to reach for all the good and beauty that exists all the while, wrapping myself safely in my home and clinging to my community.

KNOW THAT YOU ARE LOVED
Rabbi David Lyon

I can't remember the last time I sat in my backyard in mid-April, on a towel on the ground eating lunch in the sunshine. It's possible that I never have. It would take a pandemic and social-distancing to create the opening for lunch al fresco at the Lyon house. The neighborhood around me was oddly quiet, too. As I looked into the sky, I saw a Blue Jay way up high on a telephone line. It sat there for a long time without any fear of a rumbling truck down below or any disturbance around it. It had a long twig in its beak. I thought it would fly off to finish its nest building, but it didn't. Silly bird, I thought, there's so much to do and you're taking a break on the telephone line.

Then I felt oddly embarrassed. I began to learn something about myself as I continued to stare at the bird. The quiet of the day, without back-to-back meetings and urgent matters, enabled me to perch on my lawn for an extended time, too. I truly wanted the bird to fly away so I could get back to thoughts about my work, but it didn't leave. The longer it stayed, the longer I had to think about eating more slowly than before, soaking up more sun than I would have, and digesting more than my lunch, but also some new expectations.

We're all creatures in nature, but surely there's a difference. What is it? In Mishnah Pirkei Avot (3:14) we learn that Rabbi Akiva used to say,

> *"Beloved of God is man (sic) for he was created in the image of God; but greater still was the love [shown him] in that it was made known to him that he was created in the image of God, as it is said, For in the image of God made He man (Genesis 9:6)."*

Rabbi Samuel Karff taught about this verse, "It is one thing to be loved; it is another thing to know that you are loved." The difference is our awareness of our Creator, and, in that awareness, our discovery of irrefutable and unconditional love.

106

During these days of COVID-19, and all that it has come to mean, we can all find comfort in what God's love can mean to us, what love between us can help us know, and what self-love can enable us to be.

Eventually, the bird on the telephone line flew off to build its nest and to be, well, a bird. I picked up my plates and towel from the ground and finished my day with deeper appreciation of my Creator's love, greater thanks for those who are sharing this pandemic period with me at home, and increasing awareness of self-care as a necessary part of moving on from here, one day. I wish for you the same and much more.

TO BE ALONE
Miryam Kabakov

"It is not good for the earthling to be alone."
"לֹא־טוֹב הֱיוֹת הָאָדָם לְבַדּוֹ"
"Lo tov heyot ha-adam levado"
(Gen. 2:18)

I have always heard this verse as a description of the need for companionship. No one wants to be alone their whole life. Life is more fun with others! I thought of the verse as a suggestion, an observation about the human condition.

Now after three months of feeling truly alone, apart from community, I have experienced this verse on a much deeper level. I now hear it as a warning. I feel how unnatural it is to be cut off from others, from physical proximity and contact. Zoom is not cutting it. I need to welcome people into my home. I need to feed others, sit with them, share a meal, to nurture and be nurtured by them, to experience what I now know as true togetherness. The other day, a friend dropped off some pickles he had made. Even though we chatted from 6 feet apart, with masks on, I felt the power of his food nurturing me and reaching me on a deeper level than the zoom call with colleagues I had just been on.

I am lucky; I live with my family of a partner and two children. Hugs have become very important. But I know of people out there who have not hugged someone in three months, people who have had no physical contact with another human being since March. Some people are completely isolated and alone. Many people are living in a state that is simply not normal to our human condition.

From our conception until birth we are surrounded by someone, enveloped, enclosed, surrounded by a giant hug of primordial waters we float in. And upon entering our world, a baby's survival depends on touch almost as much as food and sleep. Babies who are not touched do not thrive.

I see now that adults who are not touched do not thrive. This artificial and imposed isolation is painful, it is not the way we humans are made or how we are designed. We have a deep need to be touched, to be held, to nurture and be nurtured. A screen is no substitute for skin.

Leaders in the mainstream Orthodox world often ask me, "Why can't LGBTQ people just be celibate? Better they should not act on their unnatural desires." These past few months have shown that these leaders are asking people to do something even more unnatural: to forego living a life with someone who can hold and hug them, to live in a state of being that is anathema to how humans are designed. I hope this period of quarantine has driven home to these leaders just how cruel a life of isolation is.

COMMUNITY. RITUAL. JOY: THAT'S HOW WE SURVIVED AIDS, AND HOW WE'LL SURVIVE CORONAVIRUS

Rabbi Sharon Kleinbaum

We in the Jewish LGBTQ community are feeling some déjà vu from our worst years of trauma.

Starting in 1981, the surreal became real. What had been imaginable only in the writings of Edgar Allan Poe, the annals of medieval and Renaissance history, or in the most terrifying pages of Torah, became the day-to-day reality of our lives: A terrible and unfamiliar disease appeared that no one understood but that relentlessly started to kill our people in horrible ways, while we had a government which was bigoted, hostile, and dismissive. Cause and transmission were mysterious and confusing. Stigma isolated us from each other and fear of "catching the plague" added pain to pain.

Even before we learned what HIV (or GRID as it was first known) was (do people remember when we had never heard the word "retrovirus"?), we as a community learned the power of resilience, resistance, and spirituality. Like David facing Goliath, we discovered strengths we didn't know we had. We grieved, we wailed, we fought, we became wiser, and we bonded.

And we did it without the help of our government or the larger Jewish community at first — two sources of protection that by their very definition should have been there for us. 40% of our synagogue died from that plague. We were wounded to an incalculable degree, but even wounded, we grew strong. Hell, we learned how to get along.

Although we lost so many of the community — an entire generation — we emerged from our losses with wisdom that gives us strength to deal with the spiritual illness of the Trump era and now with this newly

110

emerged illness of COVID-19 and the novel coronavirus.

We have lived through the terrifying and surreal before. We have lived through neglectful and inadequate government before. We have relied on each other's strength and the untapped resources of our spirit before.

These things we know:

The power of community cannot be underestimated. Together, we form a tribe that can survive the insurmountable. To build our strength as a tribe, we must reach out to those who are at most risk and make sure no one feels isolated or alone.

We need sanctuaries, holy places, and powerful rituals. Creating space for prayer and meditation and healing is not a luxury; it is essential for our survival. Because of AIDS, the gay Jewish communities in San Francisco, New York and Los Angeles pioneered Jewish healing services which later became normative within the larger Jewish community. A practice of reciting psalms, either as individuals or as a community, draws on the treasure of our ancient heritage and harnesses its power to heal today's anguish.

We are not defined by any virus, symptoms, or syndrome. Remember the joke that characterizes Jewish holidays like Purim which just passed and Pesach which comes next month: They tried to kill us. They didn't succeed. Let's eat. We must never forget to rejoice at our life and our resilience. Joy is an absolute necessity, not something we get around to later.

We exercise our muscles of gratitude now, daily, when it's hardest. We don't wait until we are comfortable. Even though we gathered for funerals, memorial services, and hospital waiting rooms all the time, when it came time for our Shabbat services, CBST committed to prayer and music and learning that would create joy.

Joy is an act of spiritual resistance. And making Shabbat a central part gives us the strength to face the world the other six days of the week.

It is a sin to stigmatize anyone. We Jews know what it is to be falsely blamed, and thousands of our ancestors were killed in Europe by Christian mobs who thought Jews were responsible for the black plague.

111

We LGBTQ people know what it is to live through a plague, and the stigma and the hate directed at us were often worse than the plague which killed so many of us. The CBST community knows what it takes to live through a plague. Love and compassion and support are at the center of survival. Remember to be kind and generous while being cautious and vigilant about staying healthy and keeping others safe.

We will continue being a powerful spiritual community of resistance and love. May the Holy One surround you and your loved ones and give you strength and comfort as we face the uncertainty of the times we are in. Be the reason people have faith in the goodness of others.

(This essay originally appeared in The Forward
March 13, 2020.)

COVID HAS EXPLODED JEWISH LGBTQ ACCEPTANCE ONLINE. THERE'S NO GOING BACK.

Rabbi Abby Stein

Last week, as part of a growing number of virtual speaking engagements, I had the privilege to give a talk to a few thousand Spanish speaking Jews from Latin America, through a program with Limud Buenos Aires. Among the texts and slides that I shared, I also showed a video of my own Bat Mitzvah/Coming Out celebration at Romemu, a Jewish Renewal community on the Upper West Side, titled "A Celebration of Life in TRANSition."

It was the ceremony I created to mark my coming out as a woman of trans experience in 2015. The ceremony itself was a mix of traditional naming and B Mitzvah rituals, as well as newly minted rituals focused on the (perhaps Neo-Hasidic) Jewish values of the Exodus as a Coming Out, the beauty of the LGBTQ Jewish community, and the power of living a life true to oneself. It was followed by dancing and a Kiddush.

The day after my talk to the Latin American Jewish community, I got an emotional email from an Argentinian Jewish trans woman who was tuned in to my presentation. "I have never felt so welcomed, so seen in a Jewish space," she wrote. I could feel the emotion coming through her words on the screen. "I always feel like my Judaism and my queerness, even when they are not a contradiction, don't go hand in hand. Seeing you celebrate being trans, in a synagogue, brought me to tears," she wrote.

That was just one of many similar reactions I keep getting from Jewish people from around the world, now that all community events are virtual, removing all physical boundaries.

A feminist from Sweden was shocked to hear me use feminine God

113

language when chanting the traditional tunes for Pesach Ma'ariv. She was even more surprised to learn that Hasidic and Kabbalistic teachings have a long history of feminine God Language.

A senior Russian Jew messaged me in disbelief after I mentioned my Sefaria source sheets on a talk with the Moscow JCC. "I had no idea Judaism recognizes so many genders, and that they are Rabbis who believed a person's body and soul could be different genders," he wrote with exclamation marks.

An Israeli friend I worked with at a camp couldn't get over herself after watching for the first time a Shabbat service, organized by a mainstream American synagogue, where the rabbis and cantors were all women, with live music, and where people can choose how they get called up to the Torah. "How in the world is this kind of Judaism not more common?" she texts me in wonder.

A friend who like me grew up Hasidic but is now a member of a Reform community in one of the "flyover states," joined me for a Yom Tov morning service on Pesach. He couldn't get over the "*heimish*" — the word Hassidim use for "homey" — flare he observed in our fully egalitarian service, where women are considered Kohanim (traditional priesthood) just like men. "I made peace with the fact that I either have a lively service that is Orthodox, or a church-like service that is progressive. Now I see we can have both!!!" he tells me over the phone.

When I think about the long-term impact COVID-19 is going to have on communal Jewish living, all of these experiences, and so many more, come to mind.

Until a few months ago, the majority of LGBTQ Jews had no access to synagogues where being queer was not just tolerated but treated as something beautiful. The majority of Jews outside of North America had no access to services where progressive values like LGBTQ equality and racial awareness were not just tolerated but celebrated as Jewish values, in sermons and liturgy.

As a rabbinical friend of mine told me on a long call we had, after I suggested his name to local queer Jews who wanted to have a naming celebration in shul, "You are creating an environment where people are starting to expect more. Queer or intermarried, bi-racial or Jews of color, people are starting to feel that mere acceptance is no longer enough. They want full membership and participation, not despite who they are, but because of who they are."

He is right — I am guilty as charged.

I have been saying for a while now that tolerance is for lactose and nuts, not people. People — we need to celebrate.

Now, thanks to the worst pandemic in a century, instead of spreading this message one community, one city at a time, we are spreading this message to millions of Jews at once.

I believe that when these people go back to their physical shuls, synagogues, temples, or community centers after this apocalypse is over, they will be spoiled with acceptance and celebration, and will refuse to go back to merely a "classic/traditional" world.

Because, quite frankly, the Jewish world has cracked open some boxes, and created new access points. We should not want to go back.

Let's make sure that we bring the access that a virtual community offers to the physical world!

(This essay originally appeared in The Forward
May 24, 2020.)

NEVER LIMIT LOVE
Rabbi Nicole Guzik

I went to Ralph's and above the bread section were the following words:

> *"LIMITS... Due to the huge increase in demand and to ensure that more of our valuable customers have the opportunity to purchase, we are limiting bread to 2 packages per customer."*

There were signs like this all over the store. Yet, all I could see was that word, "Limits." Yes, limit the amount of food and supplies in taking what we need. But the idea of limits extends far beyond the grocery store.

In order to live within the unknown, our minds and bodies survive within limits. Understanding there must be a limit to the energy we expend, the anxiety we produce, the tension we feel, the rapid beating of our hearts. While fear is normal and healthy, limiting our fright so that we do not remain paralyzed, glued to the couch watching the news play over and over again.

Consider these limits:

Limit the amount of harsh words expressed to a love one. We are often cruel with those we love.

Limit the anger towards our children who cannot understand why their environment has changed so dramatically. Choose embrace and understanding over rage and avoidance.

Limit the grudges against those who hurt us. Now is the time to exercise forgiveness and expansion of heart.

Limit your judgement of self. We are all in this together. Trying. Stretching. Falling. Getting back up. We are all doing our very best. Our expectations of yesterday will look very different than tomorrow. Give yourself a break.

Halakha is the Hebrew word for Jewish law. It also means "walking". We use our Jewish tradition to keep walking, understanding that each day, the path may look and feel different. But it is the commitment of family, friends, community and God that propels us forward. Devotion that knows no limits. Support that knows no bounds.

Limit resentment, bitterness, anger and fear. Limit disappointment, frustration, hatred, and hostility.

But never limit love. It will be love that allows us to remain on the curvy path. It will be love that enables our spirits to rise higher and higher. Love for God. Love for each other. Love for the stranger. Love of self.

Limit so very much.

But never limit love.

THIS PRAYER EXPERIENCE
I OWE TO CORONA
Ruth Ebenstein

What happens in our family room on Shabbat mornings would never happen in synagogue -- Five of us, davening together on the ergonomic evergreen couches with extra back support that we purchased at IKEA, brought up our condemned stairwell, piecemeal.

It would never happen at all.

At synagogue, I do not sit next to my three sons, or my husband.

There's a divider between us, a tall one with a white curtain. A *mechitza*. (We're Orthodox, the *Shira Hadasha*-partnership minyan-style kind, feminist but still seated apart.)

In synagogue, I'm habitually engrossed in *tfillah*, praying, singing, absorbing the Torah, reading line by line. I sit close to the *bimah* because I don't want to miss a word. (I've been even known to shush the chatterers around me!)

My boys are equally engrossed in how long they have to "stay in" until they can go. Eyeballing the pages remaining until they can bolt with a blessing. My oldest is nearly 14 and follows with an intelligent eye. My twelve-year-old dutifully follows the first, second, third, aliyot of the *parsha*. Even the fourth. My ten-year-old peers over his brother's shoulder, tapping his toes. My husband slouches in the front row, *talis*-less, also paying attention. Then some invisible buzzer sounds, in between *hamishi* and *shishi*, and they file out. They bolt to soccer or basketball. On good days, they saunter back in for *Musaf*, then race back to their friends. A strategic conversation ensues on manning their positions at the *Kiddush* to grab the most *PotatochipsBisliCornChipsDoritos.*

At synagogue, I am ever torn. Do I interrupt my spiritual satiety to harass them to come upstairs to pray even as I pass by my husband, also chattering away?

Most times, I don't bother.

But at home, they're all mine.

They've got nowhere else to go. Nobody to talk to, no wet grass upon which to traverse or stain their pants. The soccer ball and basketball are stuffed in the closet. And the necessity of prayer is palpable, urgent. There's a bloody pandemic outside, the coronavirus invisible to the naked eye, perhaps in the stairwell or right outside our door. Everyone needs to be protected.

The *misheberach leholim* (prayer for those in need of healing) doesn't feel hollow or disconnected. It's linked to the nightly news on Channel Twelve.

My oldest is his school's go-to guy for *hagbah,* lifting the Torah. Muscular and strong, he lifts the Torah with ease. But he's reticent and unlikely to lain.

At home, I tentatively ask him: "Do you want to read the *parsha?*"

Surprisingly, he agrees. He chants loudly, clearly. Beautifully.

My two younger sons wrap their lean bodies around me like a *talis.* The youngest toys with the tassels.

And so this pandemic becomes about something more than just face masks and alcogel and dying.

It is also about praying.

In between chocolate drops and Doritos, the twelve-year-old confesses what I know.

"Ema, that was special. And it was true. "

NOTHING IS PROMISED
Lisa Farber

Your child may have been eagerly looking for forward to celebrating a bar or bat mitzvah, and now this simply was not to be. You may have been counting the days to a long-awaited trip away, only for it to be unceremoniously, cancelled. There may simply have been a big family Shabbat dinner in the calendar, something so regular, suddenly it is declared forbidden. It's a hard lesson to learn at any age. We plan, we hope, we strive and...we expect! The old saying, that humans make plans and God laughs is often mentioned when personal plans go awry - but never have we felt this so keenly, as a community, as in these past weeks, watching our calendars empty and our everyday life drastically change.

Now as we look to slowly returning to the lives we abruptly left behind, amongst the fear and the caution, there is also a deep understanding that each activity, no matter how basic, truly is, a gift. To hug my parents, to share a meal with friends, to send my children off to school, or perhaps to even enjoy the simple pleasure of the theatre or a movie. Gratitude has been a modern hash tag and an over - used sentiment in recent years. I can't help but feel that as a word it now lacks the gravitas to convey what it feels like to have been in such a place of fear and uncertainty, and to find oneself, once again on safer ground. We need something heartier; something that acknowledges we may NOT have got to this place - that we may not have been privileged to experience this slow exit from our cocoon; something that celebrates that we are alive, well, and ready to live again. So where do I find myself turning to, so as to give words to this relief in my soul? I find myself saying the ancient prayer of *Shehechiyanu*, as I slowly inch back into the world.

> *"Blessed are You, Lord of the Universe, who has granted us life, sustained us, and enabled us to reach this season."*

120

These words, which are usually reserved for a festival or for doing something for the first time, encapsulate for me, the joy, the wonder and the recognition, that life is filled with moments that are all gifts. The newness of our old lives is deserving of a *Shehechiyanu*. For a while there, we thought that we were almost guaranteed it all, so we could "save" our *Shehechiyanu* for certain special events and prescribed moments.

But we have been shown otherwise. So I turn to this prayer.

It will be a *Shehechiyanu* moment, when my daughter can continue her VCE studies at school, and when my son can play Ajax footy again. We will all say, *Shehechiyanu* as we sit around our long full Shabbat table, surrounded by family who have not sat together for many weeks. It will be a *Shehechiyanu* moment when I can board a flight overseas, or welcome visitors from abroad to our home. So many precious moments to be acknowledged. I have found a way to express how grateful I am, with words that have been uttered by our people across the generations.

I'm no religious scholar so I hope it's ok to be reciting these words at my own discretion. Somehow, I don't see how it can be wrong to give thanks and acknowledgment to G-d for being able to once again enjoy all the bits and pieces, moments and events that we have missed during these times. To have been given life, and to be sustained to see this moment.

After all, if we have learned anything, it is that nothing is promised to us.

MY NEIGHBOR'S COUGH
Sari Friedman

I don't know if the coughing comes from a man, woman or child; young or old; tall or short; kind or crabby. All I know is he or she is close. In the apartment above or below. Maybe in the building a few feet away. These aren't like any coughs I've heard before. They seem unproductive. They sound waterlogged, desperate. Hearing my neighbor cough makes me — a mild-mannered super-nerd — want to inject hard drugs, drink till I'm sh*t-faced, binge-eat.

Before, when I went outside, escaping my tiny studio apartment felt like a marvel, glorious. Today, hearing my neighbor's incessant cough, and knowing there's plenty more coronavirus outside, I've stayed in.

I close my windows. But I can still hear through the walls. Israel has socialized medicine and quarantined people are getting food and other deliveries. The Palestinian Authority and Israeli counterparts are cooperating and coordinating resources admirably during this crisis, sharing responsibility for the whole of the region.

After a while, I re-open my windows. When they're open I can hear the warning sirens when rockets are shot toward Tel Aviv, where I currently live. When Israel's attacked, there's between 15 to 90 seconds to find shelter. So many rockets have been shot toward places I've been, in various parts of Israel, I've lost track.

I'm accustomed to rockets. Same as I got accustomed to violence when a former partner was abusive; got used to earthquakes when my California walls shook and shattered things covered the floor. I got used to muggers when I lived in dangerous parts of New York.

My studio doesn't get sunlight. But it does get fresh air, so that's precious. With my windows re-opened, though, I again hear that cough.

122

My throat is sore. That's a symptom of coronavirus, but I don't have a fever and don't think I'm sick. Maybe my throat is sore from all the things I have not said, things I have not screamed from the rooftops.

That I wish my neighbor health, but don't know what I can do to help. That I wish our increasingly polluted planet recovery… If our planet could cough, it would sound like my neighbor.

But I don't know what I should do. I wish all our governments would lead us toward sharing and peace. I wish I could stop every rocket. End the hoarding of money/resources/things. End slavery. End intolerance. End greed. End pain.

THOUGHTS ABOUT
TWO INVISIBLE ENEMIES

Jonas Kadah

Whoever destroys a soul of Israel, it is considered as if he destroyed
an entire world. And whoever saves a life of Israel, it is considered
as if he saved an entire world.
(Mishnah Sanhedrin 4:5; Yerushalmi Talmud 4:9,
Babylonian Talmud Sanhedrin 37a)

I remember when I was 11 years old and lived in Israel, walking home from school with my giant backpack. It was a scorching hot day.

After 20 minutes, I turned left to our house only to see that everything had changed - the atmosphere was different, my family was tense, and there were new faces I hadn't seen before.

There was an invisible fear of something beyond our control: Saddam Hussein had vowed to send SCUD-rockets filled with poison gas. This gas is invisible to the human eye, and since the gas doesn't smell or hurt you right away, you don't even know it's there. But the damage is catastrophic.

In school, I later learned how important it was to carry your gas mask with you at all times.

But my parents didn't get masks. Like so many people in this current COVID-19 crisis who aren't worried, my parents weren't worried.

This only intensified my fear, fear of an invisible enemy and fear of not being able to protect myself. All my other relatives and friends had stocked up on gas masks. And all this made me even more anxious. More than that, it made me scared: I felt like my life was in the hands of a crazy Iraqi dictator.

124

During this pandemic I feel the same way, except this isn't about a dictator who can push a button. Instead I face a virus that controls itself - and it is not picky. I could contract it any day.

And If I die, the pandemic will not have just destroyed my world but also my family's world. The only thing I don't fear is the hospital, because I have faith that the staff there works day and night in order to save lives - thus saving entire worlds.

I have started to live life based on the idea of *pikuach nefesh*, saving a life, but that does not make me fearless.

I take extra measures to socially distance during my job, and from my friends and extended family, and above all - my mother. My world would be destroyed if she were to succumb to the virus. My world would be destroyed if I become an unknown carrier of the virus and pas it on to her.

Life is sacred. If I were to spread the virus and someone dies from it because of me, my life would end as well, thus destroying my own world and my family's world, causing unspeakable pain.

We live in pain enduring this virus. We are in pain when we see people around us die. We are in pain when forces of evil use the situation for their own good. But most of all, this shows me that we've been unwillingly drafted into a truly global war with no end in sight.

I'm walking through the valley in the shadow of death and I am afraid.

ADVERSITY AND ABSURDITY
Benji Lovitt

For thousands of years, the Jewish people have laughed to keep from crying. The same mental exercises which allow the rabbis to debate, dissect, and interpret Torah have helped us look at life from a different perspective and identify the absurdity around us.

Whether in exile or in Israel, our people have had no shortage of adversity to overcome. Pogroms aren't funny but our ability to find humor in our darkest times give us the strength to continue towards the light.

COVID-19 is not unique to the Jewish people. Nevertheless, our experience in laughing has toughened us up and reminds us that this too shall pass.

In the spring of 2020, millions of Israelis spent weeks at home, including the holidays of Pesach and Yom Haatzmaut. These days felt strange, to be sure, but if you're going to be alone during a once-in-a-lifetime pandemic, you might as well laugh.

The following was published in the Times of Israel in April 2020.

As a result of the deadly COVID-19 pandemic, the Israeli Ministry of Health has enforced strict regulations to slow the spread of the virus. With few exceptions, the population is on indefinite lockdown.

Exceptions aside, here are the top 10 excuses to leave home:

> *10. Selling cucumbers at Ramle shuk is considered essential.*
> *9. Last-minute Daka90 package to Cyprus trumps silly "rules."*
> *8. Half an hour away from the kids outweighs possible respiratory problems.*

7. Your wife has threatened "10 more plagues" unless you return with toilet paper.

6. Guy on Facebook who claims to be a rabbi says he allows it.

5. Can't do online Pilates due to neighbors' continuous porn usage.

4. Your crazy neighbor convinces you this is just a liberal media hoax.

3. Despite all the "3rd time, ice cream" election jokes, you forgot to pick up a frozen Magnum bar.

2. Technically, it's not going outside if you "forget" your cell phone at home.

1. Sara won't let you back in until you've formed a coalition.

OLL IS KORRECT

Joey Glick

After years of sitting with an American spiritual director, I started seeing an Israeli. Whereas my old spiritual director was gentle and indirect, my Israeli spiritual director has been (perhaps predictably) strong and pointed. Last week, I told her that I was struggling to cultivate the faith that "everything will be OK." She responded, "this faith is wrong! Wrong! Do not strive for 'everything will be OK.' Strive for 'the OK-ness of everything.'"

Later that day, I was puzzling over her words when I remembered a strange story that a teacher had recently showed me. The story (first told, as far as I can tell, by Yosef Karo in the 16th century legal text, The Beit Yosef) describes a group of students encountering Rebbe Akiva weeping on Shabbat. The students were baffled. There is a commandment to cultivate oneg/joy on Shabbat but their teacher seemed anything but joyful. Sensing their confusion, Rebbe Akiva said, "this [my weeping, my sadness] is my joy." In my director's words and in this story, I felt a half-formed truth, something about a deeper OK-ness, a deeper joy that existed beyond the banks of baseless optimism and boundless despair.

That night, in the dreamy space of this emotive ambiguity, in a dreary moment of COVID-based insomnia, I found myself googling the etymology of the word "OK." I came across a bizarre history. Apparently the term was created by Boston hipsters in the 1830s as an intentionally misspelled abbreviation of "all is correct" (**O**ll is **K**orrect). When I learned this origin story, something clicked. For the first time, I found myself beginning to accept the impossibility of the world feeling "correct" in the wake of COVID. Instead, I saw myself called towards a world that is whole and misspelled, a world that is changed and pained and yet oll korrect.

THE EXTROVERT IN QUARANTINE
Joel Haber

"Are you okay?"

The message pops up on my Facebook, and then my friend continues, "You're such a social person. This must be a really difficult time for you."

Truth is, I was doing really well in quarantine. So much so that the question took me a bit by surprise (especially when a number of others asked the same thing).

I'm what you might call an extreme extrovert. I love people and being around them, at parties, events, a bar or restaurant, anywhere. So I guess my friends expected I might be experiencing what an introvert feels at a party – an "out of my element" discomfort (albeit for the opposite reason).

But I'm also a very independent person who spends a good amount of time by myself and does lots of things alone. So for me, social distancing simply provided the opportunity to be productive in my alone-time, with no "missing the crowds" malaise.

Still, the question showed me how my extroversion manifests differently in extraordinary situations.

One reason I'm so extroverted is that I like the diversity of people, getting different ideas and energies from each one. I also enjoy the social alchemy of bringing people together, turning two individuals into one golden relationship. I am the quintessential connector.

But connections don't come exclusively from physical proximity. They come from meaningful interactions, which take on multiple forms. If you read letters from the era before mass communication, you easily sense the intense emotions that maintained love bonds across miles or months of separation. That's connection.

We are blessed that our plague takes place in an age of advanced communications technology. From the outset, I began reaching out to people on Facebook or Whatsapp, just so they knew they were on my mind. I received calls from people I don't regularly speak to, who wanted to check in on me.

And I continued to organize events. Sort of. I had Zoom drinks for my birthday "party." Many friends later praised how it filled their social needs. To celebrate *Yom HaAtzmaut* (Israel Independence Day), I "hosted" a ZoomBQ, even making grilled meat deliveries (while of course wearing my mask) to the street out front, for those who lived close enough to visit within our lockdown regulations.

I also tried to use my social media posts to help those who were not doing as well as I was. In addition to sharing relevant or useful articles, I just wanted to put smiles on people's faces. I took it as a personal mission to simply be funny. One of my most popular posts came right after Passover ended.

"So glad that Pesach is over so I can get back to my normal abnormal, instead of last week's abnormal abnormal."

Close to 200 comments and reactions, including from friends of friends, told me I hit my mark on that one.

But looking back on the past few months, I also learned that connection isn't just about making people smile or bringing together disparate strangers. It's also about honesty, sharing of yourself, and providing support for those who need it. Especially those who our society too often overlooks: single adults. Addressed to them, this was (by far) my most well-received Facebook post from this period:

> *Single friends who will be spending Shabbat alone, in its entirety, without going to synagogue or having anyone to share meals with:*
>
> *I know this can be difficult, and I want you to know that we are all connected, even while apart. I will be thinking about many of you, as you should be thinking of your other friends. Not too often, but I've certainly chosen many times to do Shabbat alone. Trust me: it can truly be a wonderful opportunity to connect with the real essence of Shabbat -- genuine rest and relaxation.*

Prepare some warm comfort food for yourself, a nice bottle of wine, a good book, and a comfy bed. Sleep a lot, enjoy the silence (thanks Depeche Mode), and know that while you might feel alone, you are actually connected by the invisible bonds that tie together all of the Jewish people, across time, space and even health status.

Shabbat SHALOM to you all! I love you.

Let's all continue remembering how best to connect, and who most needs us to, even once we're fully "on the other side" of Corona.

CONNECTIONS
Laurie Gould

We are reclaiming our connections with each other and the natural world. During this difficult time of the coronavirus, having to stay inside, we are actually connecting with each other and the natural world, but in different ways. We are talking to people we have not talked to in a long time, or having longer conversations that go deeper. Maybe the natural world just said enough, stop destroying the Earth, go inside, and stop driving and producing so that I can heal, before you destroy me. Let's all take a pause and go inside ourselves as to what we can do to heal the world before we destroy her. Let's stop driving and go for a walk. Let's stop and appreciate the tree near your home that you have never noticed, or have not noticed how it changed since yesterday or last week.

I was outside singing, and the birds were singing with me. I started to sing, and so did they. I stopped and they stopped, as if to say, we are all together, we are all singing as one or we are not. The fate of the natural world is in all our hands together. We are all one planet, spinning and singing together. And there was song.

INSIDE REACHING OUT
David Karpel

"Through thought a person should be with his friend wherever he may be... for with a thought one can indeed help a distant friend reach a higher state of being, both materially and spiritually."
~ Rabbi Yosef Yitzchak Schneersohn of Lubavitch

My friends, my colleagues, students, former students, loved ones all, my soul stretches out in need of you.

Spring arrives in all its glory and we cannot share it together. We are inside.

Oh, and spring is here! Despite everything, life persists. Spring arrives this year like a drunk peacock showing off its colors oblivious to the news that someone just announced the death of a loved one. Spring just don't care. Spring is a turn on an axle, a reboot, and the birds sing louder, the grass smiles more, and the pollen colors every surface yellow. Spring is too busy making love to think about anything else but making love.

But so many people are sick and too many are dying, and the numbers increase exponentially and will continue to so for the foreseeable near future. So we stay inside.

With Pesach on the way, I can't help but think of how, about to be freed, Jews were ordered by God to stay inside, out of sight of the 10th plague, a terror fleecing life from firstborns, forcing mothers, fathers, siblings, to watch a son, a brother, a father, fall dead because of Pharaoh's hardened heart.

I'm no scholar, and no *chidush* this, but my conception of this scenario is of the more figurative bent.

When it comes to Pesach, not only is it suggested to celebrate and commemorate the holiday in the mindset of actually experiencing the very same redemption all over again, but I've also learned that we should live with a similar mindset on the daily.

What's the mindset? That we are constantly redeemed from the "Egypt" we make of our own, the fetters holding us back broken through connecting to God from our innermost core.

None of this is to say that we can escape or solve the current plague through "thoughts and prayers."

The analog cannot be stretched so far before the sound gets messed up and then the tape breaks.

My focus is this: Every day, we all struggle with our own trappings, our own prison of negative habits, or own negative thoughts, words, and actions. Right now, isn't that so much of what we are experiencing? Fear itself is a monster trapping us in bleakness. We nourish the monster with our feeds, increase our worries, threaten our own physical, mental, and emotional health.

We need to break out. We need to act even as we are stuck inside, even as what's out there keeps us in here.

Looking at the Pesach story, what steps are taken before we can be free?

Go inside. Connect from the inside out.

Go into your home, however you define home. Surround yourself with the familiar, with the warmth of whatever you call your family, your loved ones. Go to the comfort emanating from your hearth. Go inside yourself, ultimately, to what defines you, your purpose, your foundation.

And for a lot of us, now, this going inside has meant reconnecting with old friends and distant (in time or miles or both) family, and to connect more fiercely with those nearby in distance, but in the presence of whom we can no longer be safe. This may be especially true for those among us whose hearth and home is a dwelling of one, themselves, and who need this soul connection more than most of us and perhaps more than ever.

I mean, for Who/What dare we say is God in our own personal lives but

134

the very Love of those shining faces belonging to those who love us most, those who we love most?

So, when quarantine started in earnest weeks ago, I was immediately filled with a burst of need and nostalgia for friends near and far in miles and years.

I thought of friends I grew up with, friends for whom I feel deep devotion and love despite the many years we've spent apart. These men were formative to my becoming the man I am. Even now I think of them often. But now I need them, to know they are well, to know they too have gone inside to stay safe.

Surrounded by my books, playing tune after tune, hot coffee steaming in the mug on the shelf next to me, I perused Facebook, my yearbook, my memories. My friends' faces, as the kids we were, as the men and women we are now, came to me in a flood of smiles and silly faces. Coffee became whiskey, memories became as palpable as bruises. I strained to push my thoughts outward to them, picturing their places pinpointed on a mental global map, and I prayed for their health and well-being, praying that my prayer be heard, praying that I'm worthy enough to pray for such a thing...

To a core group of them, I sent an email of greetings, well wishes, and inquiries after health.

Soon, I sent another email to another group of friends.

I avoided doing this on Facebook or WhatsApp to avoid distracting myself. I went... old school.

And I promise you, the pleasure of receiving answers, the pleasure of long threads continuing for days on end, that pleasure is deep. To my core. To my foundation. It's a reaffirmation. I am here because of them. I am here for them. We will always be connected.

Like a symptom of the universe, our love will never die.

*(An earlier version of this essay originally appeared on Hevria.com
March 30, 2020)*

135

STRANDS OF BEAUTY

Rabbi Evan Schultz

Where do we possibly find comfort right now? The chasm of solace continues to widen. Our most primal mechanisms for sewing the brokenness of hearts no longer available to us. A hug is now a text. A shoulder to cry on, now an image on a screen.

Our God who created us cries out as her children are brought to their knees in fear and heartbreak. The world is being un-created right before our eyes, and we can't even hold hands as we witness it.

Yet each day we slowly adapt.

We find ways to elevate the human spirit that lies so deep within.

In our tears we discover strands of beauty in our day. From deep within the pit we can see a little bit of light from above. Entering the valley of the shadow of darkness, we hold on to a ray through the cracks.

We each have a song to sing in this moment. Each day as the sun rises and darkness looms, a melody from each human being rises above and weaves through the half-empty streets and shuttered doors.

The human spirit is real. I believe so deeply it is within us as it has been in the harshest moments of pain and darkness throughout the human journey. Love and resilience are at the roots of who we are. May that spirit that guide us and hold us through the days ahead.

CORONA SOUP
Jake Shapiro

I couldn't tell the criminals from the good samaritans.

We were all there, together, serving Tel Aviv's most destitute at the Lasova soup kitchen.

When I say we were all there, I mean we were ALL there.

Arabs and Jews. Religious and Secular. Ashkenazim and Mizrachim. Former five star generals and petty thieves, Florentine hipsters and techie entrepreneurs, Gay Arabs and old religious men.

Some groups were overrepresented (women, LGBT, foreigners). Some were underrepresented (Israelis). Some were hard to define (Jewish men wearing black kippot, tshirts, and joggers, with tattoos covering their bodies, pausing from their work to pray in the corner, wrapped in tallit and tefillin). Others' identities were more obvious (loud Americans).

We were there for different reasons. Some had court-ordered community service. Some were on university scholarships. Others came out of the kindness of their hearts. And for others, it's complicated (we'll get back to that).

The whole operation was run by one of the most intimidating and kindest people I've ever met, Ravit. She reminded me of Raz from Monsters Inc (if you know, you know).

A large woman in every sense of the word, she barked orders in a gruff voice, whipping into shape hardened criminals and soft Tel Avivis alike, chain-smoking cigarettes all the while.

Normally, Lasova is a sit-down affair, where the needy are served delicious, homemade food, and treated with dignity. Before Corona, there weren't so many needy, and many who showed up during Corona didn't look the part - but the crisis brought them to our door. Lasova went from serving 50 meals a day pre-Corona, to 1,600 a day during the crisis.

As such, we had to order pre-packaged food from outside, and distribute it through a window, constantly yelling at people to maintain two meters. Ravit tasted the pre-packaged food. "It's not tasty enough. They deserve better."

She cared so much about the people we served.

I cared too.

That's why I came. I wanted to help.

But I may have stayed for other reasons.

Mid-quarantine, Lasova allowed me to interact with others. It allowed me to go more than 100 meters from my house. There were cute girls. I felt good being there. I didn't exactly announce to my social media followers that I was there, but I slyly posted a video of me cutting cucumbers (20 seconds of the five hours that day I spent cutting cucumbers and potatoes).

Now I'm telling the world that I was there in this article.

Is it ok that I enjoyed the work? Is it ok that it made me feel good to help others? Is it ok that I got social benefits, and even a date, out of the arrangement? Is it ok for me to tell others the good thing I did? Is it ok for me to write about it here? Is it ok that I actually kind of enjoyed quarantine, while others - right in front of my eyes, waiting for my food - suffered?

I may need a few more months of quarantine to figure it out.

THIRD TIME'S THE CHARM
Karen Paul

If you had told me, 22 years ago, after getting up from four months of complete bedrest, seven and a half weeks of them flat on my back in the hospital, with no respite, no ability to sit upright, let alone stand, washing my hair in a basin over the side of my bed, desperately protecting the baby who, due to a doctor's error, did not have sufficient amniotic fluid to grow his lungs, and who died five days after his birth, in my arms, because his brain was bleeding and there was no course of treatment without tragedy, if you had told me that I would once again, 22 years later, be caught in a moment of absolute stillness, perhaps not flat on my back but confined in my space, in order to preserve my health and the health of my children, I would have cocked my head at you as if you were speaking in tongues.

If you had told me that everything I did to save my child's life would be futile, except for the lessons it taught me about resilience, lessons that came in very handy 18 years later ... not surprisingly, chai ... when that baby's father would be felled by a malevolent tumor, one that lay its scaffolding in his brain and killed him, leaving his three stunned children fatherless and his wife of 25 years a widow, I would have gulped and turned away. For in truth, no one wants to know what the future holds.

If you had told me that after I became a widow I would wake up one morning, take the train to New York to see a painting, and under that painting meet the love of the rest of my life, and that he would live five hours away and that just as the pandemic that led to our current stillness laid in we had been moving towards being together more fully and instead now we would be separated for months at a time and I once again would be caught in the tailwinds of trauma and sadness and loss, I would not have even blinked.

Because, like the rabbis who turn a potential convert away three times, to make sure they are true to their desire, once you have lived through three moments where your world has stood still, its axis no longer spinning, and you look up from your stillness – your bedrest, your grief, your distance – and recognize that, this too, is but one stroke in a painting that takes your whole life to complete – then you can take a deep breath, and wait. You can lie in that hospital bed, with the hope that your son will survive. You can care for your dying husband with the hope that his love will be enough to sustain you. And you can wait to see your new beloved, knowing that he is waiting too, on the other side of the madness, and that you need to be healthy and whole to find your path yet again.

And you learn that the world, in fact, does keep spinning, and that, with luck, there are still many more brush strokes before your painting is finished.

CRACKS & LIGHT:
A PRACTICE FOR OUR HEARTS NOW
Rabbi Shoshana Meira Friedman

In October 2018, I had the daunting task of speaking to a group of fourth grade religious school students right after the massacre at Tree of Life Synagogue in Pittsburgh.

That evening, I needed to write.

Instead, I got mad at my husband.

He had made plans earlier to see a friend, so he left the house. Seething in a fury that heated up the air a foot around my body, I called him at dinner just to blame him for my inability to write. When Yotam came home, brave and tender man, he came right upstairs to find me, and he offered that I yell at him. I did. Then he asked me what I wanted to write about.

What did I want to write about? The question was like a perfectly angled elbow digging into a muscle spasm. It pierced the anger and something in me rushed out like ice melt, like water breaking in labor, like a dam collapsing. I wanted to write about my broken heart, I wailed. About the children today and their questions. About the parts of me that have given up in the face of all the pain.

Sitting on the edge of our futon, I keened sharp, clear, long cries. In a moment of synesthesia, as when the Israelites see the thunder on Mount Sinai in the book of Exodus, I saw my cries as strong currents of water, filling the cracks in my broken heart. I saw in my mind's eye the cracks spindling out in spidery lines, continuing beyond my heart to the hearts of everyone: to my neighbors and fellow Americans both Blue and Red, to the land herself longing for health, to the dwindling wild animals and the suffering domesticated ones, to the topsoil eroding off the Great Plains

141

and to the Amazon falling. The sounds of my cries rushed through the cracks, like water flushing through a dry river bed, widening and smoothing the banks. Through the channels of grief I was connected to it all. After the torrent, there was softness. There was belonging again to life.

After decades of holding it back, I have finally learned to grieve like this, and the spasms of it have come many times over the past five years. In this regard, grief for the world is similar to grief for a loved one. It comes in waves. It is cyclical and it spirals and it is unpredictable. It has its own breath and breadth and mind. It will hit us like a wall. It will bring us to our knees.

Yet each time I feel it coming on, the worst moment is the one right before the dam breaks, when I am still straining to hold up the cement wall at all costs, when I am still pretending I can cling to the shoreline and not feel the hurt. Then when resisting itself finally hurts too much, I am swept into the water, and I ride it. I surf. I tumble into eddies. White water. And I am relieved, and blessed, and cleansed as in a mikveh – a ritual bath, a womb. I see and feel those spidery heart cracks and they are filled - with sound, with light, with water. They irrigate. They illuminate. They connect.

I am reminded, every single time, that my broken heart is only as agonizing as my refusal to grieve.

Functioning in our society, most of the time, requires holding up the dam, patching the cracks of our broken hearts enough to get us through the day. Most of us aren't at the spiritual level where we can feel our pain fully in the same moments we do our jobs, care for our children, buy groceries - especially now, when we are wearing masks and gloves, when we are afraid.

But maybe the crisis is the opportunity to reconnect, through joy and gratitude yes, but also through the shared hurt. This is the core wisdom of Joanna Macy's Work That Reconnects – the premise of which is that we must honor our pain for the world so that we can see our interconnection with new eyes, and go forth to serve.

The pace of life we were leading, as a global civilization, before COVID-19 was not sustainable. It was always going to end somehow. Most of us weren't expecting it to end so abruptly, for everyone, all at once, from a pandemic. There is tremendous loss here – loss of life of course, of loved ones. Loss of normalcy. Loss of routine. Loss of company. Loss of

142

livelihood. Loss of careers, of financial security, of graduations, of in-person communities, of classes, of familiar faces, of companionship.

It is a terribly long list.

Yet the virus connects us, too. It runs along the cracks of our humanity, linking us in spindling spidery arms of life and genetics and shared vulnerability.

May we who are living through this global moment let the cracks in our grieving individual hearts break outwards to meet the cracks in the hearts of everyone else around us, and beyond humanity to the living world that will be here past pandemics, past the internet, past any of us. May we find there a great, deep, awesome and abiding love that has been and always will be waiting for us.

COPING CREATIVELY
Rebecca Rona-Tuttle

Today is Saturday, June 6, 2020. It's been nearly three months since my husband, Rick, and I moved into our second floor "suite" in an attempt to avoid anyone in our home who might be infected with the novel coronavirus. Downstairs are my son, and our daughter-in-law, our grandson and our tenant.

We've become creative and flexible in ways we could never have imagined. We now have a small refrigerator in our bedroom. Next to it is a small table where we have a crockpot for fixing soups, and next to the crockpot, a blender where I make green smoothies each night. Originally my idea was to produce the smoothies and soup on the bathroom counter! But I was talked out of this by concerned family members.

My green smoothies are actually tasty most nights. We have fun: Rick guesses each ingredient one by one; he's awarded points for correct answers, and when his answers are incorrect, points are deducted.

We wash our dishes and utensils in the bathroom sink.

We place our dirty dishes and utensils in reusable grocery bags, carry these plus dirty laundry downstairs, out the front door, and along the concrete pathway to the back door, then into the laundry room and kitchen. Since we sometimes do this at night, I paid to have three sensor lights installed. Before that we were taking chances, walking the dishes and laundry to the back in total darkness. And since I seem to have turned falling and breaking bones into a hobby, we decided that one cost was more important than another.

Postmates delivers groceries, laundry soap, etc. and an occasional meal from our favorite vegan restaurant. These are left on our front porch, so there's no contact with the delivery person.

We wash the produce in water with vinegar on the back porch, dry it, and place most of it in our first-floor refrigerator.

We talk and text our daughter-in-law so she and our grandson will be elsewhere when we are in the kitchen or coming down the stairs.

We take wonderful walks in the evening, when almost no one is around, although we wear our masks anyway, just in case.

I'm planting beautiful succulents in the parkway and front garden, which I do around 6:30 p.m., when almost no one is walking down the sidewalk. I wear a mask anyway. My plants are my babies. I love planting them and watching them thrive. New green leaves, a colorful bud opening. Gardening is soothing, one of my great pleasures.

Luckily we have a large bedroom, large bathroom, and roomy study up here. Luckily I can work from home. Luckily Rick can do research for an academic paper, raise funds for political purposes, and talk to his many friends from the comfort of a bedroom chair and desk.

Luckily Remy, our daughter-in-law, prepares incredibly delicious meals and coffee that she brings to the bottom of the stairs for us to retrieve each day, and brings us pitchers of filtered water.

Luckily we have the cutest grandson in the world. OK Sarah, Allison, RuthE, Hershel, Mary, and friends — one of the cutest. He's three, going on four. I walk halfway down the stairs, and he stands at the gate at the bottom of the stairs. We have such fun, even in our limited way. Every time I ask him a question, he answers "Of course!" We play peekaboo. We sing and dance and play Raffi music on my phone.

(Excuse me. Remy just brought us the most delicious looking lunch! I'll return soon.)

I'm back now. Each meal is more delicious than the one before, and this was no exception.

Luckily we have wonderful family get-togethers via Zoom, and attend meetings via Zoom. I was even interviewed by our city council for a seat

145

on a city committee via a platform similar to Zoom. And of course we speak by phone with family members and friends.

Before each meal, Rick and I pray, first in Hebrew, then in English. We thank God not only for the food before us, but also for each other, Rick describing me in the most beautiful and complimentary ways, I describing him endearingly, but also making sure to mention a flaw or two. We then continue, thanking God for our family members and friends, for shelter and health, for our personal attributes and also for nature. We often name every animal we can think of, including mice and snails--except for cockroaches, wasps and mosquitos. Until now, I hadn't thought about flies and gophers. I need to consider whether I really appreciate them. Rick is a believing Christian, while I am an agnostic Jew. For me, praying this way is expressing gratitude for all we have.

I have to admit that at times I've been scared. Only one time have I been despondent. It was late at night, and I was tired. I'm 70 years old, and Rick is 80. I asked him, "Do you think we'll live this way until we die?"

Luckily, the next day I was cheerful again.

For a while I was taking breaks from COVID-19 by writing Facebook Posts. I loved doing this, especially when they were funny.

Nowadays, I can't write funny Facebook posts anymore. I just can't. I can't bring myself to write them. The combination of COVID-19 and the stark reminders of the terrible bigotry that has greatly harmed people, particularly poor people and People of Color—with an emphasis on African Americans— the lack of compassion some people exhibit, can be overwhelming. I think about homeless people and the people who have homes but are poor. The people who are hungry. What can I do when I'm afraid of coming down with the terrible COVID-19? All I can do is speak out, and write articles and checks.

Thank goodness for my wonderful husband, Rick, who calms me, hugs me, sings with me, and takes walks with me. I love him so.

RECOVERY REFLECTIONS FROM A FAMILIAR SOURCE TO HELP US THROUGH THE PANDEMIC

Rabbi Jeffrey Myers

The past 18 months have been filled with continued learning experiences, as I endeavor to serve the needs of my congregation and beyond. While we have witnessed the non-stop growth of mass shootings, we also have benefited from knowledge gained of how to help those in need.

It is horrific that we now need to have a subset of mental health professionals who specialize in mass murder therapy and recovery, but at the same time we must be thankful for the caring people who focus on this subset by selflessly offering the best practices of the day. I have learned much from them. Little did I anticipate this knowledge would also form the foundation of my response to COVID-19. While I encourage anyone who might be in need of mental health help to seek it and in no way do I offer these observations as a mental health professional, if nothing else, these cathartic words might offer hope to others.

Displacement. Nearly all of us have been displaced in some way during these past two months. Our congregation has not prayed or assembled in the Tree of Life since 10.27.18. To quote Psalm 79: "Your holy temple they have defiled." It is not yet a prayerful place, but one day, soon, with God's blessing, the Tree of Life will re-open. Until such time, we have been blessed to utilize space in a neighboring congregation, Rodef Shalom, who has welcomed us with open arms. Despite their hospitality and the beautiful facilities, we are not in our home, and people miss it.

Now, we are twice displaced, as all of us hunker down in our homes, hoping that we do not become a number in the growing list of coronavirus victims. Once again, we do not know the duration of this horrendous calamity that is cause for the newest displacement, but we recognize that this too is temporary. Just as we were in the process of carefully crafting the necessary steps to return to the Tree of Life with guidance from the appropriate professionals, we must simultaneously craft the necessary steps to return to our temporary home, again with guidance from the appropriate professionals.

I have learned during these many months that an important way to promote serenity is to engage in the familiar: retain all of the elements that were in place prior to the change of venue and the change of daily routines. The goods have not changed; the delivery system has. People seek the familiar, the comfortable, as reassurance. Anything that we can do to ease their burden is important.

Trauma. Alas, there are far too many communities around the world that understand trauma, and Pittsburgh is a member of a club that boasts of a membership far too great. We do understand trauma, and had begun to look for the warning signs in others of delayed trauma, as professionals suggest that trauma does not always display itself in the immediate hours of an event, but sometimes weeks, months, or even years later.

We were preparing for the potential new trauma at the two-year mark, when this new trauma in the form of a contagious virus hit. As best as I understand mental trauma, it is the body's inability to process external stimuli. I have learned with time how to integrate my trauma into my being, and to find productive ways to both move forward personally as well as help others do the same.

There are people who are traumatized from COVID-19 in innumerable ways. Keeping an eye out for those we care for and referring them to appropriate mental health professionals is one of the great loving acts that we can perform during these extremely challenging times. Equally important is self-care, the ability to recognize in ourselves that we must focus on our own well-being. The greater Pittsburgh community mental health professionals were overwhelmed by need, yet have managed nobly to serve our population with sensitivity. I am confident that the mental health professionals in every community are equally up to the task.

Healing. When people asked me how we have healed, I respond that we always will be healing. When a loved one would pass away, prior to COVID-19, we would mourn according to the customs and traditions of our faith. Family and friends would attend to us, and gradually we would learn to live with the new reality of the absence of our loved one. There would be reminders throughout the year of the loss, but most of us learn how to move onward. Perhaps not so much with a mass shooting. In any case, the reminders are daily and inescapable: a sight, a sound, a smell, a memory. While we do our best to move forward, it is not easy, as the reminders threaten to draw us backwards. Many families are not able to normally or formally mourn their losses during the pandemic. Some days are easier than others.

How will we heal from this pandemic? While I cannot know for certain, most importantly we cannot heal on our own. We must remain connected to those people who are important in our lives so that we can heal together as a community. Reminders will be present on a daily basis. Will they gradually fade? Only time will tell.

Hope. Despite the massacre at the Tree of Life, and despite COVID-19, I remain a hopeful person, for I have seen the good in people in incredible doses. Example after example of causeless love abounds. Approaching two years later, people from around the world continue to offer us words of condolence, empathy and love. They have reminded me that the vast majority of humanity is good. I have seen the same thing over these past two months, and it reassures me, as it should reassure you, that most folks are good. Alas that it takes a massacre and a global pandemic to bring out all of this good. Yet there are vast storehouses of good still untapped, and I remain full of hope that once fully tapped, this becomes one of the positive outcomes of a new normal for our society. Strangers caring for strangers, because it is the human thing to do. In the end, that is how you conquer a pandemic.

(This essay originally appeared on the Pittsburgh Post-Gazette
March 24, 2020)

149

TORAH TEXTS AND TOGETHERNESS:
FAMILY LIFE IN THE TIME OF QUARANTINE
Shira Hecht Koller

When life becomes disorienting, I look for frameworks that feel familiar to serve as an anchor as the ground beneath me shifts. Often, they come from our sacred texts, and act as a way to situate my own personal experience within the larger narratives of our community. Sometimes I attach to grand, epic narratives, at other times, more obscure and intimate ones.

So when my teenage children emerged Tuesday night from their 14 day mandated quarantine, to get some fresh air, meet some friends and encounter the world with fresh eyes, only to return inside the next day following a NYC-wide plea to stay home (not yet a mandatory shelter-down, but who knows what is coming), my mind kept wandering, thinking of which story this was going to be. An epic plague of Biblical proportions? Sacred temples abandoned? Rampant poverty with prophets anxiously reminding us not to forget the widows and orphans? No. These would not work to get me through the many weeks ahead.

After a few days at home, with four children ages 5-18 and my partner and I all trying to find our sea legs in these unchartered waters of a new, perplexing reality, I attached instead to the Talmudic narrative (*Berakhot* 33b) of the second century Talmudic sage R. Shimon bar Yohai and his son hiding from the Romans in a cave. While the details of the experience are quite different, the level of intimacy in the cave is what draws me in.

While inside, R. Shimon bar Yohai and his son are sustained by a miraculous carob tree and a spring of water. They sit covered in sand up to their necks, studying Torah, only emerging from the sand to pray. They live this way for thirteen years.

The simplicity and the intensity of the familial relationship and bonds forged over study and prayer is what I now feel forming around me, in

150

the cave that is my home. As my partner and I are both educators, our home has always been a place of study and learning, and creatively accessing the texts that drive us. But at this moment, it feels more critical than ever. Right now, we are at once part of a global Jewish *beit midrash* community and also a deeply personal and intimate one. There are iPads that serve as portals for tefilla, Macbooks through which the pages of the Talmud are turned, phones that serve as virtual *batei midrash*, and windows and porches from which to share thoughts and ideas with neighbors. We are – in a great place of privilege – able to be connected through these channels to thousands of others. We hear their voices, see their faces, lift one another in song, make *berakhot* and give *tzedakah* together and challenge one another through our ideas and writings. And at the same time as being part of this universal learning experience, we are also in such close physical and existential proximity to our children, that we not only hear their Torah being learned, we feel it in our bodies. It is like we are covered in the sand – father and son, mother and daughter, parent and child – enveloped and embraced in sacred words.

Of course, the ideal of the peaceful cave of study is pierced with the sounds of toddlers crying as they plea to go to the park; the tranquility of an image of solitude is punctured by chaos and flying sheets of paper – math homework, bills, college essays, book drafts to edit; until the miraculous carob tree and water emerge, we are met instead with a steady stream of dishes to wash, groceries to procure, trash to compost; emotions run high and the intensity of experience leads to navigating new rubrics of sharing space; finding a fragment of quiet feels like a miracle.

But keeping the framework in mind provides an image of intimacy that I feel grateful to aspire to. After a few days, schedules seem to be setting in, norms are adjusted, expectations lowered, children rise to the challenge, stepping up with unsolicited acts of kindness and help, those which the situation demands. The walls are adorned with the words of first grade Torah, the halls filled with the sounds of nursery tefilla, the den decorated with high school *mishmar* schedules and extra learning opportunities, the attic a place through which graduate seminars in Jewish studies are conducted, and my porch, an oasis to work on building an online Torah study platform. Our cave is being molded around us. It is what will sustain us through the next short while until Elijah the prophet tells us that it is safe to go out.

As the narrative continues, we are told that when R. Shimon bar Yohai emerged, he could not look at the world without burning it up with his

151

eyes. Such intensity of experience resulted in an intolerant viewpoint. A heavenly voice sends him back to the cave.

When we emerge from the cave, God willing in good health, and into a world that is more kind, more gentle, more fractured and vulnerable but also more connected, let us be blessed to take the intensity of our personal experience and use it to spread more Torah, more *tefilla*, more love and light to a new reality and a world that we will look at through different eyes.

(This essay originally appeared in The Layers Project Magazine on March 22, 2020.)

NOAH KNEW WHAT IT WAS LIKE
TO SHELTER IN PLACE
Rabbi Avi Killip

Noah knows what it's like to quarantine. In the most obvious and perhaps even absurd way, Noah understands what it means to be trapped inside with the entire family and all of the world's animals (Hey, we could have it worse, right?). He knows what it feels like to gather what you need, go inside, and shut the door.

In the early days of our country shutting down, I held onto this image of Noah building the ark even when he wasn't yet certain the rain would come. We, too, were stocking up on food for some mysterious future danger that we couldn't yet see clearly, that might not come at all. All we had was a vague instruction to start gathering supplies and loved ones.

Rashi tells us that Noah was a man of little faith. In Genesis 7:7, the Torah says that Noah entered the ark "because of the flood waters," and Rashi understands this to mean that Noah entered the ark too late. He should have entered because of the warning from God; instead, he waits for the water to begin pooling around his ankles. He waits until he knows that this is really happening. We, too, waited to enter the ark, waited too long before cancelling schools and ordering everyone to stay home.

But then, we didn't have the voice of God. The direction to "shelter in place" never came as a clear command from the all-knowing. Instead we heard from multiple authorities who not only offered different advice but often claimed different facts. We continue to get different information from different sources. When is it okay to leave the house? What symptoms are we watching for? Which masks are useful for what? The answers constantly change. The uncertainty is painful.

Although Noah had the benefit of a divine command, his story in scripture

153

is as confusing as our current news cycle. The flood narrative is one of the most convoluted texts in the Torah. Basic elements of the story seem contradictory or oddly repetitive: Noah is told, in one place, to collect two of each animal, and in another, seven. Genesis 7:7 tells of Noah's family entering the ark, and then they all enter the ark again just a few verses later, in 7:13. How long did the flood last? Which birds did Noah send out?

There are no simple answers to these questions. The timeline in the story is so complex, in fact, that this has become a standard text used to teach the documentary hypothesis — the idea that the Torah contains multiple narratives, from multiple authors, woven together at a later date. Yet in this moment of our lives, when so much is at stake, we long for clearer direction. We want simple answers. And even then, sometimes the message is just too terrifying to grasp. Rashi tells us that Noah "believed and did not believe" that the flood was coming. This ability to both comprehend and refuse to comprehend the severity of the situation may be necessary: we have to believe in the disaster enough to build the ark but not become so overwhelmed that we are paralyzed.

This lack of clarity is painful because there is so much at stake. The world hangs in the balance today, just as Noah's world did. For the first time in our lives, we have encountered a moment of crisis without boundaries. No country or industry has avoided this pain. No group of people remains outside of this crisis.

Those of us privileged enough to shelter in place are each Noah, holed up in our own tiny arks. We are cramped and anxious, but we are safe. The world outside the ark is not. What did it feel like for Noah to live inside his four walls knowing that the world around him was washing away? We don't have to work hard to imagine. Noah listened to the rainfall. I listen to near-constant ambulance sirens racing to overcrowded New York City hospitals.

God tells Noah to enter the ark without telling him when he will leave. One of the most unsettling parts of the order to "shelter in place" is that we don't know when to come out again. We don't know what a process of reemerging into the world will look like. And, most terrifyingly, we aren't sure what world we will find. Genesis 8:5-8 tells us that the water doesn't just disappear after the rain stops: "At the end of one hundred and fifty days the waters diminished...The waters went on diminishing until the tenth month; in the tenth month, on the first of the month, the tops of the mountains became visible." Water receding is a long, slow, incremental process. Without an all-clear message from God, Noah is forced to determine for himself when it is safe to open the doors of the ark. Like Noah, it is going to be our job to determine when we can emerge.

Even after seeing the signs of safety, Noah can't bring himself to reenter the world; he leaves only at God's direct command: "Come out of the ark... Bring out with you every living thing ...and let them swarm on the earth and be fertile and increase on earth" (Genesis 8:16-17). A small step out won't cut it. Noah and the creatures must "swarm" over the earth! We too will emerge slowly and carefully in stop and start stages, but someday there will come a time when we will again move freely around this beautiful planet.

The first thing Noah does upon leaving the ark is build an altar to God. It is this offering that leads God to make a promise: "The LORD smelled the pleasing odor, and the LORD said to Himself: "Never again will I doom the earth because of man" (Genesis 8:21). This is where our story differs from the biblical flood. The flood is a punishment, and Noah merits his own survival. Our world doesn't work that way. This pandemic is not divine retribution, and many who have died lived beautiful, righteous lives. I take this verse, this promise from God, very seriously. We are in a moment of doom, but it is not "because of man."

The story of the flood ends with a rainbow, which has been adopted as an image of hope in this pandemic, posted in windows across the city as we seek universal ways to tell each other that "everything will be okay." There is something instinctively comforting about seeing a rainbow in the sky. It reminds us that, no matter how hard the rain, there is always potential for the sun to return. And of course, rainbows appear before the water has completely dried.

(This essay originally appeared in The Forward on April 22, 2020.)

QUALITY OF LIFE
Rabbi Daniel Bouskila

It was a short but powerful meeting. It was an awkward exchange of words. It was a day when two elderly men sought to understand the meaning of life. It was the day when Jacob met Pharaoh.

Coming from completely different cultures and backgrounds, the only thing they shared in common was a charismatic boy named Joseph.

To Jacob, Joseph was his beloved son. To Pharaoh, Joseph was the economic wizard who saved his empire's economy from total disaster.

But this meeting wasn't about Joseph. It was about two elderly men reflecting on life itself.

"How many are the days of your life?' asked Pharaoh of Jacob.

Jacob replied: "The days of the years of my sojourning on earth are a hundred and thirty years, but few and unhappy have been the days of my life."

Why did Pharaoh simply not ask, "How old are you?" What wisdom is embedded in his carefully crafted question about the days of Jacob's life?

What about Jacob's response? Is there a deeper message in "few and unhappy have been the days of my life"?

Rabbi Samson Raphael Hirsch (19th century commentator) elaborates Jacob's response:

> *"You ask how many are the days of my life? I have not lived much. True, I have sojourned on this earth for 130 years, but my life was bitter and full of worry. The days of the years that I can really call my life were in reality only very few."*

156

Rabbi Naftali Tzvi Yehuda Berlin (19th century commentator) further expands Jacob's response:

> *"Even when I achieved material wealth and financial security, my life was still filled with woe and sorrow, so my successful years of life were actually very few."*

How do we measure and define a "happy life"? Is it by living to a ripe old age? Is it through material wealth and success?

Pharaoh's question emphasized days, and so did Jacob's answer. Through Pharaoh's brilliant question and Jacob's painfully honest answer, we are reminded that life is not measured through length of years or material wealth, rather through the quality of each day that we are privileged to be alive.

Pharaoh and Jacob's exchange takes on deeper meaning during these uncertain times of COVID-19. While quarantined in our homes and barraged with hourly reports of illness and death, we pause to ask ourselves "How many have been the days of our lives?" If we are blessed to survive this pandemic and come out alive, what will the next round of "the days of our lives" look like? Will they simply be about "living until 120"? Will our focus be all about material wealth?

Jacob was on earth for many years, and Pharaoh achieved power, wealth and fame. But in the closing years of their lives, these two strikingly different people joined together for only a brief moment, to remind us - as James Taylor puts it - that "the secret of life is enjoying the passage of time."

LIKE MOSES, WE CARRY
OUR BROKENNESS WITH US
Rabbi Avi Olitzky

I yelled. I really yelled. It was the middle of Passover, coming off a 72-hour Yom Tov and Shabbat span during Minnesota's Stay-at-Home order, and I was out of patience. I just could not figure out how to get through to my daughter who just would not stop protesting at bedtime, spiraling. I felt terrible afterwards and still feel terrible about it.

The next morning I sat down with all four of my children, together — they all heard the yelling. I was very candid with them: I was tired and out of patience; I didn't know how else to get through to them at that moment; I don't like that I yelled and don't plan to yell again; mistakes happen and we carry those mistakes with us through life.

I asked for their forgiveness and we all hugged.

But I have not yet fully forgiven myself. I know we're all imperfect human beings and I have raised my voice before. But this felt different. This felt like a moment of failure. I didn't yell out of anger — I yelled out of exhaustion and emptiness. And the sorry doesn't change that; it just helps us move on.

I have dedicated so much energy to teaching and "camp counseling" and cooking and cleaning and board games and legos — and truly enjoyed all of it. But in that moment, it all felt in vain; I had an out of body experience — I heard and watched myself misstep.

When Moses came down from the mountaintop carrying the first set of Holy Tablets, he encountered the Israelites dancing around and worshiping a golden calf. We're led to believe that Moses cast down and broke the Tablets out of anger. But the Midrash suggests that the Holy letters flew off the Tablets and Moses no longer had the strength or energy to support them. The Tablets fell to the ground and shattered.

We know that Moses received a second set of Tablets, but what most are not aware of is that the broken first set of Tablets traveled alongside the intact set all throughout the Israelites' time in the wilderness and beyond.

Our brokenness is sometimes caused by our lack of energy to handle a situation in the best way. However, we are meant to carry that brokenness with us. It's how we ensure that the second set of Tablets perpetually stays intact — that we own the blunder and use it as energy for when we are once again exhausted.

And that's what I'm working on. Using that moment as my fuel to do better — to be a better Abba during those moments when I am spent.

Because we are not perfect. We make mistakes and will continue to make mistakes. But all we can do as parents is strive to do the best job we possibly can.

Our children will grow to be adults themselves. We may not get to enjoy the proverbial Promised Land with our children one day, but we have to remember it's our responsibility to get them there — and have faith that as long as we do what we can, they will figure out the rest.

We will be okay. And they will be okay, too.

(This essay originally appeared in The Forward
on April 26, 2020.)

SHELTER AND LOVE, STRENGTH AND COMFORT
Rabbi Evan Schultz

Tonight after putting the kids to bed I decided to go out for a short night run. Today felt immensely hard for so many of us, shutting down schools and synagogues, churches and senior centers. Even Disneyland closed.

There was a calmness in the air and I made my way down familiar streets, lit by the windows of neighborhood homes that seemed to be engaged in their regular evening activities- the glow of television sets, families gathered around the dining room table or washing the dishes together. Cars passing by as they do every night.

The last time I felt this way was when I went out for a run in 2012, the night before Sandy was scheduled to hit. As I ran along the promenade in Bridgeport, the waves of Long Island sound seemed unnerved. The cool breeze that I felt would the next day transform into a ferocious storm. Something about that moment then felt eerily similar tonight, although I hope that's not the case.

As I made my way back onto my street tonight and turned off my headphones, I took a moment to recite the Hashkiveinu prayer.

> *Hashkivenu Adonai Eloheinu l'shalom, vhaamideinu shomreinu l'chayim. Grant, O God, that we lie down in peace, and raise us up, our Guardian, to life renewed. Shield us and shelter us beneath the shadow of Your wings. Defend us against illness and sorrow. Guard our going and coming, to life and peace, evermore.*

For a moment I felt as though I truly prayed to God, as the droplets of rain and the cool March air briefly calmed my soul. Tonight and in the days to come, may we all find shelter and love, strength and comfort from one another and from our Creator as we weather and prepare for life's impending storm.

A LETTER TO MY CHILDREN DURING A PANDEMIC

Rabbi Todd Berman

I have lived a relatively comfortable life. Other family members experienced global upheaval and the horrors of war. Your great-grandfather, who grew up in the pale of settlement, for the first time, tasted fresh milk and eggs as a prisoner of war. He served in Czar's army in the war that was supposed to end all wars. My father, your grandfather, and his brothers survived childhood during the depression to eventually fight for the United States in the Second World War. Your cousins braved battle in the jungles of Vietnam.

It's not that I haven't experienced trauma and fear. I sat in a tape-sealed room wearing a gas mask while Saddam Hussein rained Scud missiles down upon Israel. Palestinians lobbed rocks and fired bullets in my direction as I traveled to and from Jerusalem. And, of course, we have all dealt with missile attacks flowing from Gaza. I have buried friends in the wake of terror attacks and mourned at the graves of children killed by terrorists.

The most traumatic event in my life was watching the impact of airplanes flown by terrorists collapse the twin towers in New York. That event launched two wars in far off lands. Despite it all, I have never experienced the trauma of a global pandemic with all of its medical, national, and financial implications.

What can I say to you? My parental duty is to keep you safe from an invisible killer that has shut down much of the world. You may not fully comprehend the devastation of the developing international financial crises, but the impact is taking a toll on your parents.

I fear for your health, but more for the health of many you've come to rely upon. Your grandparents, like so many others, are targets of this

161

respiratory killer. As global panic sets in and airlines are shutting down, how do I tell you it will be ok?

We keep hearing that the draconian precautions only slow down the spread and that the young and healthy need not be afraid; however, as a parent to multi-aged children, it's hard not to speak with fear. Schools are shut down. Even if they are moving to online sessions, the closing of brick and mortar institutions is nerve-wracking. Events were limited to 5,000 then 2,000, and now 100. Celebrations have been canceled, and the Israel Nature and Parks Authority has suggested we not venture forth to see the budding flora and wildflowers that are the result of an unusually rainy season. The Galilee is almost full, but we are warned not to swim. We wash – hands, cellphones, and surfaces in an almost OCD fashion. Friends here in Israel and abroad are quarantined, and we have discussed what we will need to keep our lives going when we have to do so.

How do we grapple with Purim and Passover in a time of Coronavirus (COVID-19)?

There is no consolation – only vigilance.

We are warned not to embrace even the friend, but I must embrace you. My children, I can't keep the world safe, but I can be there for you.

Rabbi Avraham Yeshaya Karelitz, the famed author of the book Chazon Ish, wrote a brief treatise on faith and trust in God. He writes that sincere trust is to realize that despite what people claim, "who knows the rulings of God and His actions?" He continues that trust in the Lord is "to believe that accidents don't happen." In other words, God runs the world, and we need to have confidence that things will turn out the way they are supposed to, whether we like the results or not.

Yet, it is hard to have such faith while figuratively, or literally, wearing an N95 respirator mask and gloves.

So let's pray. Let's pray that God watches over the world. Let's pray that He guides the self-sacrificing doctors, nurses, and medical professionals in their Herculean care for the sick. Let's pray He protects those life-givers who put themselves as risk to help others. Let's pray for those who have lost jobs and who fear for their safety and the safety of loved ones. And let's pray that God helps the scientists and researchers find a cure.

More than everything, let us pray that we, as a global society, learn to help each other overcome this trying time.

(This essay originally appeared in The Times of Israel on March 12, 2020.)

WHAT SINGLE PARENTS CAN TEACH LARGER FAMILIES DURING THE CORONAVIRUS CRISIS

Miriam Metzinger

My heart is beating a bit fast, and I explained to my 14 year old carefully, speaking almost syllable by syllable to make sure that he is actually listening and understands, "I have sent you by Whatsapp my teudat zehut, my identity card. Yours is on the slip of paper beneath it. It is proof of both our identities and proof that you are my son...Damn."

"What?"

"My new address isn't on the identity card. The card proves I am your mother but the address is the Gilo address. We lived there three years ago. What if a police officer asks you why you are walking from Katamon to Arnona, but not to Gilo?"

"Who would walk all the way to Gilo? It would take 2 hours."

"There are no buses and your dad can't take you."

And then I have one of my moments when my head clears of its own volition. My mind goes from boiling with the impossibility of it all to off the heat entirely. Stop. Start again. Well if the police stop my son on the way to walking to my house and they aren't convinced he is actually visiting his mother (child visitation is one of the few permitted reasons to travel according to the new regulations) because the address hasn't been updated on my identity card (it would have to have been updated annually.

We've moved so often in the six years after the divorce), and if, as a result, my son is fined 500 shekel, which means of course I am fined 500 shekel, then I'll pay it. However, since the regulations were upgraded last week, I have lost most of my day job clients, so how am I going to pay it?

During the best of times, certain predicaments as a single parent working day jobs are accompanied but what sound like schoolkid excuses like "the dog ate my homework."They are real, but they often sound fishy because they are so complicated or bizarre. Because when you are on your own, there are so many steps needed to do basic things, because everything depends on you. And if there is one detail missing, one thing that gets delayed, the whole day can go completely out of whack Often, things get pushed off, whether it is fixing the fridge or fixing the cat, if there isn't ready cash to do it immediately.

In the time of Corona, the excuses, or reasons, seem more convoluted and yet more common. Would a policeman really stop my son walking to visit me from his father's house if the photograph of my identity card lacking the correct address fails to prove that he had a valid reason to be in my new neighborhood? Sure, most police officers would probably believe the kid and would believe a single mother might not have had the time (or bothered, depending on the attitude) to change her address on her identity card. But who knows what kind of mood they are in, whether they are eager to prove they are super-efficient at enforcing these new regulations or whether they feel like they are above trying to prove something and want to show they can afford to be nice.

Of course, there are always stories that run around, like that guy on Facebook who says he was fined 500 shekel for stepping just a few meters past the 100 meter limit. After all there isn't anything to complain about. It would be sad if I can't afford the 500 shekel since I am out of day jobs, But I can't compare it to police brutality or even basic interrogation. After all, it is reasonable to think they are taking measures to keep us safe. It has been shown in other countries that tough measures such as these measures we might have considered draconian six months ago or fascist last year, we applaud now because they keep us safe.

However, there is this feeling that, as an immigrant single mother in Israel, there may not be someone who will have my back if I do get questioned, or get a ticket or even if I end up God forbid separated from my child somehow if one of us gets infected. And there is always the concern as a society that those in power might grow accustomed to this degree of control over people's lives long after the crisis ends (and please God it will someday).

I can't imagine what I would do if the Coronavirus crisis happened five years ago in a rundown apartment in the center of Jerusalem I rented by the month to save money. I recall a particularly exciting day when my three kids and I were packed in together in our 55 meter one-room apartment when there was a snow day when they were off school and couldn't wait to go out and build snowmen. The reason the apartment was livable for three people at all was that my children, like most Israeli kids, spent much of their time playing outside. Four years ago, during a spate of terrorist stabbings in the center of Jerusalem, we were ordered to keep our kids inside, and that seemed tough, but it was only for a few hours a day for a few weeks. Who knows how long this period if social isolation is going to last?

I see my neighbors taking their children on daily strolls on small circuits surrounding the building. Many of them express that, for the first time, Saba and Savta can't help them take care of their children because of the required separation to prevent Corona from spreading. Many lament that, for the first time, they are not going to have all of their family, including extended family members, with them around the seder table.

I think this is a time that many might start to understand what a single parent with a birth family absent because of distance, indifference or death, has to undergo during normal times. Similarly, dual parent families and extended families may be able to learn from single parents during this time of widespread social isolation. I was insisting for years (yet few seemed to believe me) that yes, a seder can really be a seder with just me and my kids, even if a few of them are with their father. Yes, believe it or not, if an adult can pull off a three course Shabbat meal every week of the year, she can also prepare, charoset, maror and the rest of the seder ingredients and the meal. The kids can even help and actually enjoy it.

Yes, she can have a meaningful haggadah reading with her sons. We can even stop and tell inside jokes and laugh over them without a bunch of other people telling us to get on with the haggadah and stop getting sidetracked. So many times, people didn't understand why I turned down seder invitations when I preferred to spend a seder just my kids and I, and now many people are having to do just that out of necessity. Social isolation during the time of Corona is telling larger families what single parents have been insisting all along--yes, you can do it alone when you need to, whether it is bedtime for the kids or homeschooling. At least in some sense, all families in the time of Corona can finally find common ground, and it is a time when single-parents can be better appreciated and understood.

(This essay was originally published in the Tribe Herald.)

THE GIFT OF MY CAVE
Rabbi Danielle Leshaw

I've been contemplating Rabbi Shimon bar Yochai inside his Galilean cave for close to 25 years. It's the ancient Talmudic story to which I always return -- his 13-year quarantine, his chosen companion for isolation, and his Torah study -- all a great pull on my imagination. In my 20s, during grad school, I found the story so compelling that I wrote a Sestina about Shimon and his son and their cave experience. I recall sitting at a tiny table in a tiny grad school apartment, my boyfriend at the time cheering me on. The floppy disc that contained my masterpiece, like other things from that time period, is long gone. But I hold the memory of my longing for that cave, and realize there have been many moments in my life that I've wanted to be isolated. Quarantined. Alone with the texts of my choosing and a sacred companion.

What I never could have predicted, all those years ago, is that I'd eventually have a period in my life where I wouldn't have to go places. Where the work would slow, the errands would cease, and the tasks in front of me – food preparation, keeping house, an occasional bank transaction – would replace all other motions that had once seemed essential. The cave in our Talmudic tale is sparse, and while their domestic experience is limited, it is clearly intentional. Shimon has only the clothing he arrived in, which he is careful to preserve. He has a very regular diet, eating only from a magical carob tree and drinking from the spring of water that emerged from the sand, a gift from God. I too wear the same clothes day after day. Overalls, a soft cotton tank top. Flip flops now that the weather is finally warm. I garden and I cook and I bake, but I also refuse the sour dough starter craze, and order nothing from Amazon. My domestic sphere is intentionally limited. Shimon and his son pray, and Shimon and his son study Torah. My sacred companions, it turns out, are not unlike Shimon's. I have only my children, and I have my rabbinic library.

168

I read a page of Talmud every day. I do research on concepts that are highly particular to the Talmudic rabbis and yet universal in many ways – the notion of intentionality and what happens when there are unintended side effects associated with your actions, courageous leadership coupled with abuse of power, our tendencies to compare concepts as a means to clarify ambiguity. I read our more contemporary Jewish literary giants – dipping back into Neusner and Levinas and Biale and Adler -- looking for answers to the questions that, after two months, fill an artist's sketchpad. I unshelve books that I haven't turned to in years, but that make up a rabbi's library. I've kept them around, moved them from house to house, unsure at each interval if I should abandon them to the local used bookstores, adding to the shelves of unwanted theology and philosophy and law. Turns out keeping them was the right decision.

When the shelter-in-place orders arrived and the libraries closed without much notice, I assessed the contents of my cave: hundreds of books, two funny teenagers, one kosher kitchen, packets and packets of seeds for the garden. What is here is what is here. We will eat and we will study. And this isolation period, with its results yet still uncertain, will have provided me with a gift I've always desired.

I DIDN'T BAKE BREAD

Sarah Tuttle-Singer

I didn't bake bread or garden or learn to sew.

I didn't start doing yoga in my living room, or listening to mind-bending podcasts that made me suddenly learn how to live in the moment.

I didn't learn Japanese, or make my own soap or build a shelf.

I didn't write down my dreams when I would wake up several times a night.

Instead, I washed the dishes seventeen times a day, wiped down counters, sorted, folded, lost a dozen socks and my temper too many times to count, and took pills to try to sleep. I cried every night for my dead mother and aunt and grandparents — I cried for the summer when I turned 14 and would listen to the Cranberries on repeat back when there were still grownups, and I felt safe.

I stopped looking at maps and dreaming about pirate ships.

I forgot what day it was even when I wrote it down on my hand.

I didn't write the Next Great Novel – but I wrote a Will – even though I don't have much to leave behind.

I did try to connect with family – with friends. But some days I was squeezed into a ball, and had nothing left to give, and no room to take. I got to know the lines on my face.

I joined an online minyan every night to say kaddish for my friend's mom.

I mourned.

I prayed.

I had no epiphanies.

I drank less than I thought I would. But I ate more ice cream and cookies.

I forgot how to talk to people I don't know in person.

I threw out my back.

I found my first white hair.

I didn't leave the house without a mask.

I realized I look better some days on Zoom than I do in real life.

I let my children stay up late so we would have more time together …
and also so they wouldn't wake up so goddamn early in the morning.

I am still in the sticky middle I suppose – maybe I'll be here for a long
time even when most of you are on the other side of this.

And really, there is no way to summarize what it's like as I sit here and
think about these strange and terrible days – for all of us in so many
different ways – except for this:

I didn't bake bread.

But I am still here.

(Originally published on Times of Israel
May 19, 2020)

THE MEN IN THE WHITE SUITS

Shira Pasternak Be'eri

I wanted to show you what it looks like when the men in the white suits arrive at your doorstep, when they come to swab your youngest son, just 22, an officer in the IDF, who shares an apartment with another officer, also 22, who just tested positive for COVID-19.

But they wouldn't let me photograph. And there was actually only one of them, accompanied by a soldier in a green uniform. He didn't get into his full hazmat regalia until he was right at our door. He didn't walk through my neighborhood in his eerie, apocalyptic attire, lest he spread panic. But perhaps he should have.

I wanted to tell you what it's like to fear for your husband, who sets out every morning to work in a hospital, while you work from home (or try to work from home) in your protected ark. He's a doctor, responsible for 30 children on ventilators, who have respiratory conditions that put them at high risk for the coronavirus.

But it's impossible to convey the sheer terror of my thoughts. What will happen if his patients catch this devastating blight? What if it happens to them suddenly, all simultaneously? Will my husband have to play God, like the doctors in Italy? What will that do to his soul? Will he have to fight to save each and every one of them and confront his failures? What could that do to his heart? And will he have to treat them while not adequately protected? What might that do to his body?

Could he, a ventilation specialist, find himself in need of ventilation, in a special kind of hell — on a ventilator in a ward where the medical staff does not have time to adjust the parameters of his machine properly, or where his respiration is being supervised by a gynecologist suddenly cast as a pulmonary specialist? Could he find himself lying there, knowing what needs to be done but unable to tell the practitioners who are treating him because he has a tube down his throat? How could he survive that kind of torment?

I wanted to describe what it's like to greet your partner the essential medical worker when he comes home every day, knowing the pressure that he is under in his medical capacity, knowing that he needs your embrace, while knowing that he might be exposing you to whatever he has been exposed to during the course of the day. But there are no words for the tension caused by that ambivalence.

I wanted to tell you what it's like to worry about your daughter-in-law, the nurse, who comes home from the hospital after tending to patients, and lovingly tends to your firstborn grandson, who is teaching himself to walk while confined to home. What would happen if she were to get sick? But I simply can't allow my thoughts to go there.

Close to 30 years ago, I sat in a sealed room on the second night of the Gulf War with a 2-week-old baby, who screamed in a protective plastic tent for what seemed to be an eternity until I broke down and took him out in order to nurse him. But the filter of my gas mask blocked me from seeing him as I looked down. Quaking, I took off my mask, and with tears streaming down my face, I let him nurse.

Some 20 years ago, I was jumped in my kitchen by a workman who left me beaten and bound, wondering if I would ever see my children again, as he made off with whatever he could take from our home saying that he would return and kill me if I called the police.

But this constant, insidious, unrelenting fear is unlike anything I have ever experienced.

So I beg you, some of my ultra-Orthodox brothers, who do not defend our country other than by learning Torah, and who are now actively threatening the lives of all those around you. Please stay home! Learn from the experience of your brothers and sisters in New York and New Jersey. Abandon your prayer quorums; have only the minimum necessary number of people at your weddings and funerals. Adhere to the recommendations of the health ministry as rigorously as you would to the rulings of the sages. When the members of your community fill our ICU's because you took unnecessary risks, there will be no beds and ventilators for the members of mine. For Heaven's sake, and for the sake of all the people of Israel, stop your desecration of God's name and stay home.

173

And I beg you, my young, healthy countrymen and countrywomen, those of you who feel that the regulations are unnecessarily harsh, those of you who are taking advantage of ambiguities and utilizing loopholes so as to cavalierly continue gathering and living life as usual. In the name of those of us who are over 50, who are immune suppressed, who suffer from asthma or diabetes, in the name of our medical personnel and of my husband's ventilated patients, and for your own sakes, I implore you: Please stay home.

Because when the men in the white suits come, they may very well be coming for you. And even if you come through fine, many of those around you may suffer a different fate.

(This essay originally appeared in The Times of Israel
March 23, 2020.)

TREE STUMPS & DESTRUCTION:
THE STILL SMALL VOICE WITHIN
Robin B. Zeiger, Ph.D.

Sometimes, the most important moments arrive in darkness and silence, as the "still small voice" from within. Dreams, nightmares, and prayers whispered in silence are reminders of this still small voice. I deeply believe that our Creator is not just a force outside of ourselves but resides inside each and every one of us. And it is our charge to listen to the whispers. During February and March, I was visited by two clearly numinous scenes from my night sea journeys.

The first one arrived seemingly out of the blue, on February 15, prior to the pandemic in my home country of Israel.

I was with a patient in my psychotherapy office when I looked outside the window. I was very frightened to discover a row of perfectly cut trees. Only the stumps were left, with no trace of the branches. And somehow, I knew that an alien force had caused this type of very strange and calculated destruction. I then frantically began to prepare to run away to Iceland before it was too late. The rest of the dream was busy with details of how to escape before the alien force sent me somewhere very scary. I woke up shaking. The dream felt surreal and reminded me of the horrific edicts of the Holocaust.

I was not only frightened by the dream, but I found myself fascinated. I am a Jungian psychoanalyst and a traditionally observant Jew. Both worlds honor dreams as a gift from a deeper place. I couldn't figure out why this dream came to me when it did. Thus, it nagged at me to discover the mystery of it all.

As the pandemic spread and began to severely affect my comings and goings in my own country, I met the dream anew. I could not run away, but oh how I wished I knew how to escape this world nightmare. I began to wonder if my dream, dreamt early on in the world's story, was somehow preparing me for the alien forces of a super-virus.

But why did I need Iceland? Dreams often bring us symbolic language to understand our unconscious fears and wishes. Perhaps Iceland symbolized the farthest place I could imagine. Here I could be safe from the danger. Or perhaps its name suggests a place where I won't "feel". I could become numb to the fear and sadness.

The saddest and scariest part of the dream was the tree stumps. For this, I needed something beyond words to meet my nightmarish fear. I painted the "scene from the window of my soul." As, I read the news I began to meet all the sadness, uncertainty, and deep angst of our Globus.

Mother Nature teaches us again and again that destruction heralds rebirth. When I "showed" my art to a group of my colleagues, they sent me photos of stumps of hope. I somehow saw with new eyes all the tree stumps in my 100 meters of lockdown. I discovered the life that grows and regenerates from the stumps.

In March, a beautiful dream image arrived:

I dream about a meeting with a supervising analyst and Holocaust survivor in her 90's, I chose to call Tikva. She continues to bless the Jungian world with her work as a bright, warm, insightful, analyst and supervisor. From time to time, I consult with her. Yet, due to her age and the pandemic we were not able to meet and I missed her. In my dream,

I see Tikva with her hand on her belly. She is sitting comfortably on a chair and is pregnant I think with a girl. I am very excited and think it will be cool that she is probably the oldest person to give birth. I am a little worried about the stress of the actual birth and think they will probably do a C-section because of her age.

The dream of tree stumps and an alien force brought warning and destruction. I desperately wanted to run away and hide. Here, Tikva becomes a symbol of hope and rebirth. She has lived through a Holocaust and merited the continuity of birthing souls, as a mother, grandmother, and teaching analyst.

There is something else I know as an analyst and dreamer; our dream characters are part of our Self. My longing for the concrete Tikva heralded an important meeting with my own inner Tivka.

176

This is the Godliness that exists inside of all of us. The world is sometimes full of suffering and destruction. Yet, it is our charge as human beings created in the Image of God to meet this suffering. There is a beautiful midrash about the first human being. Adam and Chava were created back to back as one androgynous being with a 360-degree perspective. Yet, they could not "see" each other. When God separated them; they could then look at each other face to face. Human beings are the only creatures that are intimate face to face. And when we look into the eyes of the other, we begin to peek into the soul. It is from that we create the I-Thou relationship of humankind.

My first dream foreshadowed that it was not possible to run away. This pandemic has taught us again of the power of *Anima Mundi* (the World Soul). We are all in this together. Yet, the togetherness includes our Creator, who cries and laughs and hopes with us. And in the still small voice of the night, we find not only our despair and suffering, but our hope and Godliness within.

THE LIGHT AT THE END OF IT ALL
Leora Londy-Barash

The light at the end of the tunnel erases all hints of darkness in an instant. We are light-seeking creatures who are consistently surprised when blinded or blindsided by light. Looking for hope in desolate times is the essence of humanity.

Daily life in Israel has commenced. There is a sense that a ticker-tape parade was held announcing victory in the fight against this barely-understood enemy. Children have gone back to school. Falafel stands have reopened to loitering customers. Cigarette breaks have resumed and people have stopped hiding that they have been seeing their elderly grandparents (for weeks now.) Masks have also found their way under the nose in the most irresponsible fashion statement ever to be made. It feels eerie and I find myself teetering between joining the glory-shouting bandwagon and acknowledging the very large elephant-in-the-room that is a global pandemic (lurking in its creepy germy ways around the corner.) How soon we forget!

The Jewish tradition teaches us to remember that we were once slaves in Egypt. We are reminded of it by the mezuzot on the doorposts of our homes, by the tefillin that we lay between our eyes and on our arms, by the words of the Shema that we hum to sleep at night, by the kiddush on Shabbat, and by the entire holiday of liberation (Pesach,) which directly addresses and retells this memory in first-hand form. We work hard to keep the lessons of the past alive and yet here we are, only seven weeks after leaving Egypt, to receive the Torah of the return to normality. With that, we have seemingly forgotten that we were once enslaved with masks, quarantine, and the fear of ventilators.

During the past weeks, we have mourned the loss of life along with the loss of a sense of predictability. And while it is understandable why people are rushing back to the safety-net of "life before", I am reluctant to let go of this precious black gem that was hurled full force at my head. It changed me.

The beginning of quarantine came with disillusionment and anger. Anger at lost time and lost purpose. Anger about having to face the challenge of rising to the moment to give my young children security in complete tohu va'vohu. But, with the passing of days into weeks, I was humbled. The moments of emptiness became full of life. Rushing was replaced with lingering and being. There were infinite moments of stress and crying (by all parties) but there were also infinite moments of laughter, reflection and reassessment. The rhythmless days started to sing.

During this time, between the liberation of the mundane to the exaltation of here and now, we found holiness. The countless days of counting from here to there to oblivion became days that I hoped would end the moment that they started but also hoped that they would never end. The light at the end of the tunnel seems to be shining in, but a part of me is not ready to go back. I want to hold on to this holy and horrific space in time and make sure that I don't forget the pain along with the growth and engrain the lessons, the feelings and the memories from COVID-19 time into my very being.

Blessed are Your God, Ruler of the Universe, who gifts us memory, reflection, growth, and transition.

LEADING WITH TEARS OF RESILIENCE
Rabbi Morris Zimbalist

The news came on video. It was followed up by a phone call, and then a request to join a Zoom meeting. The message was expected and titled with the words "Broken Hearts, Clear Minds." The summer camp that our son loves – that our entire family loves – is cancelled for the summer.

Participants on the Zoom call referenced leadership, and I applaud the director and his staff. Without question, all involved in making this difficult decision exhibited extraordinary leadership and kept to their mission of keeping our children safe and secure, even if that meant keeping them out of camp. Many leadership decisions pose the risk of breaking hearts, but nonetheless, those decisions must be made —made with clear minds and articulated with candor. Leaders know this. Community members expect this. To be an effective, successful, and steadfast leader and to gain the trust of and experience the best from the communities they serve, leaders must hold themselves accountable for the decisions they make and how those decisions are shared. This camp director nailed it, and those listening appreciated it.

The leader of my son's summer camp is a rabbi, and I'm a rabbi, too. Not a camp rabbi, though; rather, I serve a congregation of approximately 465 families – roughly 1,200 people. Comforting the brokenhearted, raising the spirits of the heavy-hearted, and offering unrequited empathy to those who bare their hearts is part of a rabbi's daily routine. So is speaking with thoughtful candor. Perhaps this causes some within congregations across the country and around the world look to their rabbis and other faith leaders as super-men and super-women. Exemplary service to communities could give the greater membership the perception that in fact rabbis are super-human, balancing the demands of the community with the needs of their families, friends, and time for self-care.

And while some may argue that "perception is reality," ask any rabbi and I suspect you'll uncover a sobering truth – rabbis, like the members of the communities they serve, sometimes struggle with maladies of the heart, whether they are broken, heavy, or both.

One of my rabbinic mentors addressed the complex emotional role and toll of rabbinic leadership by suggesting that even when times seem unbearable and uncertain, a rabbi should reserve his or her true heart-felt emotion and never cry. Leaders are meant to be pillars of strength for the individuals they serve. No one wants to see them cry.

Perhaps that image of a rabbi rings true for some, but for me it is terribly flawed. Tempering emotion and displaying raw emotion are important for all leaders, including rabbis. All the more so, in these strange times of COVID-19, rabbis are navigating uncharted waters that put their physical, emotional, and spiritual safety at a new level of risk.

Pastoral needs are constant as loved ones are dying alone in care facilities closed to the public, funerals are attended via electronic media, and condolences are offered through any means but physical contact. B'nei mitzvah are being rescheduled, weddings are on hold, and the High Holidays are promising little if any physical or familial comforts from the past. Rabbis are home-schooling their children in both secular studies and religious values, doing their best to be dance and gymnastics instructors, working to keep their spouses or partners sane while ensuring that the dishes and laundry are done and the dogs are walked and the litter boxes are clean. And as we face summer, they must learn how to be camp directors, counselors, and specialty staff.

Leadership is not mechanical. Rather, it's complex and sometimes messy. An "ordinary day at the office" or "ordinary day with family" is anything but ordinary, "time at home" cannot be equated to "time available," and "not being okay" in many respects reflects the new understanding of "normal." Personal time is at a premium, and it is easy to lose sight of the need for self-care. Leaders must recognize this, and the communities they serve need to accept and support it, while at the same time crafting the clear message that we are in this together and we will be okay.

The genuine emotion of a leader impacts the mood of the greater community and models for others what too often we are afraid to say or express. Leadership demands emotion and, just like every person in the communities they serve, leaders should feel comfortable to freely express emotion. What kind of leaders would they be if they didn't?

Sometimes leadership requires more from a leader than anyone would have ever expected, even the leader himself or herself. No one is super-human. Even the best leaders cry, and in today's world, that should be considered a hallmark of exemplary leadership. And when coupled with resilience, those tears and authentic emotion will reveal new pathways and opportunities for the future.

(This essay originally appeared in The Times of Israel
May 22, 2020.)

IN ALL OF THE PAIN I AM REMINDED WHY I BECAME A RABBI IN THE FIRST PLACE
Rabbi Elliot Cosgrove

"Like I told you, it's an honor."

With these words, Jimmy Breslin concluded his famous New York Herald Tribune column after the assassination of President John F. Kennedy. While every other journalist covered our nation in mourning, Breslin wrote about Clifton Pollard, the gravedigger who prepared President Kennedy's grave.

He made the small big, told the human story otherwise missed, describing the call Pollard received to come to work as he was eating his bacon and eggs; the reverse hoe he used to dig the grave, and the $3.01 hourly wage Pollard earned as "one of the last to serve John Fitzgerald Kennedy." Above all, Breslin gave voice to the quiet pride Pollard felt in shouldering his duty, ending with the gravedigger's own words: "like I told you, it's an honor."

As a rabbi serving a Manhattan congregation, more than the politics or policy prescriptions surrounding COVID-19, it is the pastoral human story of our global pandemic that has been my focus these past two months. An exponential increase in deaths compared to this time last year. Synagogue members, the loved ones of members, and the loved ones of our staff family. Many have been afflicted by COVID-19. Many are what I call "COVID-adjacent" — the precipitous decline and death of infirm or elderly individuals who in normal circumstances might have lived longer, and who because of the situation are mostly dying alone.

The cruelest moments have been the stories preceding death. One man had not been feeling himself and went to the hospital accompanied by his wife of 50 years. She sat in the waiting room as tests were conducted. A medical professional came, greeted her, and handed over her husband's cell phone and personal effects, instructing her to go home: he had tested positive. All she wanted was to stay at his side, to be with him as she had for a half century, but it was not to be.

There is nothing more heartbreaking than a family conversation on whether to withhold care for a loved one, except having to make those decisions from a distance. Until this month, I have never recited *vidui* — the death-bed prayer — to a person over the phone, and I hope never to do so ever again. Death is cruel enough as it is, but nobody should ever die alone. It is not just the number of deaths, it is the nature of each person's passing that has taken a staggering toll.

As any clergyperson knows, funerals are the most intimate and moving times to be with families: grieving together, weaving the narrative of a loved one's life, and providing the mourners with the social support of the community. But for these last months, funeral traditions have been upended.

There are no public funeral services; everything happens at graveside. Funeral homes are doing the best they can given the volume. Some cemeteries limit burials to just family, some to no more than five individuals, some do not permit anyone but the gravedigger. Sometimes the rules change — you don't actually know until you get there.

In order to protect the gravediggers, mourners are often required to remain in the car as the casket is lowered. Family members stand at a distance with masks and gloves. There are no handshakes or hugs. Inevitably, one person is holding an iPhone so others can watch from a distance: a child or a sibling not present, who couldn't get on a plane or take the health risk. There is no pomp or pageantry, no elegantly crafted eulogies, no playing the deceased's favorite song.

You cannot shovel earth as we did before, because that would require passing a shovel, so you grab a handful of earth – or three or 10 – and you throw it in your loved one's final resting place. Kaddish and the memorial prayer are recited and then ... you get back in the car. The service ends as abruptly as it began. In all its unfair inhumanity, there is something deeply authentic about it all.

Shiva, shloshim, and the rest of our post-burial rituals, as the Talmudic rabbis themselves understood, are meant both to honor the dead and comfort the bereaved. But the rabbis never imagined a moment like ours when public assembly would be forbidden. Children are not reconvening in their parent's home for a meal. There is no minyan to recite kaddish.

184

Many mourners go home to an empty house.

We have tried to do our best with online shivas. A time is set, a Zoom link created and an hour spent "together." In all its stilted awkwardness, it is not without merit. Loved ones gather from the four corners of the world, from across the span of a person's life — individuals who would otherwise never make it to shiva can join an online shiva. People share memories and, more importantly, people listen and can see other's faces in a way you just can't in a crowded room. It is not the same and it is heartbreaking to think of the mourner staring at the blank screen when the Zoom session ends, but it is better than nothing.

For all the heartache, these past months have not been without moments of profound humanity. One congregant told me about the kindness of a hospice nurse who suited up in PPE to hold a phone so he and his daughters could express their love for father and grandfather in his dying minutes. At a graveside funeral, the scribbled notes a congregant was reading blew from his hands directly into his grandmother's grave. Every subsequent speaker then placed their notes into the grave after speaking. Another congregant arrived home after burying his brother to find 10 physically distanced members of our synagogue standing outside ready to daven with him so he could recite kaddish in a minyan.

I am heartbroken that the pace has not permitted clergy to check in on the bereaved with greater frequency. Clergy need to reflect on how to better care for congregants even as we are off to respond to the next passing. We are far from perfect and I ask for patience and forgiveness as we try to do our best in this dark hour.

And in all of the pain I am reminded why I became a rabbi in the first place. To be brought into the confidence of people's lives with their humanity at its most raw; to be extended the opportunity to let the wisdom of our tradition ease a person's sorrow; to be present to remind people that even when they are most isolated, they are not alone. These months have been filled with the most trying, exhausting, and rewarding stretch of my pastoral career.

Like I told you, it's an honor.

(This essay originally appeared in The Forward
May 4, 2020.)

185

TORAH

FIVE TORAH PORTIONS: INSIGHTS FOR PANDEMIC AND POST-PANDEMIC TAKEAWAYS

William Liss-Levinson, Ph.D.

On Shabbat, April 25th, we read the double Torah portions of *Tazria-Metzora*. They yielded much fertile ground for parallels and metaphors for our COVID-19 pandemic, with insightful themes of designated experts being the sole determiners of the biblical plague of *Tzara'at* pertaining to diagnosis and treatment, issues related to isolation/quarantine, etc. If we look at the NEXT 5 Torah portions that followed, I think that there are some themes for all of us, both while we are very much still in the midst of the pandemic and for the "post-pandemic" period, as well. The ensuing 5 Torah portions were: *Acharey Mot; Kedoshim; Emor; Behar; Bechukotai*, which can be translated as: **AFTER DEATH; HOLY HUMAN BEINGS/SEPARATED ONES; SPEAK; FROM ON THE MOUNTAIN; WITH [MY] STATUTES**.

Now, and certainly **AFTER** the most intense period of infections and **DEATH** (*Acharey Mot*), we must take a very sober look at what we have learned and continue to learn from the deaths of all the **HUMAN BEINGS** felled by this virus. And what are the medical, psychological, social and spiritual lessons from those who have managed to survive after periods of **SEPARATION** (*Kedoshim*), isolation and often critical medical interventions.

We need to understand that they **SPEAK** to us in a commanding voice (*Emor*). It is a voice that demands of us - as individuals, cities, states, countries and as a global community - to honestly acknowledge what we have learned and how we will commit to effecting changes for those things that are under our control.

The intersection between climate change, emigration, immigration, refugees seeking asylum, poverty, slavery, hazardous working conditions, housing densities and housing inadequacies, water and food

187

inadequacies and concomitant hunger and starvation, and health care and healthcare inequities, shout to us as if **FROM ATOP A MOUNTAIN** (*Behar*). It is like the Midrashic interpretation that when God spoke to Moses and the Jewish people at Mount Sinai, at that moment in time, ALL the world heard God's voice. What will we do to meet these varied challenges that are really the forever plagues of our societies?

It is not simply whether there will be a resurgence of the virus or when will we have a vaccine and what will it result in on a short term and/or long-term basis. COVID-19 will come and go and other pandemics will certainly arise, as scientists have been telling us for decades. And yes, it is dramatically important when and how we "re-open." But it cannot be about "returning" to life as we knew it, to some idealized past "normal." The bigger issues are: what do we want our world to look like moving forward based on what we have learned?; what **STATUTES, POLICES, AND REGULATIONS** (*Bechukotai*) do we need?; what personal behaviors do we need to change?; what forms of leadership in times of crisis speak to the types of leaders we need at all times, even in the "best of times."

Psalm 33 is recited as part of the morning service on the Sabbath and Festivals. In verses 13-14, it says: "God observes from Heaven, and sees all of humanity. From God's dwelling place, God oversees all inhabitants of the land." Whatever your concept of God, it would do us all well to feel that we are under a lens. There is much for us to do to rid ourselves of inequity, bias, hunger, famine, poverty, hatred and disdain for science, facts and expertise. The mitigation, management and - if we are so lucky - elimination of COVID-19 at some point, will be insufficient for us to self-proclaim that WE are rid of the plagues of our own creation. We CAN do better and we MUST do better. We owe that to ourselves, to those who have died, to those who have survived, and to generations to come.

TERUMAH: TOGETHERNESS
Rachel Chabin

"And let them make Me a sanctuary that I may dwell among them."
–Exodus 25:8

A year ago this month, I celebrated a belated bat mitzvah with one of my dearest friends from university. As neither of us had ever formally marked such a milestone in our lives, we chose to embark on a project of learning to mark our growth as Jewish women, as well as the strides we had made during our four years of college. When the day arrived, we were overwhelmed by the sheer amount of love emanating from those around us who had gathered to mark our achievement. It was a celebration of accomplishment, of Jewish identity, of growth, of lifelong learning, and of Torah itself.

In the last weeks and months, our places of gathering and celebration have been shuttered, with the threat of spreading contagion from person to person outweighing any impetus or obligation to come together in person, whether for occasions joyous or solemn. To say that Jewish communal life has changed radically is to state the obvious: without access to synagogues, *minyanim*, and *tefilah b'tzibbur*, Jews have had to grapple with the question of what Jewish identity and observance might look like during isolation.

For me, this shift entailed a loss of the community structures I had come to cherish and rely upon, with the Beis community switching to remote engagement and my Hadar year fellowship drawing to an abrupt end ahead of schedule. And while my friends and colleagues began to adjust to virtual *chevruta* sessions and Zoom *kabbalat shabbat*, I found myself bewildered, lost, and unable to connect to any virtual community offered to me. Despite all of my walks to the park and around the neighborhood, I broke down in tears one Friday evening after a virtual *kabbalat shabbat* left me feeling more severed than connected. "I miss Torah," I managed to tell my fiancé. "I feel like I'm locked in a cage and the Torah isn't here with me."

189

There was no other way to say it. It did not matter that I had my books with me, my Talmudic dictionaries waiting patiently on their shelves, and generous *chevrutot* behind their computer screens beckoning me to study with them; I felt utterly torn away from Torah, with a profundity that can only be called heartbreak. I will not pretend that this feeling has completely gone away, or that I believe any virtual learning can be a perfect substitute for the rhythm of a bustling *beit midrash*. But in thinking about what the holiday of *Shavuot* represents, I began to consider another perspective.

Make no mistake: the Torah, more than anything else, is a blueprint for existence in diaspora. The time spent in the land of Israel is brief, and mainly occurs only before "Israel" was the name of a person, much less a place. Our forefathers spend moments of their lives in the ancient land of Canaan, but the bulk of the Five Books of Moses is spent abroad, in Mesopotamia, Egypt, and the Sinai Desert. Departure and movement is one of the Torah's principle motifs, and in fact the Chumash ends before the Israelites ever cross the Jordan into what will be their new homeland. Our forefather Avraham, considered by rabbinic tradition to be the first Jew, is said to have discovered God at the age of three, and forged on to worship an unrecognized deity utterly alone, joined only by his wife and immediate descendants.

And what is there to learn from this journeying? What can we gain from knowing of our ancestors' seemingly endless wanderings and crisscrossing pathways through time and across the deserts of the Middle East?

Last week, I had the pleasure of reading the *d'var Torah* of the friend with whom I celebrated a bat mitzvah. She wrote beautifully about the essence of *shemita* and *yovel* agricultural cycles and the virtue of preparing yourself for leaner times, so that when they arrive, you are not left bereft. And crucial to this process, she said, is leaning on your community when you most need support. "Judaism cannot be done alone," she explained when she summarized her essay. "You taught me that."

It's true. As a student leader in my university's Hillel, I constantly worked to make sure other students felt that they had a place in the Jewish world should they want or need it. I was emphatic to the point where "Judaism cannot be done alone," was as much a mantra as a *hashkafa*, and I tried to impart it to any Jewish student willing to listen.

190

But if Judaism is meant to be communal – filled with the richness and vibrance of crowded sanctuaries and populated study halls and overflowing *shabbat* tables – where could we find a sense of togetherness in an era of isolation?

More than ever before, I believe the answer lies in God's commandment in Exodus 25, to build a sanctuary so that He could dwell among the wandering Israelites throughout a generation of homelessness. It's one thing to build a shrine to a deity in order to connect to them, but what the Torah offers through this commandment is precisely the opposite: God sees His nation cut off from Egypt, the place they once called home, and still decades away from crossing the Jordan River, and decides to live among them.

This is the God Avraham encountered, says the *midrash*, as a small child surrounded by idol worship. This is the God that accompanied Yitzchak and Yaakov as they traveled from land to foreign land. This is the God that spoke to Moshe Rabbenu at the burning bush, when no one else was around to see. "*This is my God, and I will honor Him,*" cried the Israelites after crossing the Red Sea. "*This is my father's God, and I will exalt Him.*"

The festival of *Shavuot* commemorates the giving of the Torah at Sinai. Before a thundering voice could proclaim the Ten Commandments to the Israelites, our ancestors made a promise to keep the laws of the Torah with a timeless statement of confidence: "*We will do, and we will listen.*"

And why did they listen? Why were they ready to follow the laws of a Torah they had yet to see or understand? I believe they did so because while they might not yet have known the Torah's contents, they were intimately familiar with the God who offered it to them, the God who brought them forth from Egypt, sustained them with heavenly bread, sweetened the desert oases they encountered, and protected them with pillars of fire and clouds of glory in their wanderings through the wilderness.

This God had been with them since the time of their forefather Avraham. This God, who offered the Israelites protection through their journeys at every step, had no desire to be aloof, uninvolved, and distant from the affairs of daily life in the desert. This God watched God's children sojourning through the wilderness and, rather than turning a blind eye,

191

asked them to build God a home among them, so that He could dwell with the ones He so loved.

It is the Torah of this God that we accepted upon ourselves at Sinai, and that we extol on our holiday of *Shavuot*. The period of counting the omer between *Pesach* and *Shavuot* commemorates our journey from Egypt to Sinai – a journey through which God accompanied us every step of the way. And no matter what community we have surrounding us, whether in a packed synagogue or in a quarantined bedroom, the God whose Torah we accepted still dwells with us there.

VAYAKHEL-PEKUDEI: COMMUNITY IN THE TIME OF CORONA

Rabi Yael Ridberg

It is impossible to count the number of moments this past week where I have seen the creation of virtual communities online in response to the COVID-19 closures and shutdowns all over the world. The sing-alongs in apartment complexes, the free yoga classes, opera from the Met in NYC, rabbis teaching, families sharing, children learning, organizations meeting, and religious services streaming.

These convenings have been filled with the qualities with which the Torah imagines a sanctuary is built: *nediv lev* and *chacham lev* – generous and wise hearted people, bringing their gifts to the larger effort of making a sanctuary, and through which they can feel the divine presence.

With this week's double Torah portions of *Vayakhel-Pekudei*, we come to the end of the book of Exodus, as well as the end of the process of building the *Mishkan* (Tabernacle), crafting the tools and creating the clothing for the priests and the *Kohen Gadol* (The High Priest).

The Exodus text echoes the concluding words of the mythic tale of creation: *"And Moses saw all the tasks, and behold, they had done it as God had commanded them* (39:43), which sounds very much like, *"And God saw all that God had done, and behold, it was very good"* (Gen. 1:31); thereby making a connection between divine and human creativity.

The details are simultaneously mind numbing and intense, physical and spiritual manifestations both of God's presence and the people's faith. The Israelites have brought their willing hearts, their wisdom, skills, talents, and possessions to the creation of a sanctuary that for all intent and purpose, is not literally for God.

The text is clear that God will dwell "among the people," so why did the people *need* this sanctuary? This generation experienced and witnessed God's work in the world. The miracles that Exodus relates are all symbolic of Divine power shared with the Israelites. What could a portable sanctuary truly add to their faith, and their perception of God's presence?

Perhaps it is as simple as the need to transform a miracle based association with God into a more personal spiritual connection. This possibility is evidenced by the entire process of building the *Mishkan*. *Everyone* is invited to contribute because *everyone* is potentially impacted by the power of ritual and convocation.

How similar to this week's activities online. The platforms that only a short time ago we might have derided for their manner of *disconnect*, we now can see also can create intimacy where there seems to be none. When a picture I posted to social media after an impromptu wedding I conducted at the County Clerk's office of the couple and I bumping elbows and wearing masks invited more "likes" than I have ever received in response to something I posted, it was as if the couple had 900 people sharing in their joy instead of just the three of us and a witness.

The command was to build the Tabernacle, and God would come to dwell among the people. But a better rendering of the command might be, "build me a sanctuary, *such* that I will come to dwell." Something intimate is created by the acts of generosity in our day. The small sanctuaries built this week online enabled all aspects of life and invited the Divine to dwell among us.

The mythic story of creation in Genesis might also be explained by a divine instinct to want for human-divine connection, *such that we might experience God's presence* as we make our way in the world. The *Sefat Emet* (Rabbi Yehuda Leib Alter of Ger) taught that the *mishkan* was to be a place of testimony. It was to be a place where people would come to *testify of the experience of God*. Once people gave of themselves to build the sanctuary (likened to God creating the world), the root of testimony could grow in their hearts. *That* is when God could come to dwell among the people.

As I watched my children engage with their classmates and teachers through Zoom, the kids were so happy to see one another, the teachers were nimble and creative in their lesson plans, and it was clear that something sacred was happening.

194

Upon the completion of the *mishkan* Moses blessed the people (39:37), much like God blessed the Sabbath day upon the completion of creation (Gen. 2:3). The exact words of these two blessings are not recorded in the Torah, only the statement that they occurred. But *Midrash Tanhuma* (Pekudei 11:9) offers the imagined words of Moses to be: "May God's presence take root in the work of your hands."

When we feel God's presence (if we do), it is not usually because of a physical structure. It is more likely that we have opened to the possibility of authentic connection, and/or that we have contributed something meaningful of ourselves. When we experience those moments, or recall them later, we point to all the conditions that made it *possible* to experience the sacred – and then we feel blessed. May it continue to be so.

VAYAKHEL-PEKUDEI:
STAYING HOME WITH GOD
Yoseif Bloch

In a normal year, the Sabbath on which we read the double Torah portion of *Vayakhel-Pekudei* is something of an island in time. It comes as the pageantry of Purim is fading, while the intense preparations for Passover have not yet begun in earnest.

There's not much new in the Torah portion itself, although it occupies the last half-dozen chapters of the Book of Exodus. Essentially, the Jewish people do what they have been told, to build a house for God at the foot of Mount Sinai. The theme is simply about coming together for a common purpose, men and women, rich and poor, architects and artisans, leatherers and laborers. At the end, God rests His Presence upon the people. It's fitting for a portion that begins with: *"Vayakhel Moshe,"* "And Moses gathered all the Israelite assembly." The term *kehilla* — congregation, community — comes from the same root.

Of course, that's in a normal year, which this year has most assuredly not been. In 2020/ 5780, *Shabbat Vayakhel-Pekudei* was the first Sabbath without our *kehilla* -- our friends, extended family, neighbors. Our synagogues, schools and study halls were shuttered, as we were locked down in our homes. Some of us wondered: How can we approach God without our regular *minyan* (quorum)? How can we pray? How can we study?

Personally, I took comfort in two rabbinic sources.

First, the Mishna, from *Avot (Ethics of the Fathers)* 3:6:

> *Rabbi Halafta ben Dosa of Kefar Hanania said: When ten sit together and occupy themselves with Torah, the Divine Presence abides among them, as it is said: "God stands in the assembly of God" (Psalm 82:1).*
> - *How do we know that even five? As it is said: "This band of His He has established on earth" (Amos 9:6).*

196

- *How do we know that even three? As it is said: "In the midst of the judges He judges" (Psalm 82:1).*
- *How do we know that even two? As it is said: "Then they that fear the Lord spoke one with another, and the Lord hearkened, and heard" (Malachi 3:16).*
- *How do we know that even one? As it is said: "In every place where I cause My name to be mentioned I will come unto you and bless you" (Exodus 20:20).*

Second, the Tosefta (*Sukka* 4:3), citing Hiller the Elder:

> *Wherever my heart lies, there my feet take me. [Thus God says:] If you come to My house, I will come to yours; if you do not come to My house, I will not come to yours, as it is said: "In every place where I cause My name to be mentioned I will come unto you and bless you."*

This is a Divine promise: if we go to the study hall and synagogue when we are able, God will come to us when we stay home to protect the elderly, the vulnerable and those who care for them. Even if we are five or three or two or one, God will meet us wherever we may be.

VAYAKHEL-PEKUDEI: AND THEY ASSEMBLED
Rabbi Tamara Cohen

And Moses said *dayam*, enough.
Enough: enough.

Stop, withdraw,
bring/do/perform/gather   no more.

Let the silver glare of a silent sanctuary,
the gold blue of a plane-less sky
the garnet sheen of an empty concert hall
be our sacred offering,
meager gifts of absence from wise and less wise-hearted people.

Please God let our ceasing be enough.
Let our hospital beds be enough.
Let our slow awakening to the interconnectedness of every living being
be enough
Let a pillar of stillness rest at the entrance to every home and prison.
Let this plague pass over us, enough of us.
Enough.

SHMINI 5780: TRAGIC OPTIMISM
Rabbi Barry Leff

I can't decide whether I'm getting used to our new coronavirus reality, or whether the sense of "unrealness" is getting worse. Maybe both at the same time.

For some people, the costs of the novel coronavirus are very much in their face. Some people, including members of our HNT community, have lost loved ones to the disease, or live with the frustration of loved ones having the disease, hospitalized, and being unable to be by their side. Others have had, or now have it themselves. Many have lost their jobs and are terrified about the future. Some are healthcare or other essential workers, exposing themselves to danger on a daily basis to take care of the sick or allow us to have food on our tables.

In our community we're fortunate that most of us are not directly living with the real costs of coronavirus. Many of us are able to work quite comfortably from home, some are retired and don't have to worry about working. But everyone is impacted by the coronavirus, at least psychologically. Our world has changed. Our routines are completely disrupted. Simple pleasures we took for granted, like having friends over for Shabbat dinner, or going out to a concert, are denied us. And that takes a toll.

A rabbinic colleague, Sue Fendrick, posted something on Facebook that captures how many people feel:

> *I heard many people independently say–after feeling it myself–that yesterday they just hit a wall, felt the sadness and stress at a new level or for the first time, etc. My mom said that she experienced the same thing among her friends and contacts.*

I'm a big "let's name it" person, so let me just name this: It's not about weeks anymore. We're no longer counting in weeks, we have now been doing this for a month.

In that month, we've learned that this is going to be many months, very possibly over a year, of substantially dealing with (in a variety of ways) the impact of COVID-19 on our lives and our communities and most of what we take to be the normal way things work, and the planned and imagined trajectories of what we expected to be in front of us in the next year or two.

In the beginning, there was the adrenaline, the gearing up, the WTF, the figuring out how to cope, for now.

Now we're at the beginning of the very long and uncharted middle.

A Kaiser Foundation poll from early April found that 45% of all Americans feel their mental health has been negatively impacted because of coronavirus related stress and worry. And that number was up significantly from a poll taken in early March.

What can we do to preserve our mental health? How can we cope with the stress, the worry, the uncertainty?

We need to tend to our bodies, our minds, and our souls. The three are inextricably connected.

I'm not going to dwell on what to do for your body. It's the things your doctor tells you every time you go in for a physical. Eat healthy, take your medication, get some exercise. Exercise is especially important in these times when we're either not working or working from home and living a more sedentary than usual existence. Exercise, even just a walk in the fresh air, with proper social distancing of course, reduces stress hormones in our system.

I'm also not going to dwell on what to do for your mind. Our minds need exercise too, and there are all sorts of ways to stimulate the brain beyond spending 5 hours a day on Netflix.

But what about our souls? How do we nourish our souls, which is probably the real key to maintaining one's mental health in a difficult time?

200

It's by cultivating the right attitude. An attitude of "tragic optimism."

Tragic optimism is a term coined by the famous psychiatrist and Holocaust survivor Victor Frankl, z"l, in his book "Man's Search for Meaning." It is also, perhaps, the quintessential Jewish response to adversity.

As Frankl describes it, tragic optimism is an optimism in the face of tragedy that allows for

> *1) turning suffering into a human achievement and accomplishment;*
> *2) deriving from guilt the opportunity to change oneself for the better; and*
> *3) deriving from life's transitoriness an incentive to take responsible action.*

In an oped piece in the NYTimes on using tragic optimism to cope with coronavirus stress, Emily Esfahani Smith described a study of the well-being of young adults in the wake of the 9/11 attacks. None of the students in the study lost loved ones in the attacks, but they did report feeling distressed, as I think all of us felt. The study found some of the students were much less likely to be depressed. What was the difference? As Smith describes it,

> *What set those resilient students apart was their ability to find the good. Unlike the less resilient students, the resilient reported experiencing more positive emotions, like love and gratitude.*
>
> *But that didn't mean they were Pollyannas. They did not deny the tragedy of what happened. In fact, they reported the same levels of sadness and stress as less resilient people. This finding comes up frequently in psychology research: In general, resilient people have intensely negative reactions to trauma. They experience despair and stress, and acknowledge the horror of what's happening. But even in the darkest of places, they see glimmers of light, and this ultimately sustains them.*

Frankl did a study more than 60 years ago in which he pinpointed a critical way to find those glimmers of light. Frankl reported on what he called "unemployment neurosis." People who were unemployed who were depressed, feeling they were useless, that their lives had no meaning. Frankl determined that these feelings were the result of two erroneous

201

assumptions: 1) that to jobless meant you were useless; and 2) that to be useless means your life has no meaning.

Frankl wrote:

> *Consequently, whenever I succeeded in persuading the patients to volunteer in youth organization, adult education, public libraries and the like – in other words, as soon as they could fill their abundant spare time with some sort of unpaid but meaningful activity – their depression disappeared although their economic situation had not changed and their hunger was the same. The truth is that man does not live by welfare alone.*

What keeps people going isn't denying the tragedy of the situation or finding a way to be "happy." It's about finding meaning. And meaning in context is NOT about understanding the ultimate meaning of life. It's about having meaning in your day. Doing something you perceive as useful.

This week's Torah portion, Shemini, like everything we've had so far in the book of Leviticus, has a lot of stuff about sacrifices. Sacrifices in general reflect a sort of tragic optimism – there's the minor tragedy of the sacrifice, giving up something we value, but it's accompanied with the optimism that this is a path for repairing damage we may have caused in our relationship with God. The tragedy has meaning.

In this week's parsha we also see Aaron's response to a horrible tragedy – the death of his sons. The very same day his sons died, he continued in his job as Kohen Gadol, bringing the sacrifices that it was his right and responsibility to bring. Yet he was clearly also in mourning. The Kohanim were supposed to eat the goat of the sin offering, and instead Aaron had it burned. Moses was angry with Aaron -- he said, "Why didn't you eat it? It's most holy, God gave it to you to remove the guilt of the community!"

Aaron's response was,

> *They brought their sin offering and their burnt offering before the LORD, and such things have happened to me! If I'd eaten the sin offering today, would the LORD have approved? (Leviticus 10:19)*

Aaron was clearly in mourning. He was clearly troubled. And yet the great meaning he found in his work allowed him to carry on.

202

Throughout history, Jews have responded to catastrophes with "tragic optimism." After the destruction of the Temple, yes, we mourned, and we still mourn on Tisha b'Av, but we also affirmed a belief that future redemption will come, we found comfort in our community and in our rituals.

When the Jews were given the choice of convert, die, or leave by King Ferdinand in 1492, most didn't simply give up and convert or die. The people left. Giving up their material comfort, their homes, they surely experienced tragedy, but they also clung to hope, saw a glimmer of light, that in a new place they could find a way to remain faithful to their God and rebuild their lives.

Frankl wrote his book after surviving the horrors of Auschwitz and other concentration camps. He found that even in the most dire of circumstances, there are ways to find meaning, often by performing acts of service for other people.

My favorite Jewish example of tragic optimism is a pair of holidays coming up later this month. Yom HaZikaron and Yom Ha'atzmaut. If you haven't lived in Israel during those holidays, you can't really understand them. Yom HaZikaron is Israel's Memorial Day. Here in the Diaspora the day is mostly ignored. We'll have a community celebration of Yom Ha'atzmaut, but do nothing for Yom HaZikaron. In Israel Yom HaZikaron is a huge deal, way more than Memorial Day in America. The nation stops for the sounding of a siren, just as on Holocaust Remembrance Day. Schoolchildren all have solemn ceremonies to attend. Cemeteries are full of people visiting the graves of loved ones who gave their lives to defend Israel. Yet at sundown we go directly from the mourning of Yom HaZikaron to the celebration and barbeques of Independence Day. Yes, we mourn. Yes, we remember those we lost. But the tragedy gives way to thanks and optimism.

I am grateful that my mental health does not seem to have been adversely affected by the coronavirus crisis, and for that I thank you, the Herzl-Ner Tamid community. I have as much meaning as ever – even more than ever – as we navigate these difficult times. I'm grateful we live in a time when technology makes it possible for me to continue much of my rabbinic work even in a time of physical isolation.

Throughout our history, Jews who are in difficult circumstances conclude both the Passover seder and the Yom Kippur prayers with a message of hope – l'shana ha'ba'ah birushalayim, next year in Jerusalem. Next year at peace. Next year in a better world.

Next year in a world where it is safe to have our joyous seders physically present with friends and family.

Amen

TAZRIA-METZORA
Rabbi Tamara Cohen

On the quarantine trampoline my son and I jump high and fall down
bouncing
my knee aches but I jump again
here in this caged circle we are safe and can forget.

He is shirtless and I am shedding hat, mask, gloves, jacket.
He is a superhero, fast and wicked , and I an ancient priest,
pomegranate bells tinkling at my ankles and the words "clean, clean" on
my lips.
I lift my arms as he calls out "make me jump higher" and I have been set
free over the open field,
wings spread wide and dappled with the sticky blood of the slaughtered
ones.

I rise over house and yard, make-shift hospitals, border crossings shut
down, and I land
softly at the entrance to the Tent of Meeting, join the long spaced-out line
of the lucky ones, head-shaved, lips covered, waiting for the holy
pronouncement, for the relief of a prescribed guilt offering, for male
lambs without blemish and choice flour, 3 tenths of a measure.

The big blue house in which we dwell is being torn down.
Its stones and timber, its caretakers and sick, it's pretense of justice,
all the coating on the house. We will jump under the white wisp of
Iyyar's moon
until we tire or collide, seeking expiation, healing, the wild hope and
sacred will to cease long enough.

TAZRIA/ METZORA:
WHO'S INSIDE AND WHO'S OUTSIDE
Yael Hirsch-Biderman

The two parashot "Tazria" and "Metzora," that we read together this Shabbat, are found at the heart of the book of Leviticus and deal exhaustively and, perhaps too graphically, with a multitude of situations that fall on the spectrum between purity and profanity and the actions we are to take to deal with these states. These parashot and the issues that they raise are of the kind that most of us would choose to skip over out of lack of interest and our own discomfort. It seems that in more ordinary times it's difficult to find a connection between the text and our lives today.

But a close reading may lead us to seek the human story within the parasha's seemingly endless rules surrounding 'nida' (female purity rituals) after giving birth, leprosy, disfigurement of garments or in the home. Along with all of this, the scripture describes the priest's role in handling the various situations ranging from impurity to purity.

Biblical scholar Jacob Milgrom, who has studied these issues extensively, argues that the sequence of examples given in the parasha are meaningless in and of themselves, however, the spectrum between impurity and purity in various circumstances or settings as it relates to people, and to women in particular, is a constant reminder of our choices in life, and the possibility of change and movement through ritual action. These possibilities range from looking within ourselves to turning outward, between closeness and distance, and between death and life.

What is it like for the woman who safely gives birth and immediately afterward becomes 'impure'? What is it like for the leper when the priest sentences him to another seven days of isolation? What is the experience like for those moving between these two extremes – pure and impure –

206

when some such movements involve a dramatic transitional ceremony? Do these transitions free them and allow them to move through a kind of natural dynamic of life? Or do they carry traumas and difficulties with them back into the "safe space" of purity? Is this system of laws supposed to benefit the individual or is it intended to organize and institutionalize social order?

Traditional and secular Jews are usually disconnected from the tension between impurity and purity, but it seems to me that some of these biblical processes may relate to some social insights that are relevant today.

The distinction between who is inside the camp and who is outside, as well as life experiences that force us to confront mortality, or that evoke intense fear may require a recovery process in order to return to our normal routines. Common to all of the situations described in the parasha is that they could happen to any one of us. It's not about them and us, but rather about our constantly-changing reality. Just like our current situation, there is no telling who will "become impure" by getting infected, and as such will have to "dwell outside of the camp," by going into quarantine. This uncertainty engenders mobility in the private and social spheres. This dynamic also raises important questions like: Where do we place the woman or couple who has just given birth in this context? What place do we give to the sick and elderly who need us and may live in constant fear of death? What is the place for bereaved families who have had a horrific encounter with death and face the continuous dialogue of life in the here and now?

In Israel, we find ourselves in this special time, the week between Holocaust Remembrance Day and Yom HaZikaron (memorial day for fallen soldiers) followed by Independence Day. In addition to these commemorative days, the coronavirus pandemic and the resulting crises, demand of us as individuals and as a society to take responsibility and seek those who are outside the camp – those whose encounter with death is unbearable, those who need care, support, warmth and recognition of their situation.

Tazria – Metzora are difficult parashot, but at the same time they ask us to take a hard look at reality and to touch life itself – between the body, the walls of the house and the clothing and to examine the situation. To touch, to see, to pay attention – and not to ignore.

It seems to me that the COVID-19 pandemic allows us to experience a bit of what happens to those who had to leave the Israelites' camp. But the view of life from the outside is not always negative. It allows for the process of restarting, of rethinking. Leaving the camp also gives us an opportunity for self-introspection. Sometimes it allows for quiet and gives us an excuse to take a break from the constant noise of life. It seems to me that these days we are all trying to figure out how to re-enter the camp – that is, how to go back outside to our familiar routines, with careful and measured steps and, most importantly, safely. Perhaps during biblical times, the ceremonies and leadership of the priests provided solutions for those whose time had come to re-enter the camp and get back to their lives and routine. And we should expect our leaders to show us the way professionally and confidently, step by step, back to a safe routine during this new reality.

(This essay was originally published by
Binah: The Jewish Movement for Social Change
April 24, 2020)

TAZRIA METZORA:
WHAT WE LEARNED
IN SPIRITUAL QUARANTINE

Rabbi Charlie Savenor

Reports about infection cascade across the page. This invisible menace adheres on skin, clothing, and household surfaces. It's not clear where the disease comes from or how it spreads, only that it must be contained and the afflicted quarantined.

One might easily expect that this scenario depicts the current reality of the Coronavirus unfolding outside our windows and on our TV screens, but this dismal picture comes directly from the Torah portion, *Tazria Metzorah*. The only thing missing are the sirens in the background whose shrill alarms pierce the silence of New York City's now empty streets.

Mah Nishtanah: On all other years, this almost overlooked Torah portion most commonly beckons us to comment on how we care for the sick or prevent the damaging effect of gossip.

But on this Shabbat in 2020, the contemporary relevance of this ancient text surges within our consciousness with the ferocity of a riptide. Looking at these chapters like we never have before, we stand united spiritually despite being separated physically.

The Torah deals with a biblical malady called *tzara'at* that is believed to be similar to leprosy. For the afflicted, this condition impedes everyday life in the Israelite community. When the symptoms erupt, the Torah gives clear guidelines to the priests of that day: "He shall be impure as long as the disease is on him. Being contaminated, he shall dwell apart; his dwelling shall be outside the camp." (Leviticus 13:46) Serving as much as a government official as a pastor, the *kohen* is called upon to separate the afflicted from the community.

It is logical for us to surmise that the rationale for this quarantine is to shield the community and the afflicted soul from one another. Yet commentators across the generations note that the procedures in place do not sound entirely medical in nature.

If this detailed sacred source is not protecting public health, then what meaning does it hold for us? The Torah and Talmud link this affliction to the ethical failings of gossip, so the quarantine amounts to something akin to a social "time out."

By contrast, Rabbi Samson Raphael Hirsch asserts that this physical separation is not about time served but rather time away: "During this period of isolation he will contemplate changing his ways and will reconsider his past behavior. Thus, he will come to a change in his attitudes and undertake to improve his character, and, as a result, he will emerge from the test stage in a pure state." In his eyes, the seven-day quarantine constitutes a sabbatical in the truest sense of the word. The separation represents an opportunity for internal growth that is more than skin deep. Walking back to the camp, the *metzora* is supposed to look at oneself and the world itself differently.

In some strange way, this biblical quarantine reminds me of *shiva* -- the prescribed week's period of mourning in Judaism. Sadly, *shiva* during COVID-19 has been conducted amid shelter in place. Both experiences disrupt our daily lives and conclude with a transitional moment when it's time to reenter society.

When my father died nearly 25 years ago, from the instant he breathed his last breath through the end of *shiva* was a surreal and numbing blur. After a week of remembering, crying, laughing, eating, and embracing, the concluding ritual was to walk around the block to symbolically reenter the normalcy of communal life.

What I didn't expect was that crossing the threshold of our door would be a life changing experience. In the matter of just days, the world looked different. Certain priorities and sources of anxiety were put into perspective. In short, a clarity had emerged about what matters.

One day, hopefully soon, when the COVID-19 virus has been defeated and the sirens are silenced, the moment will arrive for us to make a symbolic walk around the block to re-enter normal life.

Before we take that first step, let's consider what we have learned about ourselves and our community since the beginning of March. The world we left behind faced serious challenges: political polarization that eroded civility, the environment, homelessness, food insecurity for the poor, racial inequality, sexism, xenophobia, and the plague that won't go away, namely Antisemitism. Looking out my own window, I realized that for the first time since the Pittsburgh synagogue massacre 18 months ago there hasn't been a police car parked outside the synagogues across the street.

With the beginning of social distancing, we have witnessed a sense of solidarity that we haven't seen since 9/11. In addition to humanity's circling of the wagons, this ferocious virus inspired us to reach out to old friends, let bygones be bygones, eat family dinner on a daily basis, and acknowledge medical professionals, grocery staff, and teachers as the unsung heroes that they are.

At our finest hour during this dark chapter, we have achieved clarity about what matters.

Unfortunately retaining this clarity is extremely challenging as *Midrash Genesis Rabbah* observes: "In time of trouble, people vow; in time of relief, they return to old habits." The rabbis understand that clarity evaporates quickly if it isn't intentionally integrated into our souls.

Rabbi Hirsch writes that the quarantine of the biblical *metzora* reveals the "discrepancy between the life that he leads in the world and the life that he is called upon to lead." The same can be said of us today.

While shelter in place enables us to reflect on life's priorities, the biggest challenge is retaining the clarity that has emerged within us. When tomorrow comes, will we build on what unites us to tackle humanity's current and future challenges or do we go back to our tribal and frequently petty divisions?

Before walking across the threshold of our doorstep, do we truly want to go back to "normal?" I don't.

(A version of this essay appeared in the NY Jewish Week
April 22, 2020)

BEMIDBAR:
LESSONS FROM THE WILDERNESS
Rabbi Robyn Fryer Bodzin

This year, we practically skipped *Sefer Vayikra*, the book of Leviticus. Most Jews did not join together physically as a community for the entire time we should have been reading *Vayikra* each week in synagogues around the world. For this third book of the Torah, we were not able to see each other's faces except through a screen, or give each other hugs, which I miss very much.

I find it ironic that Jews were not permitted to join together in sacred space during the weeks when we learned in the Torah about how to live with centralized sacred space as a focal point. So much of the *Sefer* is about the *Mishkan* (Tabernacle) and its accompanying sacred duty which could only be done in that one particular place.

While we missed *Vayikra*, we know the holiness described in *Vayikra*. We know how to lead holy lives because we inherited a different kind of Judaism where communal gathering is but one focus.

This Shabbat we pivot and begin *Sefer Bemidbar* with *parshat Bemidbar*. It is the book of the Wilderness.

The Israelites had a destination. They were going to the Promised Land. It is a bumpy ride, but they get there every year. This destination was promised to them by God, as it was part of the covenant.
Unlike the Israelites, in COVID-19 time, we don't actually know where we are going. We don't know what to expect on the other side. I am not convinced we are going back to where we were before and of course that makes most of us uncomfortable.

It could be that for some of us, it feels like we have already been wandering aimlessly for 40 years since COVID-19 began impacting daily life here in Toronto. Days never end when you are isolated with young children at home or when you don't or can't work, and can't currently figure out your purpose or meaning.

If we look to the Israelites as examples, we know the journey will be bumpy, and we also know that most of us will survive along the way. While the journey was sometimes arduous for them, the Israelites make it to their destination. But us? We are living in undefined terms and most of us know at this point that it is going to be a very long journey.

There is so much that we thought we would need on this journey. While we were caught off guard and unprepared back in March, many of us have discovered that, actually, we need very little and we can adapt. Manicurist? Hair Stylist? Car? Big box shopping? Continuous gastronomic tour of vegan restaurants? Apparently I can do without all of those.

God? Meditation? Daily exercise? Check-in texts and conversations with friends and loved ones? Those I need and value deeply.

One of the lessons of these last two months is that as much as we may be missing and yearning for our pre-coronavirus lives, we actually can live much more simply than we might have thought, before our world turned on its head and the words isolation and quarantine were inserted into every single conversation.

In the wilderness, the *midbar*, the people did not know what each day would bring. The only thing they knew for sure was that the sun would rise in the morning and would set at night. So too for us.

I doubt we will be physically together again before *Sefer Bemidbar* ends. So for the next 10 weeks as we read *Sefer Bemidbar*, we will accompany the Israelites as they go into survival mode. But this year we will follow the weekly adventures in the Torah as examples of how to survive.

The first example comes right at the beginning. As the *parsha* begins with a census of the people, I invite you to count as well. Count the people in your lives, count on the people in your lives, and be one of the people that others count on during this unknown wilderness that we are all trekking through alone, but together.

(This essay first appeared in The Times of Israel
May 21, 2020)

213

HOLY DAYS

SHABBAT

THE GROWING IMPORTANCE
OF SHABBAT IN QUARANTINE
Akiva Gersh

We're now well into our third week of quarantine here in Israel and it's getting harder and harder to distinguish between one day and the next.

It used to be, what now seems like a lifetime ago, that days were defined by their unique schedules. As an Israel educator/tour guide, almost every day was a different adventure for me, traveling the length and breadth of this glorious country every couple of months. While my wife's work schedule is more constant, our kids' lives mostly set the rhythm and pace of our day-to-day life, making each day different and distinctive — *chuggim*, *Bnei Akiva*, playdates and the like.

And now, every day is the same. Intensely the same.

No going to work for me (for there is no work to be done.)

No school, after-school activities, youth movement, or seeing friends for my kids.

It's become easy to forget if it's a Tuesday or a Thursday because, essentially, everyday has become a copy/paste of the day before it and a foreshadowing of the day that will come tomorrow.

Yes, my kids, like most kids, are filling up their days in quarantine with a collage of interesting, diverse and meaningful activities (exercise, gymnastics, YouTube art videos and learning Arabic, to name a few), but the flow and feeling of each day is basically the same. Especially for me who, because my wife is working (online) during the day, is solely responsible for making sure that our kids wake up at a somewhat reasonable time, are periodically fed, keep up with their quarantine activities and leave the house once a day for our daily walk (no further

217

than 100 meters, of course). And while there are those sweet moments, those fun moments, and those deep family bonding moments (like campfires with smores and spontaneous dance parties), as the week goes on I feel like I'm waking up every morning to live the same day once again. And then somewhere in the midst of the amorphous cluster of days, Shabbat comes.

And despite the fact that there are aspects of quarantine that feel like a never-ending Shabbat, blurring the line somewhat between the six days of the week and the sanctified seventh day, there is still something powerful about transitioning from the mode of weekday quarantine to Shabbat quarantine. Even more powerful than during normal weeks and normal times.

First and foremost is putting our phones down and shutting off the screens and giving ourselves a very necessary and healthy break from the onslaught of (and addiction to) Coronavirus updates, videos, charts, numbers and articles. During these past few weeks I have been vacillating between shedding tears as the seriousness of this pandemic and its effects intensifies and breaking out into loud laughter from the latest funny meme I receive on Whatsapp. Temporarily disconnecting from the world has never been more important to give ourselves a rest from the emotional exhaustion this pandemic (coupled with unrelenting media) is causing and will continue to cause for the foreseeable future.

Shabbat also helps us to remember, while not pretending there is no pain or suffering in the world, that there still is great beauty in the world. That there are countless reasons to be happy and feel blessed to be alive, both in general and in this time specifically. To take one day of the week and focus specifically and intently on that which is not broken in order to recharge and rejuvenate ourselves so that we can face another week of a world that indeed does have darkness in it, and have the strength and the ability to confront it and transform it.

More than ever, Shabbat provides an anchor of familiarity in these days of the very unfamiliar. An experience of something normal in these times of the very abnormal. The rituals of Shabbat act as a comfort to help us realize that the world as we know it, or knew it, is not entirely gone. The candles, the prayers, the songs, the wine, the challah, the food, the family time, the games, the downtime, and the naps all combine to create a refuge and a sanctuary from a world that is, let's be honest, scary right now.

At the onset of the past two Shabbats spent in quarantine, and I imagine the same thing will happen this Shabbat as well, I suddenly remember that we are not stuck in a repeating 24-hour cycle of time. That there still is a forward movement of time taking place. That what we are going through right now is just one chapter, albeit a very challenging one, of a long story that is still unfolding for the Jewish people and for all of humanity.

But, as in the past, this too shall pass and we will one day (hopefully soon) return to days that are filled with their individual tones and colors while never forgetting these unique times that we are experiencing right now.

(This piece first appeared in The Times of Israel
April 2, 2020)

A TASTE OF THE WORLD TO COME
Rivka Begun

"This world is like the eve of Shabbat,
and the Olam Ha-ba (World to Come) is like Shabbat."

I couldn't stop thinking about that phrase from the Talmud as I sat in my mother in law's kitchen in Mexico City baking her family's blintz recipe. The world to come would be an endless Shabbat, eternity of rest and connection. I wondered how close we were. Inside, I felt like the world was ending. Sleep had become a rarity during Corona times, interrupted by anxiety, bad dreams, and disrupted schedules.

We were the lucky ones during Covid. No deaths in our immediate family, no major financial issues to grapple with as we watched friend after friend get laid off, their names filling out Linkedin notifications until their news became equally as upsetting as the news on the television.

I'd kept Shabbat in a past life. Some people experimented with drugs in college, I experimented with religion. I had left a lot of my more stringent religious practices in my past and the loss of those rituals didn't fill me with regret, only a sweet nostalgia for a world that I had been a part of and that I still maintained a tremendous amount of respect for.

Shabbat, however, was different. I had sweet nostalgia for those moments, but I also had a fierce longing for it. The loss of that ritual hit me harder than my loosened Kashrut rules and my lost moments of prayer.

When I stopped keeping it, I missed the feeling of being in a calm bubble as the rest of the world used their Saturdays to catch up for Monday. I missed the chance to put down my laptop, light Shabbat candles and return to an elevated time where the present was clear in front of me. I missed taking walks with my friends around our college campus, discussing Torah in our own electricity free world while life continued to spin around us. When I stopped keeping Shabbat, my weekends changed. My Friday nights and Saturdays went by as if they were any other day, a little less writing, a little more time outdoors. The time had lost it's glimmer, the sun didn't quite hit the same on a weekend without Shabbat.

Then Corona happened. My husband and I had already planned a trip to his family's home in Mexico City for March, and when we arrived at the vibrating mess of a capital, our flights back home were canceled. We were stuck in Mexico City, away from our apartment and our daily distractions, and committed to a quarantine in my in-law's house.

I hadn't spent so much time inside since I had kept Shabbat. It was difficult at first. At night, I couldn't sleep, haunted by my uneven anxiety breathing, thinking of the future and of loved ones working in the medical field. Eventually, it got easier.

On quarantine Shabbats, my mother in law brought the laptop outside and we sat on chairs under the stars, listening to her rabbi lead *Kabbalat Shabbat* from his home. We tried to separate our weeks from our weekends by lighting candles and reviewing our highs and lows of the week, moments ranging from the excitement of a new freelance opportunity to the terror of a pandemic related panic attack. On Saturdays, we brought towels to the backyard and read, grateful for the small garden that now felt like a big blessing. On Mondays, the week would begin but a hint of Shabbat would remain. We had nowhere to drive to, no obligations taking us away from the heart of our current lives-the home.

Outside of the oasis of my in-law's home, Mexico in particular was falling apart. A government that initially denied the need for social distancing, lack of testing and infrastructure, and extreme economic disparity meant that chaos raged around us as we calmly lit candles in the house, made challah and discussed the books that we hadn't had the time to read previously. Inside, we dealt with normal in-law fights, the natural conflict that arises when a new person enters a family dynamic for the long run.

Despite all of that, we felt grateful. My anxiety attacks subsided, and I gradually felt the calm that I had always associated with Shabbat. I realized that even on Mondays, while the Shabbat candles were unlit and our meals consisted of more tacos and tostadas than challah and kreplach, my sense of fortune, of the opportunity to spend time together, and to take a step back from the world that was constantly pushing us forward, was a taste of the Sabbath, a taste that I had sorely missed. I secretly thanked God that this difficult moment for the world had brought me back to Shabbat, that in a moment where I felt the world was ending, I again was able to find a taste of the world to come.

COVID-19: OUR COLLECTIVE SABBATH
Rivka Hecht

COVID-19 brought with it a collective global Sabbath. We felt it even more poignantly each Friday night and Sabbath Day. Here are three short COVID-19 Sabbath experiences, connected to our textual sources.

1.

הִשְׁבַּעְתִּי אֶתְכֶם בְּנוֹת יְרוּשָׁלָ ִם אִם־תִּמְצְאוּ אֶת־דּוֹדִי מַה־תַּגִּידוּ לוֹ שֶׁחוֹלַת אַהֲבָה אָנִי: (שיר השירים
פרק ה פסוק ח

King Solomon's Song of Songs promises the daughters of Jerusalem that they will find their one true love.

On Friday night, under corona lockdown we began our Sabbath Meal in our apartment in the alleyways of Jerusalem. As we dined, we heard our Airbnb neighbours across the hall singing King Solomon's Song of Songs about love, my all time favorite. And thus began our *Sabbath Sing Off Fest*. The boys sang, and then we sang. Sometimes we listened to solo or duet, sometimes we sang in unison. It was truly beautiful. We sang Hebrew songs and English songs; Hasidic songs and Jewish songs; and everything in between. Some with lyrics, and some soulful melodies without words. What moved me of course was the promise of love to blossom once again in the streets of JeruSalem & the World, with the rising & healing of Men & Women; but beyond that, I was in awe of the power of song - the pen of the soul - to penetrate the walls and doors that divided us and to unite us in solidarity as we dined at our respective meals. We never met our weekend neighbours, but the songs we sang bridged the gap of social distancing in ways it couldn't have penetrated had we opened our doors and invited them in....

2.

תנו לה מפרי ידיה ויהללוה בשערים מעשיה
Give her to enjoy and pleasure in the fruits of her labors (Proverbs, 31)

222

Nature will keep flowing as we adapt to this new age. On Friday night during corona lockdown, as we sang to the "Woman of Valour" the אשת חיל, I felt like we were singing to Mother Earth - Let her be, let her flow, let her nurture, let her heal, let her grow...May we become Humans of Valour אנשי חיל to truly merit our Mother Earth and her bounty, the coronation of creation.

3.

עץ חיים היא למחזיקים בה ותומכיה מאושר דרכיה דרכי נעם וכל נתיבותיה שלום

It is a tree of life to all who grasp it, and whoever holds on to it is happy; its ways are ways of pleasantness, and all its paths are peace. (Proverbs 3:17-18)

For as long as I can remember, the Torah Scrolls felt alive for me - a living beating heart ♥ that protected and united us in a way that transcends reason. As a little girl, my siblings and I would play near the Ark of our community Synagogue and I would imagine the internal workings of the Home of the Torah Scrolls - the mystery, warmth, wisdom & answers. Whenever a new Scroll is dedicated and brought to its Home, I'll be the first to purchase the holy letters and invest in this timeless investment for body & soul, and then dance with emotion as we carry Her through the streets under Her canopy with music and dance to welcome Her to our world and to Her new home. Recently, under corona lockdown I found myself tearing up when thinking of how alone we all are, but also how very alone our Torah Scrolls must feel too. As tradition has it, a huge part of institutionalized Judaism is the reading from the Torah Scroll twice a week, as well as the weekly Torah portion on the Sabbath Day and on the Jewish Festivals. However, for the most part, institutionalized Judaism in community gatherings has been cancelled due to COVID-19, for now the real, crucial & critical test is to be a Jew at Home, inside; to truly internalize the Torah teachings ונשמרתם מאד לנפשותיכם. May we truly merit the physical & spiritual protection and healing in mind, body, heart, soul & spirit so that all of our Homes can reunite again with eternal & internal life, balance, joy, peace & harmony, through the Torah of Life.

PURIM

THE HOPE IN THE FREEZER
Miriam Aronin

In the Greek myth, curious Pandora opens a forbidden box, unleashing sickness, death, and all sorts of evils on the world. Yet one thing remains inside the box: hope. As illness, despair, and uncertainty swirl around us today, I have tried, like Pandora in the myth, to hang onto a little bit of hope.

Unlike Pandora's, my hope is a very Jewish one. And it is not in a regular box, but in an icebox.

The last week before we began to shelter in place in Chicago, we prepared for Purim as usual: learning megillah readings, laying out costumes, and baking hundreds of *hamantashen*. For the first time, my daughter could even shape a few of the triangles all by herself. We passed out the finished *hamantashen* to nearly everyone we know. In person. (Knowing what we know now, it could have been a terrible disaster, but luckily it wasn't.)

Then came shelter-in-place orders around the country, and then Passover. Every year, we have seders and spend a few days with my parents in the New York area. I save our last few *hamantashen* in the freezer to share with them before the holiday begins and we stop eating chametz.

This year, of course, we did not go to New York. Instead, we held our seders online, by Zoom, including more widespread family members than usual. The lovingly hand-shaped *hamantashen* — including a few that my daughter made herself — stayed in the freezer. We could have eaten them before Passover ourselves, but we didn't. Instead, I pushed them to the back of the freezer, and we symbolically sold them with the rest of our chametz, buying them back at the end of the holiday.

Our freezer has gotten very full lately. Besides the usual leftover muffins and soups, it is now packed with precious ice cream, frozen vegetables, and favorite breads from rare grocery runs or particularly successful deliveries.

But however tight the freezer space, I am not taking out those *hamantashen*. Not until I can share them safely with my parents or other family members across the country.

If that does not happen before we bake *hamantashen* again next Purim, as winter turns to spring again, I will add a few of next year's *hamantashen* to the stash. And more the year after that, if necessary.

However long it takes, I will do what I can to stay safe and to safely see my family again. And when I do, I look forward to sharing with them a batch of stale, freezer-burned hope.

WE LOOKED TO THE WORD OF GOD

Aayisha and Jacob Gold

It was the night of Purim at Anshe Emet Congregation in the Lakeview neighborhood of Chicago, our family's synagogue. We took our 1-year old son, Asher, dressed as an owl, while my husband Jacob was Mordecai and I was Queen Esther, this time with a "twist": both in Purim happy-ending warrior garb. At the synagogue we were surrounded by many groups of congregants of all ages, all engaged in the epitome of communal festivity.

Even before Purim, our family used Shabbat dinner on Friday nights as a way to create community and Jewish light in a physical, temporal, intimate way that built relationships and meaning by making the sabbath holy together.

Not long after Purim, the pandemic hit our lives, as the saying goes, "gradually and then suddenly all at once." It became more and more clear that our son's 1st birthday had to be cancelled... just a few weeks later the clamor for "zoom Seders" seemed on their face to evince comfort with a "new normal" but rendered them unrecognizable in so many ways (yet in their increased brevity, all too familiar...)

Under the day to day reality of "Shelter in Place" we were forwarded many ways to participate in virtual film festivals, charity concerts, conferences, etc. At the time we could not help but face the reality that our daily life under lockdown was become a very different way of being from which to project ourselves out into the virtual Jewish *kibbitzsphere.*

For some reason, maybe the sense of a voice calling to us, we decided not to beat back against the tide of isolation, stuffing our weeks with onscreen substitutes, alongside the constant hammer of new statistics: the number of cases, of deaths, recoveries, miracle cures, and many measures of disparity as the plague swept across the nation. These joined, moreover, by regular FaceTimes with elder relatives anguished at not being with our little cutie.

There were many nights spent looking into each other's eyes with confusion and uncertainty trying to figure out what to do next. Instead, we decided to use these circumstances to go inward and find answers to the persistent questions about our uniquely Jewish family and its destiny; questions that the conviviality of our outwardly social permanent Purim Masks likely obscured.

We were reminded that just as the original Passover was spent alone together household by household with lamb's blood on the door post. The first ancient Jewish families of the global Diaspora who had these same feelings of confusion and uncertainty but they heard the voice of God who guided them when they were strangers in a strange land.

Many times we've asked ourselves, "What does this mean for our family and families? Why is this happening at this particular stage in our lives? Will the torch burn-out?" No, we found a much better narrative by holding on to our faith; practicing daily and becoming better Jews for the future of our children, ourselves and community.

We know that Jewish life is full and constant with reminders of community's strength. It also offers us perhaps overlooked legacies of insight through isolation. Within the confines of our apartment, we found our space inside Noah's Ark; with the Essenes at the Dead Sea; in Bar Kokhba's caves; or as a latter-day Moses and Tzipporah with their children, fleeing to Egypt on that dreadful night of pursuit and *bris milah*, looking to *shamayim* (Heaven) until the dawn.

PESACH/ PASSOVER

TO PHARAOH
Alicia Jo Rabins

I never understood
why you couldn't just
let my people go, even as
the plagues approached,
even when holding on now
meant losing everything later.
Now I get it. It's terrible
to separate, to say goodbye
and watch the world drift away
like a sailor leaving shore--
alone, and who knows
for how long? No one
belongs to anyone, Pharaoh,
you were wrong about that.
And yet the opposite
is true too: we all belong
to each other, which is
what makes it so hard
to let our people go.

SOURCE OF HOPE
Rabbi Lisa B. Gelber

While preparing for Passover, I unearthed notes for the blessings my wonderful colleague and friend Rabbi Cindy Enger and I crafted for *A Journey Towards Freedom - A Haggadah for women who have experienced domestic violence* (FaithTrust Institute, 2003). Alongside traditional, longstanding blessings we introduced this formula for blessing - *nazmin et m'kor hatikvah l'kirbeinu*/Let us invite the Source of Hope into our midst. Creating text for those who had survived Pharaoh in many forms, we imagined blessings as hands extending in togetherness and community, purposefully rooted like a wellspring in the enduring thread of our tradition. Seeing Gd as source of hope seemed apt for a gathering to navigate the journey from slavery to freedom. Reminding ourselves of the promise of hope, communally sourced dispelled isolation, loneliness and alienation. Using blessing to place the holy, sacred and generative at the center, we made space to nourish and welcome, release and celebrate.

Many feel unsafe and unsettled this year as we prepare to experience Passover. We cannot help but ask *when will it end?* Without a crystal ball or even a Magic 8 Ball, no one can say when we will find relief and return to the rhythm of the past. We don't know what post COVID19 life will look like. We must know it is out there. A new, more gentle rhythm awaits us. We can imagine the possibility of celebrating abundance and rejoicing in the fruit of the vine. Inviting the Source of Hope into our midst, we can embrace this moment on our journey at this time in our lives.

For some, this year offers the invitation to celebrate with more people than ever before. Many will connect with family and friends via zoom and Facetime before, during or after *seder*. Faces and voices, images and videos placed at the center of the table - in our midst - offer hope, hope for connection, hope for continuity, hope for adaptation and hope for the future. Make space for photos of family members and friends like family who used to sit among you, those whose recipes inspire your meals and

231

wisdom guides your lives. Just as our ancestors held onto hope for the future, so too must we remember what we have alongside what is missing.

This year let us invite the Source of Hope into our midst so that we may tap into whatever we need to hold us on our journey towards freedom.

SALTWATER, PARSLEY,
SADNESS AND HOPE

Rabbi Evan Schultz

I can't remember the last time, if ever in my life, I felt such an overwhelming sense of sadness. Mourning the deaths of people I have never met, praying for doctors and nurses whose names I do not even know. Heartbreak for those who lie alone in hospital beds, and tears for their families who don't know if they will ever return home.

We have full license to be sad right now. There's nobody telling us to cheer up, or that it's all going to be ok, to look on the bright side, or that there's some good in all this.

Certainly I know many of us are trying our best to find the small blessings in this. More time to be at home or to connect with old friends. Communities have come together in such powerful ways despite being physically apart. The virtual world we have created has given voice to so many people, filling our homes with beautiful new music, songs, imagery, and words. And I know the earth itself is finding respite, blue skies in cities that most days are covered in smog, animals returning to habitats claimed years ago by human beings.

Yet I think we would all give it up in a heartbeat to save a life, to ease the horrible suffering of those who have contracted this relentless virus. To save businesses shuttering their doors and return jobs to the millions who have lost their livelihood. But sadly there's nobody to negotiate with. No evildoer or terrorists that we can send our powerful army to go and fight. No legislation that can make this virus go away. No Pharoah that can let our people go.

I'm thinking a lot tonight about the imagery and symbolism of Passover.

233

Only days away, her story feels so very vivid to me right now. How can I not equate this sadness I feel to the salt water that we place upon our seder tables? How can I not connect my own tears with those shed by my ancestors? The salt water - the tears, the sadness, the enslavement, the sense of loss. It has never felt more real than it does right now.

I pause and think for a moment about the ritual of the salt water. We each take in our hand a tiny sprig of parsley. A thin, flimsy, fragile, barely edible sprig of parsley. Embedded within those tiny stems and leaves are Hope. Rebirth. Springtime. Light.

That's all we need to carry us through right now. A fragile, delicate, beautiful sense of hope touched by God herself. We hold it between our fingertips, and as it dances through the bitter waters, it remains intact. We offer a blessing. We taste the mixture of light and bitterness upon our tongues. We keep telling the story. We move forward through the wilderness, carried by one another, by the profound beauty of hope, the love that carries us amidst the sadness.

PASSOVER, CORONA AND BIRTHING A NEW WORLD

Daniel Sherman

It is a pleasant, though dark evening here in Israel as I sit down to review my thoughts for yet another Passover. The moon—almost full—glows faintly through a clouded sky. No stars can be seen. On the one hand, it is a lovely early spring evening. On the other, we are strangely bonded together in our isolation, sensitive to the darkness, and conscious of the angel of death flitting in our midst.

I wonder if the skies were clouded and dark that terror-filled night prior to the tenth and final plague, when each Israelite family painted their doorposts, hoping that their home would be spared? Were the night stars to be seen when each family made its fateful decision to journey—poorly prepared–out of the narrow places to freedom?

We are living in darkened times in Israel and in the world. There is confusion and fear. Tectonic shifts—political, economic, ecological—lead many to question the most basic of premises upon which they rely. Spreading its shadow over all, our world is convulsed by a pandemic that came seemingly out of nowhere.

In all of this, there is an issue, raised so eloquently (in his own way) by Bogart in Casablanca "the problems of three little people don't amount to a hill of beans in this crazy world." A corollary is that one person – or two, three or more people—are seemingly helpless in the face of this crazy world's problems. How can one person's voice be heard — how can one person's actions be felt — within today's frantic, threatening world? Why does one life matter? To whom can we turn?

Our leaders, either seemingly corrupt or ineffective, provide little confidence that there is a safe way forward. And on the global stage, "the best lack all conviction, while the worst are full of passionate intensity."

What, then, is each of us to do?

Every year I revisit a seldom-told story from the exodus that touches on these issues. Here is this year's telling as again I dip my foot in waters before they are split.

In the traditional telling of the Exodus story, a people-in-the-making is oppressed, threatened and, ultimately, freed by great forces that swirl around it. It is a story in which individual agency has little role.

But a closer reading—and one informed not only by the Haggadah— shows us that it was only through the courage and initiative of individuals that our freedom was won.

You see, according to rabbinic tradition, when the Israelites, ill-prepared as they were and chased by the Pharaoh and his army, arrived at the Red Sea, Moses was at a loss. What were they to do? The people panicked and despaired.

Floundering, Moses began to pray for guidance.

But Nachshon ben Aminadav, heeding the call to move forward, boldly stepped into the Red Sea. He pressed on, as we are told told in the Babylonian Talmud (Sota 37b), until the waters covered even his nostrils.

Others leapt in after him.

According to this Talmudic rendition of the story, God chastises Moses, "My beloved are drowning in the stormy seas, and you are praying?"

"But what shall I do," asks Moses?

To this, God answers, "You lift your staff and spread your hand over the seas, which will split, and Israel will come into the sea upon dry land."

It was only then—and only following Nachshon's willingness to enter the waters before they had split—that God parted the sea.

Miracles, it seems, represent more of a partnership than we tend to think.

In Tehilim (Psalms) 69:3-16 we can hear echoes of what must have been Nachshon's fears and his realistic assessment of his predicament. "I have sunk in muddy depths, and there is no place to stand; I have come into the deep water, and the current has swept me away . . . Let not the current of water sweep me away, nor the deep swallow me, and let the well not close its mouth over me." Nachshon, though, did not allow his fear or a loss of confidence to stop him.

So my questions to you: Can we advance ourselves to safety and freedom—laying the groundwork for peace and a just society — when we have so many real doubts and fears? What are the risks if we do not? And why is this so important now?

Regarding safety: as we are being reminded constantly these days, we each are inherently limited. We may improve our position, we may protect ourselves temporarily, but our lives remain rounded with a sleep. As the Hebrew poet Rachel wrote "A person may yearn, yet his legs fail him."

What then must we do? It appears that the best for which we may hope is to live a good life within our own mortal limitations. To remain aware of our mortality, but not paralyzed by it.

So many of us carry a debilitating, sense of despair at our ability to shape our future and to take proactive steps towards building the communities and societies within which we want to live. Many have come to believe that we are threatened on all sides and lack an ability to move ourselves into a better position—to change our world. We seek guidance from a leadership that seems unable to give it.

It is as if we are dug-in by the shores of the Red Sea.

But perhaps the future really is in our hands. In the context of Israel, isn't this the crux of Zionism: that we make our own future? In a broader context, isn't this essence of the story told by all peoples who seek to create just and free societies: that you and I, through our actions — or our lack of them — change the world?

Another Midrashic tradition (Numbers Rabbah 13:11) holds that Nachshon was rewarded for his actions, including having the honor of fathering the messianic line. According to the story, then, our very redemption is linked to Nachshon's — and perhaps our own–basic willingness to step forward and act.

237

These indeed are dark times. But as I look around me, I find encouragement in the audacity of so many who strive — with decency, commitment, love and a humble awareness of their fragility — to birth daily a better world for themselves and those around them. Each in his or her own way struggles against the crushing isolation of our moment. Each in her or his own way guides the way forward through the narrow places.

This Pesach, I will be thinking of Nachshon striding into the waters and, through his actions, helping to make them part so the people could pass through on dry land.

(This piece first appeared in The Times of Israel
April 5, 2020)

JUDGING THE BOOKS BY THEIR COVERS
Anne Gordon

It was before masks. Before masks were worn, and longer before masks were decorative, but not functional. Before they were discarded altogether. And before they were worn again.

We had alcogel. The 6-year-old had orange ducky gardening gloves from a visit to his grandparents last summer (they have a lawn and a yard and the great outdoors to plant vegetables). He wore those gloves to remind himself not to touch his face. Which worked. Mostly.

It was a couple of weeks before Passover, and all non-essential stores were about to close indefinitely, so we were headed to the bookstore. I had 300 NIS on gift cards that were about to expire -- holiday mini-bonuses from a previous employer, for use at an assortment of establishments. I'd thought I was so smart, so prudent. I was going to spend those gift cards on the homewares we needed for Passover. Though, in the end, that didn't work.

I've been an adult for a lot longer than I've felt like one. And I've been glad to host Shabbat and holiday meals throughout. But never the seder. Growing up, the family seder expected all the sisters and the cousins and the aunts. Thirty-five people, crowded on tiny folding chairs, rented every year, along with long board tables, to overflow a deep Brooklyn basement. Even when the family shrunk -- I mean, grew, and spread out, as those cousins began hosting their own seders -- the Family Seder was always It. I hadn't been there for long decades, but it was the prototype, and I always celebrated with buzzing family... a crowd around several tables. Not this year. Even if we were all willing to be cocky (and we weren't), there was no way we were going to risk bringing plague to Savta, well into her ninth decade. So I was hosting seder for the first time.

Or not quite hosting. We'd be two at the table - me, and the 6-year-old. And I'd gotten it into my head that we needed a regal table -- all the fixings, to make the holiday feel real.

Which meant I needed dishes for Passover. And silverware. A seder plate. A matzah cover. I sat on websites perusing their wares way into the night. I made decisions. And I tried to buy, with those clutch gift cards, saved for just such a rainy day. Except that the stores wouldn't accept them for the online purchase. "Get with the program," I shouted in my head. "There's no other way to make a purchase right now!"

Which brought us to the bookstore. In person. Before the shops were closed indefinitely. Before that money expired.

I rounded the English section. And the children's books. Frog Yoga seemed perfect for a child doing so much sheltering at home. I found the card game "Set," figuring we'd play over the holiday. But what to do with the rest of the funds? I scanned cover after cover, author after author. I was taking too long, tense to get moving, as others entered the store. This one looked quaint, that one gaudy, another homey, another slick. I read a bunch of blurbs. And I bought some books.

It was almost Shavuot before I took note of the fact that I'd brought Barbara Kingsolver's Unsheltered home. Serendipity? Divine Providence? Either way, the book suited; the gift card well-spent. Kingsolver's writing is exquisite. Also startlingly prescient. With a 2018 publication date (I checked), she was not interpreting our coronavirus current events. But what vulnerability there is in her fictional collapsing home that does not protect its residents -- "unsheltered," while we shelter at home, all of us vulnerable to the outside. "Without shelter, we feel ourselves likely to die," she writes. Indeed. With my terror of this virus of unpredictable effect, had I read that on the back cover and found it relatable? If I did, I don't remember it. I might have just gone for the author's familiar name. Or maybe I liked the cover photograph of a passageway through a series of open doorframes, with light and shadows and at least the illusion of roominess in an old American house that is impossible in the rooms of my Israeli apartment.

"Without shelter," writes Kingsolver, "we stand in daylight." In the novel, it's a literal statement, as a roof crumbles and a family reveals itself. It is also a figurative statement, in a tale of a couple of rationalists who find solace in each other, as science begins to have its day. For me, being outside these days -- running forward and breathing deep -- carries a whiff of setting forth unsheltered, losing the fear of contagion, no longer feeling the threat of death.

Yet we remain sheltered, with masks and alcogel. Also handwashing and two meters of distance, as needed. With shelter, we feel ourselves protected -- not impervious, but taking care. We keep each other's company, me and the 6-year-old. We color (I work). We exercise and listen to music. We read. And we see the daylight streaming through our windows, waiting.

WHAT IF OUR ONLY SEDER GUEST THIS YEAR IS ELIJAH?

Rabbi Dr. Bradley Shavit Artson

Many of us celebrate our Seder meals that launch the festival of Passover with a wide array of special guests: beloved family, special friends, colleagues, some dear souls who don't have other commitments that night. We gather, a ragtag representation of one big tribe, the Children of Israel. Around a crowded table, we share a magical evening, re-enacting in our gathering the event that makes us a people in the first place: leaving Egypt together, crossing to freedom together, dancing in freedom together.

But we won't be together this year.

The surge of the Coronavirus, a plague not mentioned in the comprehensive list of biblical plagues, has forced the whole world to shelter and to separate. Guess who's *not* coming to dinner? Pretty much everyone!

For most of us, this social separation is unprecedented. Finding a place to share a seder might feel pressured, and can sometimes feel forced, but we all seek or offer invitations. We all reach out to our broader circle of care, and we aim to find a place to join with others to celebrate Pesah and its tale of freedom in community. Almost every synagogue and Jewish community offers to connect hosts and guests so we don't have to hold a Seder alone.

Is it even possible to hold a Seder alone? Turns out, it is and it isn't.

It is possible to hold the Seder alone, according to Jewish law and custom. The Haggadah, the rabbinic script for enacting this ancient story, does not require a *minyan* (a quorum of 10 adults) for the Seder to proceed. In fact,

242

the only difference numbers make in the ritual is that there have to be three present to recite certain lines in the *Hallel*/psalms of praise responsively. None of the other prayers or songs require a minimal number of participants. If one is alone for the Seder, it is even proper to recite the *Mah Nishtana*/Four Questions to oneself!

In fact, the Haggadah goes out of its way to remind us that everyone should give themselves the gift of a Seder:

> *Therefore, even if we are all wise, all understanding, all old, all knowledgeable in Torah, it is still incumbent for us to retell the story of the Exodus from Egypt. It is praiseworthy for everyone to expand and embellish the story.*

On the other hand, it is also not possible to hold the Seder alone. Every Passover, without exception, we throw open our doors and extend an invitation to the Prophet Elijah, the harbinger of redemption.

According to Biblical tradition, Elijah never died. He wanders the earth, appearing from time to time, reminding us not to give up on better days ahead, messianic days.

After the meal and final blessings, Jewish tradition asks us to set aside a fifth cup, the Cup of Elijah, and to invite Elijah into our homes, insisting that redemption, liberation, wholeness is on the way. We dare not surrender.

This year, as we recline in our chairs, sheltered and separated, we will remember that better tomorrows are coming, that this virus will not keep us isolated forever. Just as Elijah reminds us that we have a role to play in the advance of redemption, so we affirm that we all have a role to play in containing this pandemic, in rolling it back, and in caring for each other along the way.

This year, in addition to opening our doors, let's open our hearts as well – to the healthcare workers who are tending the sick and the suffering, to the volunteers and aides who are tending to our loved ones who are old, who have special needs, who require additional attention. Let's open our hearts to each other, as we struggle against separation and loneliness, as we fight off disappointment and despair.

243

Elijah is our guest of honor, especially this year. As we open our doors, we affirm that no one is ever truly alone at a Seder. All of our people around the world, all of our ancestors who forged a path of endurance and light, all of our sages, poets, pioneers and visionaries will be with us. Along with the family and friends who can't sit around our table, or crowd into our usually overstuffed room, they will be in our hearts, in our souls, in our song.

Let them in. Embrace them with all we've got. Know that redemption is coming. There will be better days.

Elijah's Visit Passover 2020
Mark S. Freedman

There is so much noise in this sequester of silence
Too much space in these space-less rooms
Little comfort on couches of recline
Clocks which denote no measures of time
Calendars with pages that need no turning
Will we wander to the end of days?
Look to the spirit inside your anguish
Whose family is lost like yours behind the front door.

FREEDOM FROM ISOLATION, FREEDOM FOR CONNECTION
Rabbi Lisa B. Gelber

As we move into the ninth week of life outside our synagogue building, I am acutely aware of the changes that emerged to maintain physical and spiritual safety. As synagogue community, we are physically distant from one another even as we see and sit together via computer and other screens. Many of us have adjusted to receiving food via delivery (others were experts from past practice!). People share practices for mask making - from shirts and socks - and where to order on-line. I practically jumped for joy when I saw a basket filled with packaged masks at the grocery store. In some moments new practices bring relief, in others they hi-light frustration. This differs from person to person and from moment to moment in ourselves.

Last week my daughter crossed the threshold of our apartment for the first time in 6 weeks. She had not wanted to go out and I did not push her. But Saturday was such a beautiful day and we thought it worth putting on our bandana/masks and heading out into the street. We walked around for an hour, noticing people's masks, especially the creative and fun ones! and those who were not wearing masks. We offered thanks for the sunshine on our faces and enjoyed visiting the little sprout down the street in front of a tree to see how much it had grown.

The next morning, I noticed my daughter's doll wearing a mask that had not been there before. Influenced by our outing, she used a piece of fabric from a stuffed animal she once made (and from which she had apparently borrowed some stuffing a while ago) to create a mask for her doll. Watching and listening, she internalized this trip into the outside world and did her part to recreate safe space. She did not worry that she did not have a doll sized mask. Instead, she took apart something old to create

246

something anew.

In some ways, that is the message of *Pesach Sheni* which occurs today on the Jewish calendar. *Pesach Sheni*/the 2nd opportunity at Passover arises to address the need of those who missed the Passover commemoration in its rightful time because they were *tamei*/unclean. Being *tamei* represents a space of temporary alienation. In Numbers 9:6-7 we learn of those who, because of their proximity to a corpse were not fit (in biblical terms) to participate in the Passover offering. A similar approach to death appears in parashat *Emor* (Lev.21ff)). These men express their frustration and disappointment at being barred from the Passover sacrifice at its rightful time, 14 Nisan. In response, God creates the opportunity to offer the Passover on 14 Iyar. Thus *Pesach Sheni* is born.

Pesach Sheni reminds us that even though we cannot always fulfill our responsibilities at their precise time, we may be gifted another opportunity to commit to freedom and our own redemption. As an outgrowth of Passover, this is a lesson about adapting over time and writing ourselves into the story in new ways. A second chance at the path to freedom invites us to retell our story.

Just as we mourn those taken from us by COVID19, so too do we mourn the loss of physical proximity, restaurant meals, the spontaneity of laughter experienced without the mute button and so much more. Even as we exist in this place of separation and unknowing, the potential for another path exists. There is a new story out there for us to tell, one in which we take our *matzah* and our bitter herbs and internalize again what it means to be free. In this retelling, we put a mask on our doll to demonstrate that all of us deserve to be cared for with kindness and attention to safety, and that shifting our practices for the time being are normative and part of everyday living at this time.

Our world is transforming before our eyes. It is up to us to remain connected, to practice being agile in the way in which we encounter the world and those around us. We recently returned to our Shabbat morning *davenning* together, now in our on-line sanctuary. Next week, we will commit to a weekly service to wrap our proverbial arms around one another and bring strength to those saying Mourner's Kaddish. While prayer by zoom may not fit the image of the shul of your (recent) past, it is born of our commitment to freedom from isolation, freedom for connection and freedom to recreate something anew. Come and be a part of our transformation, no mask required at home.

LEARNING TO LIVE
WITHOUT THE EGGS
Rabbi Alan Abrams

I couldn't believe it. There were no eggs.

Here it was, days before Pesach, the holiday where nearly every dish I cook — matzah balls, matzah brei (not to mention the Seder plate itself!) — requires eggs. But our grocery order came without the eggs. Chicken came. Beef came. But the humble egg? Nada.

All during the Pandemic Pesach week I was obsessed with eggs. There seemed to be none to be found in all of Jerusalem, but we did have a bit more than a dozen left over from the previous week. Could we still make Pesach, could we still be redeemed? I looked at the remaining eggs and wondered. I carefully decided to use fewer eggs in my matzah balls so we'd be able to have matzah brei a couple of mornings. I felt so grateful every time I took a bite of that matzah brei. I was so grateful that we had enough eggs. But I thought that my gratitude was centered only on the fact I was getting to eat that egg, but, later, I would realize that the greatest gratitude came from an egg we didn't get to eat at all.

I associate Peasch with an abundance of eggs -- with abundance in general. Pesach was by far my favorite Jewish holiday growing up. Other people, as I only learned as an adult, dread the eating practices of Pesach (especially matzah, which can be so "binding" of the intestinal tract), but I always looked forward to it. The Seder meal always had matzah ball soup. We had a choice of gefilte fish or chopped liver for the appetizer. And dinner was a choice of beef roast or turkey. And there were potatoes, lots of potatoes.

And of course, Pesach comes in spring, this reminder of new life and new green. But could we celebrate new life amid a pandemic, when so many people are dying? Could we have abundance without eggs?

248

"Teach us to number our days," says the Psalms (90:12). What does this mean 'to number our days'? A common image in popular culture is of a person crossing off days on a calendar, perhaps the days before the person will be released from prison.

There's no doubt that the self-isolation so many of us faced during the pandemic can feel like a prison sentence. But this pandemic sentence was one without a known end. How long would we have to stay inside? How long before we could see friends and family in person again? How long before we could have childcare again? There was nothing to count. Except the eggs. I felt angry looking at them. Why did I have to count them? Why did I have to face this deprivation, especially amid the holiday of abundance?

When Seder came I was worried. Would it even feel like Pesach without guests? Was it really worth using up one of our precious eggs for the Seder plate? Would our four-year old daughter even feel interested enough by a guest-less table to just want to sit there with us?

But she did. She remembered that she had made a haggadah in her Gan pre-school the year before and went running off looking for it. And my heart kept when she helped me to fulfill the Torah's command to "teach your children" about the practices of Pesach by asking the two of us questions. "Why is there an egg?" she asked, looking at the Seder plate. Because of spring, we said. To remind us of new life, we said.

Why does the Torah urge us to number our days? The Psalms verse continues, "so that we gain a heart of wisdom." But how does counting our days bring wisdom? In my work as a spiritual care educator I urge my chaplain students to carefully make note of the things they do, of the things they learn, and, especially, the things they accomplish amid the difficult circumstances of pain, fear and uncertainty that the people we talk to in their hospital beds are experiencing. Claim your learnings, I urge my students. Claim them so they count.

During the pandemic Pesach, I counted many eggs, but none counted more than that one egg on the Seder plate when my precious daughter asked about it. In that moment there was abundance. There was joy and celebration. Maybe even there was a feeling that I was getting a little closer to the source of holiness and wisdom. And that I was finding a reason to keep numbering my days.

249

In This Strange Springtime
(Passover 2020)
Jessica Levine Kupferberg

Let's play hide, not seek.
Let's love each other from afar
Let's hope kindness never peaks
As faces mask uncertain hearts
Let's save each other softly
And flatten curves when we're apart.

Let's mutter can you believe and I can't even
Swallow shards of cancellation's broken plans
Let's call to say how have you and gosh it's been forever
Rub long-missed voices against our cheeks
With the backs of latexed hands.
Throats ache from growing lists of names we whisper
Prayers floating past our gardens, over seas
Arms reach out to be picked up by our Father
But we're the children of our mothers
When it's difficult to breathe.

Let's yearn for what we never even noticed
Let's learn now what we know we should have known
Let's celebrate old freedom when we aren't
Let's extend translucent tin cans, home to home
Flicker flashlights of concern from bedroom windows
Gasp at wildflowers like expensive art
Scrub our tears clean, bleach resolve and wipe the news down
Let's breathe in deeply with our lungs
But exhale with our hearts.

Let's play hide, not seek.
Let's love each other from afar
Let's pray kindness never peaks
As we need the end to start
Let's save each other desperately
And cling though we're apart
Let's breathe in with our lungs
But exhale with our hearts.

Seder Night
Joyce Friedman

Why is this night different than all other nights?
In the sky, it's Super Moon Time,
Brilliant glow of radiance above the horizon on my
Front lawn.

It's Super Seder time,
The once in Many Lifetimes Passover
Where our families are on screens
And we eat alone in front of our seder plate.

It's Super Wild Time,
We are cells in the body of the planet
Gone bad,
Yet continuing to love, to sing.
To stretch, to listen
And to comfort one another
From afar
On a screen
On a phone.

There is no normal
Yet
It's Ordinary Spring and the
Buds are greening,
Birds are nesting,
My grandsons are blowing bubbles
And making sand cakes in the
Blue sand box.

Alone Tonight for Seder
Rabbi Aaron Weininger

When I stay home tonight, I will be alone but not lonely.
For ancestors who left Egypt will be with me.
I feel their tears reach my eyes even as my hands can't do so freely.
When I stay home tonight, I will be alone but not lonely.
For family by birth and by choice will be with me.
I yearn for the commotion of Seders past while using Zoom technology.
When I stay home tonight, I will be alone but not lonely.
For partners in abusive relationships will be with me.
I realize staying home for them is painful even as it gives others safety.
When I stay home tonight, I will be alone but not lonely.
For teens managing life in the closet will be with me.
I believe in their power to live fully into who they are meant to be.
When I stay home tonight, I will be alone but not lonely.
For kids (and their exhausted adults) will be with me.
I imagine question upon question born out of beautiful curiosity.
When I stay home tonight, I will be alone but not lonely.
For workers facing job instability will be with me.
I recognize these uncertain times create a deep anxiety.
When I stay home tonight, I will be alone but not lonely.
For those who have no home in which to stay will be with me.
I know my words are inadequate unless my action matches to change reality.
When I stay home tonight, I will be alone but not lonely.
For healthcare providers and chaplains will be with me.
I pray for well-being, peace, and care to envelop them regularly.
When I stay home tonight, I will be alone but not lonely.
For friends with illness of body and soul will be with me.
I see their struggles for hope to bud, yearning for spring to revive each
and every tree.
When I stay home tonight, I will be alone but not lonely.
For I am with them and they are with me.
I feel and yearn and realize and believe and imagine and recognize and
know and pray and see.
Hope will fill my table, and may it give each of us a sense of being free.

This Year
Laurie Pollack

I am on lunch break,
my laptop upstairs with the cat.
I sit on the steps of my rowhouse
it is a sunny day
an old man walks by
carrying a small plastic bag
of groceries
minutes later
a young woman, cellphone in hand
keeping her distance.
I tell her "hi"
she says "hi. How are you?"
I say "fine"
that word no longer taken for granted

I return to my Kindle book
I am rereading "Diary of Anne Frank"
for around the 6th time in my life
And I feel grateful for my life
How she would have loved
to go outside from her hiding place
whenever she wanted to
and sit in the sun
near a tree
looking up at the sky
greeting neighbors
unafraid of them
being greeted without hate

I am grateful for my life
and I breathe in
thankful for air

Why is this year different
from all other years?

This year we have
a President
who thinks the

Easter Bunny
will bring the cure.

This year
we attend seder
only with immediate family
who live in the same household

This year we may leave our homes
only for purposes
that sustain life

This year
Elijah stays
six feet away
outside the door,
waiting.

A Post-Quarantine Dayenu
Rabbi Sarah Marion

When this quarantine ends, and we never again take a single hug, handshake, or human touch for granted....*Dayenu, it will be enough.*

When this quarantine ends, and we return to the rushing, swirling, spinning world with a newfound appreciation for slowing down... When life resumes, but, this time, with more room for rest, laughter, creativity, connection and play....*Dayenu, it will be enough.*

When this quarantine ends, and we mourn the loss of school days, play dates, family vacations, but we focus, as well, on the tremendous life lessons that our children learned throughout it all....*Dayenu, it will be enough.*

When this quarantine ends, and we look our doctors, nurses and healthcare workers in the eye and thank them, from the bottom of our hearts, for putting their lives on the line so that we could live....*Dayenu, it will be enough.*

When this quarantine ends, and we use all that we have learned to ensure that we are never again so woefully unprepared for a global health pandemic....*Dayenu, it will be enough.*

When this quarantine ends, and we don't stop protesting, organizing, lobbying - doing whatever we need to do - until affordable, accessible and adequate health care for *every American* becomes a reality....*Dayenu, it will be enough.*

When this quarantine ends, and we understand the incredible ways that quarantining millions to avoid one plague has exacerbated countless others - plagues like domestic violence, poverty, racism and greed, just to name a few... When this quarantine ends, and we re-focus our attention and our energy towards abolishing all the other horrific plagues that still pervade our world....*Dayenu, it will be enough.*

When this quarantine ends, and we realize that going back to "normal" is not what we should want or hope for....*Dayenu, it will be enough.*

When this quarantine ends, and we live each day of our lives with more fullness, more compassion, more gratitude, more purpose and more joy than ever before....*Dayenu, Dayenu, then it will truly be enough.*

DAYENU

Ruth Messinger

At our seders we sing Dayenu, enjoying the tune but perhaps not clearly focusing on the words. We list things God [or the eternal force] did for us for which we are grateful — taking us out of Egypt, splitting the Red Sea, giving us our Torah — and then we belt out a refrain that says, for each thing, that "it would have been enough".

Complicated, because really it would not have been enough. Yes, we are grateful for receiving each gift, but not necessarily satisfied. We are who we are because we escaped Egypt AND got the Torah AND got Shabbat.

We want to develop a practice of being grateful on the one hand, but not satisfied, because as long as the world is the way it is, we should not be satisfied.

So perhaps *dayenu* means that we should take a moment to celebrate each small victory as if it were everything, and acknowledge that in our song, because maybe it is in fact the most we are going to be able to achieve.

But we should <u>not</u> <u>be</u> <u>satisfied</u>. We should finish the refrain and then look to the next step in the struggle, reminding ourselves that there is more for us to do.

If it is our responsibility to partner with God [or the eternal force] to work for justice, there will always be another step. Perhaps we will be able to take that next step more easily precisely because we stopped to celebrate where we were.

> *If we were to provide food and shelter for everyone, meeting all their basic needs but not protect them from discrimination and oppression, it should not be enough;*
>
> *If we were to free people from discrimination and oppression, but not protect their right to free speech, it should not be enough;*
>
> *If we were to protect people's right to free speech, but not release those*

256

*unjustly jailed and not allow others access to our country, it should not
be enough;*

*If we were to release those unjustly jailed and open our borders to those
fleeing oppression, but not free our earth from pollution, it should not
be enough;*

*If we were to free our earth of pollution, but not empower all people to
be and do and love as they choose, it should not be enough.*

There is much we can do, then, to meet human need; to speak truth; to
listen to others with compassion; to fight economic injustice, sexism,
racism, homophobia and anti-Semitism; to organize, march and vote to
affirm our values; to volunteer our time and our money; to realize our
power to effect change; and to honor our visions more than our fears.

In each instance, it will, and will not be enough. In each instance we want
to feel grateful, to feel blessed, enjoying what we have and celebrating
what we have done.

And in each instance we will then turn our energies to the work that
remains, hoping we can do more, not because we are greedy but because
we are hopeful and we remain committed to healing the world.

An addendum in the midst of the Covid 19 plague:

*If we are sheltered in place, but so many others have no place that
provides shelter and so are triply at risk, it should not be enough;*

*If we are fortunate enough to retain our health or have the best medical
care, but others are toiling on the front lines without adequate
protective equipment, it should not be enough;*

*if we are able to identify those leaders who are giving us grim but
accurate scientific information, but too many others are being fed
poppycock by dangerously manipulative people in positions of power, it
should not be enough;*

*if we emerge from what may be months of quarantine and home
schooling and zoom, but fail to change our leaders, expand health
coverage, care for those who are still in danger around the globe, and
plan better for future disasters, it will not be enough.*

257

My Four Questions for Passover
Rabbi Aaron Weininger

1. Our hearts are broken. How will they reach neighbors while keeping six feet apart?
2. Our skin is broken. Will our poor hands endure more washing at the Seder?
3. Our matzah is broken. Must we go hide and seek the afikoman alone?
4. Our souls are broken. Do we have it in us to celebrate this season?

O God of Bravest Responders and Costco Shoppers, of Zoom Muters and Facebook Live Producers:

With broken hearts, may waters part in their cracks for us to find dry ground and dance with distance.
With broken skin, may our hands find healing in loving acts of kindness toward ourselves and strangers.
With broken matzah, may our decisions lead us to flatten the curve of illness.
With broken souls, may our song have space to rise and reach souls who lived before us in the quest of freedom.
We are broken as we ask. We are mending as we answer. Be with us, Holy One, as we ask and answer tonight and every night. And let us say: Amen.

To My Seder Guests
Aurora Mendelsohn

Next year we will run out of Passover mixing bowls from cooking for crowds, so we'll just keep rewashing them.

Someone will ask us if they can join us two days before the seder and we'll say yes.
There will be a mountain of coats.

Next year we will get that old table out of the garage and clean it off and make it fit in our awkwardly re-arranged living room to make space for you all.
We'll forget who we asked to bring the extra folding chairs so we'll scramble with a few wheely desk chairs.

We'll run around the table during the fun songs.
It will be so loud.
I'll have to settle you all down to begin the next part.

Next year you will taste the produce of my garden, our local maror.
Next year the table will groan.

You will all jump in with your comments and talk at all once
and I will not moderate, but sit back with delight.
Our elaborations on the story will be worthy of praise.

It will smell like fresh asparagus and flowers
And artificially flavored fruit slice candies.
and red wine.

Next year we'll find more typos in our homemade family Haggadah.
And no one's favorites will be skipped.

Our house will ring with your song.
Then, we'll laugh at inside jokes in the kitchen as we clear up together.

Next year it will be Jerusalem here for an evening again.
I will greet each of you like Miriam and like Elijah
And I will hold you and kiss you as you enter and as you go.

What are the most fitting questions to ask at a Corona Seder?
Ittay Flescher

Every year at Seder, I put a bowl of questions on the table and invite every guest to pick one to ask before *Ma Nishtana*. In 2020, there were more seders than any other Pesach night in Jewish history, as families that usually gathered together, had multiple small ones. These are the questions that were most on my mind as had the smallest seder of my life in Jerusalem:

> * What innovations to Jewish life that have occurred during this pandemic do you wish to see remain, once it's safe to congregate in your community again?
> * If the fight against the coronavirus is a war, it's the first one where all of humanity is on the same side. Has the past month brought you closer or further apart to people in other countries?
> * If you had to spend one Seder with a representative of an ideology that you disagree with, who would you choose?
> * From the Haredim in Israel to the Chinese in Australia, the coronavirus has given licence to people with existing prejudices against certain groups to amplify their animosity. On a night when we are called to "remember the stranger for you were once strangers in Egypt," what can you do to combat stereotypes and hatred in your community?
> * Many Jews are suffering tonight, being forced to have a seder alone, or without their most beloved family members for the first time in their lives. How will you support these Jews after the chat?
> * If you are doing this seder alone, what do you want others to know about your experience?
> * Numerous surveys have shown that the Seder is more practised by Jews than any other ritual. How do you explain the popularity of Pesach over other festivals?
> * What's more important, History (what actually happened) or Memory (how we interpret the event today)?
> * Pesach is one of the few festivals where Sephardim and Ashkenazim practice the rituals in different ways. How does where you came from influence your Jewish practice today?
> * If you could only choose one option, would you rather Israel be a Jewish or democratic state?
> * Would people be more generous to each other with or without religion?
> * If you were given a million dollars to promote freedom which

you had to spend in one week, what would be your plan?

* If Eliyahu HaNavi shows up outside our door without a face mask, should we let him in?

* How long do you think it will take before the word "corona" returns to just being the name for another Mexican beer that is forbidden on Pesach?

YOM HA'ATZMA'UT/ ISRAEL'S INDEPENDENCE DAY

LONGING TO DREAM AGAIN
Rabbi Ezra Balser

Tonight began in a similar way to the first night of Passover I showered and got dressed for a glorious night. On Passover I donned the white *kittel*, the robe I was married in and the robe I will be buried in. Placing my arms in it, buttoning up and tying the belt, I was ready for redemption. Tonight I chose a short sleeved white button down shirt to wear with my blue jeans in honor of Israeli Independence Day/Yom Ha'Atzmaut. Every year I make these same preparations.

And yet, this year was so obviously different. While my wife, Laura, and I would have hosted sizable Seders for our community on Passover during normal times, in the epoch of the pandemic, it was just the two of us, with only our newborn daughter on the monitor across the table. Laura and I worked our way through the highly ordered retelling of our ancient liberation story. It was celebratory, sure, but it was truly quite sad and strange.

I absorbed that sadness, figuring I could handle it, as we are all shouldering new and difficult burdens during this time, and moved on. But as our modern day to celebrate our national liberation approached, as we neared closer and closer to Yom Ha'Atzmaut, I could feel myself beginning to crack. In the recent years, we have hosted a large barbeque and a celebratory prayer service with a song filled and soulful Hallel. This year I knew there would be none of that.

While the fall holds what we often call the High Holidays, our days of the Spring season are the real Holy Days for me. Passover grants me the opportunity to be grateful for the ancient birth of our people. And we imagine what it might be like to return to our homeland and honor that divine love of liberation with the paschal offering that the Torah describes.

Yom Ha'Atzmaut is a day of pure joy. We have returned to our homeland. We no longer need to imagine what that is like. Our dreams have come true. Rav Shagar describes our miraculous return as something that was so utterly unexpected, that even though it is actualized and completely real, it is like living in a dream. We pinch ourselves and ask, "is this real?!?!" We are the lucky few of our people throughout our history that get to walk on clouds and live in our dreams.

I have told close friends and family members this week that this day is going to be hard for me, something I was not willing to admit, even to myself, about Passover. And it has indeed not been easy. This afternoon, sitting on the couch with my 3-month-old daughter watching the official torch lighting of the Yom Ha'Atzmaut ceremony on Mt. Herzl in Israel, I sobbed. Every time one of the 12 torchbearers told their story and ended with "for the Glory of the State of Israel," tears came out. Could it be glorious without being able to sing and dance together? The word for glory, *tiferet*, also can mean beauty or splendor. Could it really be all that beautiful without being able to grill our celebratory meal with friends huddled around as I placed the pargiyot on the grates? And tonight, as I began to sing Hallel with Laura, it was hard to not concentrate on the tears that were welling up inside. These two holidays are not just not meant for isolation, they are barely even possible in our current state of distance from each other.

This year, in many ways, I have woken from my dream. On Passover, I was no longer imagining what it would be like to eat lamb in Jerusalem, but rather just praying to eat our brisket next year with real people around the table in Chicago. And tonight, I could not fully celebrate our national liberation while caged in my home.

I was left this year to mourn my inability to imagine and my powerlessness to dream. Just as the smells of the paschal offering would ideally waft through the neighborhood of my imagination, so too the joyous songs of Yom Ha'Atzmaut should be heard and danced in the streets.

"They who sow in tears, in glad song will reap," the Psalmist writes. This year I have had enough tears. I pray that next year I will live to sing again, imagine again, and dream again.

(This piece first appeared in The Times of Israel
April 29, 2020)

COUNTING
THE OMER

LAG BA'OMER:
APPROACHING THIS DAY WITH FIRE
Abrielle Fuerst

Remember when the world shut down after Purim?

Well yes, of course it did. Purim has always been a time of insanity. When scholars wear sackcloth and orphans become queens and we are whoever we wish for an evening, presuming we aren't too drunk to remember it. A time for changing fate.

Pesach was always meant to be the *Yetzia*, the leaving. From the moment I picked up medication priced with the same exact year of the Exodus. Pesach was going to be the moment when we took matters into our own hands and lost it, when we cried and spilled blood and then God came and saved us, and it was always going to be grand and glorious.

Well. Perhaps Pesach was the next step of a journey, as the Exodus itself preceded forty years of wandering with its own tribulations. Pesach was when we began counting the omer (which for me was an extension of the days in lockdown), because we knew without a doubt we would all sing together come Shavuot, just as Miriam sang *Az Yashir* at our first cumulative redemption.

I had never considered the omer as a time of mourning. Rediscovery, yes. Refinement, absolutely. Something vague about the promise of pancakes and cheesecake and midnight ice cream parties if I completed it.

And yet. Amidst it all, amidst the days of working on ourselves and rising from the depths of grief and degradation, one day at a time… amidst the holy light at the end of the tunnel that we *know* awaits us at the foothills of Mount Sinai, amidst the knowledge that each day is one day better than the one before it, the omer has always been a time of grieving. A time when weddings are suspended. A time for mourning battles failed and

266

lives lost to plague and illness, a time for cradling the repercussions of our choices. What does it mean that time set aside to change for the better and redefine ourselves is not a time of simcha, but actually of heartache? Does it mean we cannot really change without surrendering the memories and the moments and the souls that are lost in the process?

Tonight is lag Ba'omer. That was the line I read this morning, on a Facebook status. Ah. A mental box to be checked off. One number instead of another.

You know, lag Ba'omer isn't the end of it. It is a break. It is the day when the deaths stopped, amidst a plague that killed thousands. (And if you do believe that plague held the repercussions of not treating each other respectfully, what does it mean now that *rebbeim* (rabbis) across beliefs are holding hands in unity?) There is a symbolism to it; three is strength and four is God (*al shlosha d'varim haolem omed*, on three things does the world stand), and tonight, the thirty-third day, antecedes four weeks and four days completed.

What does it mean that we approach this day with fire? That we know we'll grieve again and fight again and keep walking through it, and so we take this day to pause and play and get married? That we embrace this moment not merely to regroup and hold our losses, but to forge the most joyous and sacred lifelong changes?

I believe Purim changed it all. I believe Pesach was a step as deep as the oceans that were redefined for us back then, and as profound as the mountain. I believe tonight, we will set the world aflame. And dear God, by that fire let us forge the strength to wield the fragments of our souls in healing.

267

REFLECTIONS OF OMER DURING COVID – 19

Rabbi Aaron Gaber

April 12

On the second night of Passover, we started counting the Omer. In ancient days, farmers would bring an omer of barley to the Jerusalem Temple, it was a signal of new harvest. From the Torah, we learn that we count 49 days and the 50th is Shavuot. The Israelites would go from slavery in Egypt to Revelation at Sinai. Today, we continue counting off the days from Passover to Shavuot as a period of new opportunities and ways to see how our world can expand. In Jewish mysticism, each week and then each day in the week are given particular *sefirot*. Today is the 3rd day of the Omer. The first week is *Hesed* (Loving kindness) and the 3rd day of the counting week is *Tiferet* (Beauty, Compassion). So today would be *Tiferet* in *Hesed* (Beauty of Loving kindness).

Love is often given with the expectation of love being reciprocated but when we add *Tiferet* (compassion), we recognize that compassionate love is given without expectation because like *Tiferet* which is connected to all the other sefirot, so we are truly connected to everyone else in the world as well. When we reach out to another, we suddenly feel uplifted because we brought a smile to another's face. So many of us are "stuck at home" and feel disconnected. Can you share your compassionate Loving kindness with others by just calling someone up to say hello? Can you check in on a neighbor that you do not know well and make sure they have everything they need? If so, this will be the moment you will be uplifted because you helped another.

April 13

The name given to today, the fourth day of the Omer, is *Netzach* of *Hesed* (Endurance in Loving Kindness) *Netzach* means endurance or eternity.

Is love enduring? Does it last forever?

An early meme making its way around the internet was that after this quarantine there would be an increased need for either divorce lawyers or midwives.

Enduring Love doesn't happen by itself; it takes discussion, reassurance, and people communicating clearly with one another about their needs and their desires. Enduring Love also means accepting the flaws of another just as we accept our own flaws.

Physical distancing has created a need for us to better use our words to communicate with our loved ones, our co-workers, and the people we interact with online and in person (from a distance). We are learning to be even kinder to each other.

Spend a few minutes today reassuring another of your love for them and how important your relationship continues to be.

April 14

Today is the 5th day of the Omer. In this first week, we are examining various understandings of *Hesed* (Loving Kindness) through the *spherot* assigned to each day. Today is Hod of *Hesed* often translated as humility in loving kindness. I believe we can also translate Hod as acknowledgement. As you can see from the picture of the *spherot*. Hod stands next to *Netzach* (endurance or possibly victory). They serve different purposes, but both are placed on the chart like the "feet" of a metaphysical person. The job of feet are to take us from one place to another as directed. So *Netzach* could be the characteristic which helps us jump or climb over objects while Hod helps us to get by the object in another way.

There are various leadership styles in this world. There are those who have a personality that dominates the room, and everyone suddenly pays attention. There are also those who walk into a room and no one notices them until they start to speak with a quiet authority, and everyone takes their words to heart. There are also situations where both styles are needed in some combination.

Today, Hod in *Hesed* is a challenge for us to approach the world with humility and acknowledgement that not everything is within our control. However, with quiet authority and compassion for others, we can shape

269

the world around us.

I wish everyone a Hag Sameach as we complete the Passover Holiday tomorrow and Thursday!

April 17

Today is the 8th day of the Omer. Today we begin the second of 7 weeks of counting the Omer. This week's characteristic is *Gevurah* translated as strength, discipline, judgement. On the chart, it is parallel to *Hesed* and often they serve as a counterbalance to each other but what happens today when they are combined? Today we have Loving kindness in strength/judgement. When I think about loving kindness in *gevurah*, I think about what it takes to get a job completed, what do I have to do to accomplish a goal. And those tasks are not always fun nor are they ever easy. I try to stay away from judging another for his/her flaws or just passing blame to another without first owning my own responsibility.

During the High Holidays (Rosh Hashanah and Yom Kippur), we often speak of *Din* and *Rahamim*, judgement and mercy. We pray that God will move from one throne to the other and give us the benefit of the doubt and grant forgiveness. In our world, we are often confronted with choices of judgement and mercy. We make judgements all the time. We judge those who cut us off in traffic; elected leaders on the job they are doing or not doing; or even our children on the way they take care of chores in the house.

We just completed Passover, a holiday devoted to escaping slavery, escaping the *hametz* of our lives. The day after Passover is a time to start again. How will we start this new period of time?

I would like to suggest that we use Loving kindness in strength/judgement as an opportunity to give one another the benefit of the doubt. To step back for a moment before criticizing another and reflect on whether our critique is really about them or about covering up some flaw that we have and want to hide. It is easy to blame another; it is more difficult for us to own up to our own flaws. Take a breath before judging another and decide whether you do it out of love and desire for them to be their best selves or just to over our own failings.

Shabbat Shalom.

April 19

Thanks to my cousin <u>Anita Simon</u> who inspired me today because she was looking for the other days of the Omer. I have not written every day because of Shabbat and holidays. I started this daily writing in public because I always say to myself that I will write for each day of the Omer but then something gets in the way and I do not. It is like counting the Omer, every day you must count. You are allowed to count the next morning without a blessing but if you miss a day, then the count is done. This year, I decided 3 days in that I would write most days but would probably not write on Shabbat or holidays or when I am too squeezed for time as I am already feeling for this week, but Anita inspired me.

So that is my explanation for yesterday, the 9th day of the Omer which was *Gevurah* of *Gevurah*. (Discipline of Discipline) which could be seen as being a bit OCD, but I see it as it is giving me strength to keep doing what I need to do. Make my endless to-do-lists for each day and although it never gets smaller, it is still there to remind me that my job is not to necessarily complete the job to the nth degree but to always be involved and to keep doing it.

For today, the 10th day of the Omer, it is *Tiferet* of *Gevurah* (compassion/beauty of discipline/strength). Compassion is so important, especially today in our world. I am watching with growing concern as we reach that critical moment where we have been stuck at home for a month or so, this dreaded disease may be plateauing and there are more discharges from the hospital than admissions (at least in Philly area). This is not the time to lose our focus and open the world without careful consideration and compassionate thought because the danger still lingers even if it is not as horrific as it could have been for us or for those in areas where Covid 19 is still very small. It is time for us to demonstrate the strength of our convictions and the compassion for our fellow person by continuing to be diligent and maintaining our patience. Let's make these decisions together in a way that brings the greatest good to the greatest number of people.

April 23

Today is the 14th day of the Omer. *Malchut* of *Gevurah* (Nobility of strength/discipline) My apologies for not writing much this week; it has been busy. I have spent much of my week helping to comfort those who lost a loved one. Multiple Zoom *Shivah* minyanim, zoom meetings about

271

where we are and what we might be doing. Working with students via Zoom. Watching the news as we try to figure out a world that is shifting before our eyes because of this pandemic.

What will I do for the Jewish High holidays? Worrying about going out into the world and potentially being exposed to Covid 19? Where would I self-quarantine in a full house?

I will say what everyone is thinking (and many are saying). This pandemic is horrific, and it really sucks in so many ways. Now what?! Today's Omer characteristic reminds me that we should work on recreating the healthy habits we had in the time before the pandemic. Healthy discipline bolsters self-esteem.

What healthy habit will you adopt today in our "new" world? How can we support you in that new healthy habit?

April 27

As the sun sets on the 18th day of the Omer, it is dedicated to *Netzach* of *Tiferet* (endurance of compassion/beauty). As we get further into our shelter at home, we may be becoming more frustrated and stuck, we may also become angrier and more hopeless. This is the time for us to become more compassionate and to fill the world with more beauty. In this time, it can be very tough, and we may even feel as if we are getting to the end of our rope. Take a few moments for yourself with some cleansing breaths and know that you are doing your very best.

Take a few moments and call someone, let them know you care for them and love them.

I am dedicating this message to the Doctors, nurses, EMTS, techs and first responders who are caring for those who are sick. They are doing such important work and need our care now and in the future.

I also dedicating this post in memory of Dr. Lorna Breen, who dedicated her life to serving others. May her memory be a blessing.

May 14

Today is the 35th day of the Omer. I have not written for a couple of weeks for many reasons, mostly because it has been tough to do so. Today is *Malchut* of *Hod* or Nobility in humility. In my life, these are the best leaders. The people that I would follow no matter what are the ones who walk with humility and walk very tall. The essences of humility and modesty is dignity. There are many people in this world who outrank me, who know a whole lot more than I do and who have more experience. Leaders may have all three, but they remind each of their folks that they have something incredibly important to contribute. These leader's humility and modesty increase our dignity. Micah 6:8 teaches

> *"God has told you what is good, and what the Lord requires of you: Only to do justice and to love goodness, and to walk modestly with your God; Then will your name achieve wisdom."*

Today, I express my gratitude to those I consider to be my leaders, my role models and those who take their communities to places of compassion and wisdom. Take a moment to express your gratitude to them as well. Together we will achieve wisdom not because someone "lords" it over us but because they enhance all of us.

SHAVUOT

UNDER THE MOUNTAIN, EREV SHAVUOT
Rabbi Paula Mack Drill

It is Thursday morning before Shavuot, and here I am, encamped at Mount Sinai, preparing to receive Torah. It occurs to me that I know the reason for and the outcome of the preparations and the waiting. But in that long, long ago moment when my ancestors were literally encamped b'tachtit ha-har, under the mountain, they knew nothing at all about what was to come. My ancestors, released slaves, no doubt hot, tired and hungry after forty-nine days of wandering in the wilderness, were told to prepare, to be pure, to be ready, but for what? They did not know. At least I know that we are preparing to receive Torah.

In these COVID-19 Shelter-at-Home weeks, I am encamped at home, identifying with those Israelites slaves in the desert. We are preparing, we are ready, but for what? We do not know what we are waiting for. The pandemic has created for us a liminal moment with a twist: we are in-between; we have left something behind but have not begun the full transition to what is next. We have no idea about what is next.

In the Torah, we gathered, בתחתית ההר, standing under the mountain. Midrash imagines God holding the mountain like an upside down funnel over the heads of the Israelites, declaring, "Accept this law or here will be your grave."

And we Midrash readers cry, foul play. We insist, "We were not coerced into accepting Torah! We excepted it gladly, enthusiastically. נעשה ונשמע (We will do and then we will learn) and all that, after all."

It occurs to me today, this 49th day of counting the Omer, that there is another way of understanding God holding that mountain over our heads. Perhaps it was not about coercion at all. Perhaps, like all stubborn humans, we needed time to learn our lesson.

275

I imagine God, the Pedagogue. God speaks sternly, but patiently, "Listen, you slaves. I understand you are stuck. You are living lives devoid of any sense of your agency, your potential, your very reason for being created which is to partner with me, your God. So stand here a bit with this threat over your head - this mountain can bury you or you can think about accepting something new, eternal, basic yet so complex that you'll never tire of it. It's your way out of the immediate threat, but it is also your way forward to a better human experience, married to me, God."

And today? Standing under the mountain of COVID-19, literally just past the peak of the curve as the numbers of sick and dead grew, doubling and tripling daily, and now tracing back down to form the other side of the mountain. This morbid COVID-19 curve is the immediate threat over our heads. So we put on masks and gloves and meet via zoom. We stay home and support essential workers. But will we learn to accept something new? Will we accept our agency and recognize our purpose? Will we partner with God, an open-ended offer that God has never withdrawn and we have never accepted?

The ultimate question of the pandemic is whether we can become something better and new or just return as soon as possible to our enslaved mentality. When I receive Torah tonight, let it be new. And let it remind me of my full complete human capacity.

SHAVUOT 2020: DO WE DARE NOT DREAM?

Rabbi Tamara Cohen

There is more that makes us One than death

More that runs between Wuhan, Tehran, Milan, Seoul and New York, than tiny droplets of breath that sicken or simply fall to the concrete or cobblestone, sand dune or grassy plain.

There is the beating heart
There is the wide expanse of blue, periwinkle, black

There are the winged singing creatures of flight and the red worm soil workers under foot, the fuzzy buzzing pollinators busy on the azalea's blooms, there are the glowing pulsing jelly fish rising and falling in the deep sea, the resting volcanos and the paddy fields, the mangroves filtering and protecting with so many reaching fingers.

Some say Mount Sinai was lifted up above the Israelites and the mixed multitude of freedom seekers and the Holy One's voice said accept the Torah or face your grave.

It is above us, isn't it? The Great Death we will bring upon our children's children and already right now upon the ones who cannot as easily hide from leadened water, carboned air, exploitation, the cruel value placed on the pigment of skin.

Some say it was just one word the Holy One spoke which was heard in seventy languages and the word was Anochi, I AM.

Do we dare to dream a land where every citizen and non-citizen alike can say Anochi and be heard and safe, where A big proud divine I am, a full of possibility and life I am, like the I Am a Man block letter signs of the

277

1968 Memphis sanitation strikers, like the Am, Anochi stolen from George Floyd and Toni McDade and Breyonne Taylor and Ahmaud Arbery, the I Am, Anochi chipped away by white supremacy and state violence that destroys lives and makes it almost impossible to be a black man following bird calls in a Bramble, listening for each sweet and singular sound?

Do we dare not dream and not only dream but commit to organize?

Do we shut our eyes to mountain and Torah made greater through action, or do we reach out to our masked and unmasked neighbors believing another Pharaoh can fall, believing another Pharaoh will fall, believing it is not too late to choose life, to know there is more that makes us One than death?

Let us carry hope like a basket of red pomegranates, fresh green olives, and harvested barley, let us invite the gleaners to take all they need from our fields, let us count the days and make the days count, let us allow our hearts to dream of revolution while we cast our eyes on the possible and let us begin walking now on the slow winding pilgrimage towards change.

Some say it was just one letter the Holy One spoke at Sinai, the silent Aleph of breath.

SHAVUOT AT HOME:
LEARNING ALONE, WITH(OUT) GOD

Akiva Mattenson

These days, I am learning alone. Quietly, for hours at a time, staring at digital copies of sacred texts. Soon on Shavuot, others may find themselves in a similar position: without their havrutah, learning the books they have available in their homes, quietly and alone. Our sages have words of comfort for such people: Hashem's presence is there, his warmth and closeness filling the emptiness, because wherever his name is mentioned, there he dwells (Mekhilta de-Rabbi Shimon b. Yohai 20:21; Mishnah Avot 3:7; Mekhilta de-Rabbi Yishmael – Ba-Hodesh 11; Talmud Bavli Berakhot 6a).

But these days, those words of comfort simply don't ring true for me. Instead, I turn to a less familiar sentiment also found in Mishnah Avot. One who sits and learns alone is like one who upholds the whole torah; or in other versions, Hashem allocates a reward for those who sit and learn alone (Mishnah Avot 3:3). The prooftext? A verse from the book of Eikhah: "Let him sit alone and be patient, for God has laid it upon him" (Eikhah 3:28).

In the mishnah, the 'it' of the verse's second half is interpreted to refer either to the earmarked reward or the weight of the whole torah. However in context, the 'it' is a burdensome yoke of suffering. The larger context reads as follows: "It is good to wait patiently till rescue comes from Hashem. It is good for a man, when young, to bear a yoke; let him sit alone and be patient, for God has laid it upon him. Let him put his mouth to the dust – perhaps there may yet be hope" (Eikhah 3:26-29). The whole thrust of these verses expresses the visceral experience of a God who is not there, a God for whom we must wait, a God who may not return. Indeed, the uncertainty of the final verse is highlighted at Talmud Bavli Hagigah 4b: "When Rabbi Ami reached this verse, he cried: 'Let him put his mouth to the dust, perhaps there may yet be hope.' He said: 'all this and only perhaps?'"

279

This mishnah does not pretend to offer the comfort of God's presence. To the extent it offers comfort, it is a comfort deferred to a future to come when the stores of reward will finally be shared. In its other versions, there is only the recognition of the tremendous difficulty of learning alone, weighty as the whole of the torah's charge. The painful absence of God from this picture is made more explicit, in the elaborated version of the mishnah found at Avot de-Rabbi Natan A 8:

> *Someone who sits and studies Torah alone – his reward is collected in heaven, as is said, let him sit alone and be patient, for God has laid it upon him." They offered a parable: to what is this similar? To a person who had a small child. He left the child and went to the market. The child rose, took a scroll, placed it between his knees, and sat and studied it. When his father returned from the market, he said, "Look at my young son whom I left when I went to the market! What did he do? All on his own, he learned [what to do]: he took the scroll, placed it between his knees, and sat and studied it!" Thus, you have learned that even the individual who sits and studies torah alone – his reward is collected in heaven.*

But the passage from Avot de-Rabbi Natan does not simply confirm the mishnah's picture of learning alone. The parable suggests that it is precisely God's absence which draws the learner into their learning in the first place. Like the child in the parable faced with the absence of his father who turns to the bookshelf for comfort, for something that reminds him of his father, the one who learns alone turns to Torah to fill the gap left by God's absence and create some kind of intimacy with God, however meager and limited. I do not know when God will return from the market; but until then, I have the comfort of God's scrolls.

To begin with, these scrolls offer comfort for what they contain. The child does not merely glance at the scroll; he sits down and reads it. In reading the Torah, the words of God, we attain a certain private closeness with God, as the contours of who God is and what God cares about are vulnerably disclosed therein. That books have this capacity to present the selves of their authors and preserve their likeness and figure is a point beautifully articulated by Rabbi Nahman of Breslov (1772–1810) at Likutei Moharan §192:

> *There in the book of the sage, a likeness of the sage is imprinted and depicted. For these statements and letters that are imprinted and*

280

inscribed in the book are the intellect of the sage and his soul and a sort of figuration of his face. Thus, his intellect and soul and face, which are his very likeness, are within these letters and words. Therefore in each and every book, the likeness of the character of the sage who introduced those statements is found. For in accordance with his likeness, i.e. the intellect, soul and face of the sage, the letters of the book are inscribed. For if the sage had a different likeness – i.e. a different intellect, face, and soul – he would have introduced and inscribed different letters in the book in accordance with the intellect that he had, which was his likeness. Thus, in each book there is a likeness of the character of the sage.

For Rebbe Nahman, the fabric of language woven in the book is a kind of imprint or trace of the singular and unique self that shaped it. This singularity is given a threefold name: intellect [שכל], soul [נשמה] and face [פנים]. He does not here articulate what he means in speaking of these three facets of the unique self, but we might take this semantic openness as an opportunity to reflect on their possible significances. The intellect may point to a certain singularity present in the novelty of the ideas brought to light by someone. The conceptual web and interpretative schema they develop introduce a singular lens with which to inspect the world – one that may draw from the efforts of past thinkers or bear certain similarities to other novel creations while nevertheless maintaining its absolute uniqueness. Meanwhile, the soul could point to that emotional thickness which confronts us in another human being: the sadness that they carry, the joy that slips into their laughter, the shame, the affection, the frustration in the clenched fist. All of this emotional richness bursts forth in an absolutely singular way from them — again, bearing names we attribute generally to our common emotional worlds, but always pushing forward an ineluctable particularity. Lastly, we might take the face for that most vulnerably intimate of bodily configurations that carries a certain style of vitality with it, that suggests to us a life and a way of being not reducible to a bundle of disparate activities, habits, peccadillos, and so forth, a configuration that as it were brings a unity and integrity to bear on this singular array.

All of these facets of the singular self embed themselves in and imprint themselves upon the book that we find before us. At once, we are confronted by a host of creative and novel thoughts that bespeak the intellect of the author; we sense in the tone of the text a certain emotional vibrato that echoes silently throughout and discloses the soul of the author; and we feel the face, the style of vitality, in the lexicon and syntax as it forms upon our lips and becomes flesh and full-bodied with a certain indescribable taste and color that we come to associate with the author. Thus in reading, we maintain a certain intimacy with the self that stands behind a text as we engage their singularity as intellect, soul and face. If we extend Rebbe Nahman's insight about authors and sages to the divine author and sage, what emerges is a picture of Torah as bearing the imprint of God's very self. In some ways, this is the picture that emerges from a striking passage at Shir HaShirim Rabbah 5:11:

> His head is the finest gold (Song of Songs 5:11) – 'his head': this is the Torah... The finest gold – these are words of Torah... His locks are wavy – this is the ruling line [on the parchment]. Black as a raven – these are the letters. Another take: His locks are wavy [תלתלים] – heaps upon heaps [of laws] [תילי תילים].

Continuing the elaborate hermeneutic transformation of the male lover of Song of Songs into God, the passionate lover of Israel, the author of this midrash suggests that God's head is nothing other than the Torah. To use Rebbe Nahman's language, the Torah presents us with the weighty intellectual and emotional heft of God's head and the singular face that is always part and parcel of it. Here, the Torah is perhaps more than simply a pale reflection of God's singular self; it is the very flesh of God's body. In reading the Torah, we are privy to a moment of profound intimacy with God's very self.

What's more, in this midrash God's being is not bound up simply with the intellectual, emotional or even linguistic singularity of the text of Torah; it wends its way through the physicality of the scroll, its ruling lines of parchment and the inky letters that glide atop them. We find here a second comfort in the scroll: the comfort of its feel. The child does not merely sit down and read; he places the scroll between his knees. Here too, in the experience of the book *as book* we come into a space of intimacy with God. For those bibliophiles among us, this experience is not unduly foreign. As Jean-Luc Nancy has written, "Even touching books communicates to the reader particular impressions: the weight, grain, or suppleness through which one thinks one can discern the inflections of a voice or else the fluctuations of a heart."[1] Thus, in the whole experience of engaging with the books of Torah – in holding them in our palms, in slowly piling them haphazardly beside us as we sink deeper into their folds, in breathing in the *tzurat hadaf* of a page of Talmud, and of course in thinking their thoughts, feeling their feelings and lapping up their turns of phrase – we attempt to hold God close and tarry with God for a while in a moment of intimacy.

282

Still, it is an intimacy that always carries with it a reminder that God is not here, still walking the market, looking for something important we suppose. Such is the intimacy of reading: an intimacy that lives in a certain solitude, a vulnerability of author to the gaze of the reader that nevertheless holds the author apart and still distant. As Rebecca Solnit writes, reading is "living in books, through books, in the lives of others that are also the heads of others, in that act that is so intimate and yet so alone."[2] Or, as Rebbe Nahman writes in the same teaching:

> *And it is like ink, for even though the image and likeness have truly been depicted therein as was said, nevertheless it remains merely an image and likeness and not truly the thing itself. So too, even though the statement depicts the likeness, nevertheless it is nothing but an image and likeness, i.e. the lowest rung of its being – the statement. Understand this.*

So for now, I learn alone. And I learn, because I am alone; because right now, God is not here with or for me. I hope you come back soon. But until then, I will spend some time in your library, reading your books and thinking of you, longingly.

Endnotes

1. Jean-Luc Nancy, *On the Commerce of Thinking: Of Books & Bookstores*, trans. David Wills (New York: Fordham University Press, 2009), 40.
2. Rebecca Solnit, *The Faraway Nearby* (New York: Viking, 2013), 60–61.

SHAVUOT WITH 20/20 VISION

Marilyn Russell

I have been fortunate during stay at home orders because there is a State Recreation Area not far from my home in Los Angeles that remained open and I could exercise and enjoy a photography hobby while effortlessly social distancing. However, as word got out on social media about this haven, it became increasingly congested and less possible to social distance.

I was still able, though, to experience Shabbat services via Zoom. But the image behind my eyes throughout this time was of the (Jewish) doctor with the dark, haunted eyes, being interviewed on 60 Minutes during a brief break from a long emergency room shift in a New York hospital. All he could say was "Stay home, New York." Though he was the image behind my eyes, I couldn't begin to imagine what he was seeing behind his eyes, what his vision was of the emergency room he had just left, the same one to which he was about to return.

Shavuot, our happy *chag*, arrived, and although Zoom Shabbat services had initially seemed awkward and distracting, by Shabbat Shavuot I had become comfortable and had eventually located my screen in the same room where I normally *daven* at home. As I rose for the Amidah and *Hallel*, I realized what an amazing experience it was to be davening at home, in my usual place, accompanied by my rabbi and congregation.

An hour before the end of Shabbat Shavuot, I noticed my phone had received a text, but waited for the end of Shabbat, enjoying the sweetness of the holiday a little longer. The message was from my city, announcing a curfew due to civil unrest resulting from the brutal taking of George Floyd's life.

Throughout our history, Judaism has challenged us with entering prayer as a holy space, often a joyous space, yet never one of denial.

Shavuot 5780 (2020)
Cantor Vera Broekhuysen

If a Torah comes out of the Ark
and there are no arms to receive it,
does it still sing our people's song?

That question's stalked me,
in a spring scented with
lilacs and fear.
Singing together, impossible –
instead, I stay up nights,
trying to (re-)create the same voice-hours of
my choir, banished from our building
for safety's sake.

Disease's sudden onslaught
made impossible the accustomed
circuit of Ark to person to breath to song to siddur
to touch to kiss to grasp the
smooth curves of the atzei chayyim
and bend to breathe in parchment, and the sweat
of a tale long read and longer told

Now a new hakkafah,
the circuit of bed to coffee to computer to mic cord to capo
to constantly moving fingertips where new calluses
lift their edges almost as fast as they form,
to contact lens case as I pluck sight
from my red eyes at day's long end
(and really, am I still their cantor
if I only exist from the shoulders up?)

Oh, we circle.
We hover, wingspans apart,
waiting for the wind to shift,
for an unthinkable gift of grace -
a vaccine, a decreasing R,
the world waking up one morning and
putting on their damn masks –
that we may cease our treading air
and touch down

285

and huddle together once more for comfort.

There were birds at Sinai too.
Their profuse praise filled the air
outside the tent flaps,
which opened (like my back door)
so that Israel could spill forth, sleepy, unshowered,
dress tunic on top,
pajama pants and bare feet below,
to see God's love break the sky open

to say "YES" back before we'd properly processed
Na'aseh v'nishma:
Covenant first, coffee later.

This year, like I did that first thousands-year-morning ago,
I will take it. I will say "Yes" back before I know
the "how" to receive this
Torah that is quarantined from our touch
but not our need

And when my children ask me, years from now,
"How did the scroll survive, unopened for so long?"
I will pause with them between the lilacs
and say, "My darlings, it opened.
In every home."

WEARING A VEIL
Rabbi Claudio Kupchik

On Shavuot we celebrate God's giving the most precious gift, the Torah, to Israel at Mt. Sinai.

I want to discuss today what happened after that momentous event, after the thunder and lightning had ended and Moses was getting ready to come down the mount. The Torah tells us:

> *"So Moses came down from Mount Sinai. And as Moses came down from the mountain bearing the two tablets of the Pact, Moses was not aware that the skin of his face was radiant, since he had spoken with Him. Aaron and all the Israelites saw that the skin of Moses' face was radiant; and they were afraid from coming near him. But Moses called to them, and Aaron and all the leaders in the assembly returned to him, and Moses spoke to them. Afterward all the Israelites came near, and he instructed them concerning all that God had imparted to him on Mount Sinai. And when Moses had finished speaking with them, he put a veil over his face. Whenever Moses went in before God to speak with Him, he would leave the veil off until he came out; and when he came out and told the Israelites what he had been commanded, the Israelites would see how radiant the skin of Moses' face was. Moses would then put the veil back over his face until he went in to speak with Him." (Exodus 34:29-35)*

After his encounter with God, Moses face was shining and the Israelites were afraid of that radiance. Because of their fear, they didn't want to come near him. Moses, our great prophet and leader, understood what was needed and covered his face with a veil.

Today we are again afraid to come near each other. It is not because of a divine radiance, but because of another kind of fearsome force, the COVID-19 virus. Being afraid to come near each other is painful. We need and crave social contact, we are social creatures, we need to be close to each other. One of the most popular Hebrew songs, based on Psalm 133 is "הִנֵּה מַה־טּוֹב וּמַה־נָּעִים שֶׁבֶת אַחִים גַּם־יָחַד:" How good and how pleasant it is that brethren sit together." Few things are as beautiful and pleasant as sitting together as families and as communities to share good times and instead of doing that these days we need to take distance from each other.

In this time of crisis, we need to follow a great leader, perhaps the greatest leader ever, Moshe Rabbenu, Moses our teacher. Moses wore a veil, he covered his face in order to be able to interact with the people and diminish their fear. We need to follow his example and wear masks when we go out and about and where we might be close to other people. Wearing a mask is perhaps the simplest and most effective way of showing people we care for their feelings and their health. Wearing a mask might also be the best way to slow the spread of the virus as well, as recent studies comparing the infection rates and outcomes in different places suggest. In early March 2020 NYC and Hong Kong both had single digit cases of COVID-19. Latest figures show 16,410 deaths for NYC compared to 4 in Hong Kong. While other factors might be at play too, the early use of masks in Hong Kong might have helped prevent the rapid spread of the virus.

Using masks in public might be the best way we have right now to protect another of God's precious gifts, our lives.

May the memory of our loved ones, all who helped us become who we are and enriched our lives, inspire us on this Shavuot day to do what we can to enrich and protect our lives and the lives of others.

May we all soon be able to sit together and enjoy God's precious gifts in good health and without fear of the virus, but for now let us all wear our masks with pride, knowing that we are following the steps of the greatest leader, Moses our teacher.

POEMS

QUARANTINE
Jamie Wendt

The street is desolate, early morning
and no matter the time of day these days.

I pull open my embroidered curtains
like the doors of an ark,
but instead of Torah scrolls on the other side,
the sleeping windows of strangers stare solemn,
where, later in the day, I will find
neighbors standing in lonely doorways
with mugs of coffee,
cats rubbing against ankles.
Our homes become museums
of saved things we stare into
to find our previous lives.
But it is early

April, the buds are slow to open,
and yesterday, snow softened
our Chicago street, kissed narrow paths
between buildings. Next week
when the season changes,
a child will draw apple trees with sidewalk chalk,
press her painted rocks
in the dirt of neighbors' gardens,
her street becoming her gallery.
Trees will bend to her, nod and shelter
nests of new life.

Our hands placed against living room windows,
we watch the sun rise and lower for the first time
with our children wrapped in blankets like tallit
as we are gifted time, a closer look
at the waiting world.

FOR YOU

Rabbi Sonja K. Pilz

Yesterday, I was joking with your father
As both of us were riding a subway car
Not touching
Anything.

We were wondering aloud
If this is the first of many.
If we were to tell you one day
About a world of concert halls

Bars, churches, and synagogues,
Parties, classrooms, swimming pools,
Movie theaters, park picnics,
Writing circles, and orchestras.

Most days, I feel fine.
Others,
I don't even know how to get through.
Then we talk about germophobes,

The stock market, strong states,
Three months' rent, political violence, and PTSD.
On yet other days,
I am staring at my growing belly,

Which is probably also just me getting fat.
And I find myself praying,
That you may become a warrior,
Born in silver knight's armor,

Impenetrable.

ARRIVING LATE TO MYSELF
Rabbi Aaron Weininger

I arrive late to myself
The needs pile high
Like a snow-capped mountain
On my last trip down the slopes
More like last week's laundry of unfolded whites
Who's kidding, mixed load
Who knows when I'll travel next
Or leave the house.

Because
I keep stumbling on
Work
School
Art Projects
Dishes
Laundry
Zoom
The Known
The Unknown
Privilege
Gratitude
Hope
Because I have a roof over my head
Work to do
Food to eat
Clothes to fold
Kids to love.

I arrive late to myself
In pursuit of a
Deep breath
Walk
Bike ride
Meditation
Prayer
Phone call with a friend
I give myself a harder time for not Doing It Right
Which only makes me later.

292

I arrive late to myself
As I arrive on time for others
Will you stick with me six feet apart
When I trip down the mountain?
I'm on my way
To arrive to me and to no one's judgment
Whenever I do.

Dedicated with love to all who are parenting
in every way possible at an impossible time.

PANDEMIC POEMS
Laurie Pollack

Today May 27th

Today May 27th
we are nearing
the summer solstice
and even at 8 pm it
is still not dark.

Today the rose bush is
filled with pink
blossoms.

Today the wax beans
broke the
surface of the black soil
with small light green leaves
reaching up.

Today the grass is
could use a trim,
today the chives and parsley
are doing well.

Today the
cherry tomato
vines sprouted
tiny green and white flowers,
some day soon to be
small round red fruit.

Today after checking the garden
 I did not leave my house again.

Today the weather was hot and steamy.

Today the US
death toll
from COVID-19
reached

100,000
unique
sacred
precious
human
lives.

Memorial Day 2020

Rose Tree Park
Memorial Day
trees are green
shadows and sun
air feels soupy humid
sitting in our car
keeping away
from others
who pass by
walking the trails
or sit at benches,
always
in distinct family groups.

We eat our
take out
pizza from Pinocchio's.

I tore the cardboard box into
two plates
we forgot to buy drinks
so we share a bottle of
leftover warm Coke.

the fries are warm not hot but
that's okay.

Our masks pulled down
to eat.

Mary turns on
her IPod to a tune from
the movie "Dirty Dancing"

295

and we get outside and
stand on the pavement and
then for a moment we
hug and dance
two women moving to
music,
our feelings unmasked,
no distance between us.

Today I made a mask

I had loved the images of
dolphins on the blue teeshirt
but there was a stain
I had been unable to erase
so out it went
into the black bag
to be stuffed into the
metal clothes donation
kiosk
outside the supermarket
after work when I got around to it.
But then the world ended.

I like the shirt's bright blue color
so I chose it from the shirts in the bag
as the one to slice up
to make a no-sew mask
for wearing to the supermarket.
The stain will not matter
because it will go
on the side I wear inside
over my mouth,
and the dolphins will show
on the outside.

Life Sustaining

I hear the song
playing halfway down the street
and I exclaim to Mary:

WHAT? The ICE CREAM man???
and she says: oh good!
yes yes get me
a cone and I grab a mask quickly
and my wallet and run
to catch him and
get there in time
lining up behind a family
and it gets to be my turn and
yes he is really there
inside his truck
wearing a mask too
and I
ask him
how much for a vanilla cone
and he says two fifty and
I hand him a five and
say two vanilla
and he hands me the cones
with a gloved hand
and I run back home
before they melt
and then
almost the same as
a normal warm afternoon
in May
we lap up
life sustaining sweetness

Masks

"I can't breathe"
He said.
They choked him.
I breathe
Inside a mask, it is true
but I have enough air.
We have suffocated we have choked
We have strangled we have stolen the air.
"Don't kill me"
He said
They killed him

We have lynched
We have enslaved
We have segregated
I breathe
Inside a mask, it is true
But I have enough air.
We have lied
We have hated
We have stifled
We have crushed
We have turned away.
I breathe inside
The mask of whiteness
It is true
But I have enough air.
I have had enough!
"I can't breathe" he said
I have had enough
We have killed strangled
Smothered asphyxiated
I have had enough
I don't want this mask of whiteness
That lets me breathe
That suffocates you
I have had enough
I want a world
With no more masks
With clear air for everyone

"ADONAI LI, V'LO IRA..."*
Rabbi Marci N. Bellows

Lo.
Aval, lo.
Ani M'fachedet.
I Am Afraid.
I Fear.
Fear. Fear of death.
Fear of my own death. Fear of the
Death of my child my husband my
mother my father.
This virus. The people who do not
Fear enough.
The people we entrust to take care of
Us who do not care about us.
Fear of so much we still do not know.
Fear of so much still to come.
Fear of wrong choices. Fear of stepping
Out. Fear of leaving safe boundaries.
Fear that I am paralyzed.
Fear of others. Fear of all that could
Be. Fear that this will never end.
Fear that I am irrational.
Fear that I am exactly Right.
Fear that One Small Mistake is all it would take.
Fear that others' lives are in my hands.
Nevertheless,
B'yadecha, Adonai, afkid ruchi,
B'eit ishan v'aira.
V'im ruchi g'viati,
Adonai li, v'.....

(inspired by writing session with Stacey Zisook Robinson)

* *"God is mine; I shall not fear." Excerpted from Jewish liturgy.*

INTO THE ARKS
Jessica Levine Kupferberg

In multitudes of landlocked arks
Bright screens burn–
Dazzling diamond windows
Connections across the winds
And the dark.

Listen to the
The brays of boredom
The roars of uncertainty
The squeals of hungry bellies wanting snacks
Again and again.
Huddle close;
Stay apart!
Two by two and seven by seven and each by each
All aboard for a bumpy ride:

Take only your close family with you.

We did not heed the warnings.
We were not ready
For the churn,
The day by day and night by night
Bordered and clockless
Zooming in on
Our anxieties and inadequacies
And maybe
Maybe

Love.

Remember that when the first flood ended,
Waters' retreat a slow dance back and below,
Elderless–
They didn't know what they would find when
They opened the door.

Who will be our raven
And then our dove

To tell us when it's safe again,
And what of our olive branch,
Brittle reed of hope to stick in our beak
After the deluge of alone retreats–

And what will be our rainbow:
A warning or a blessing?

It all depends on us.

(This poem originally appeared in the Times of Israel
March 22, 2020)

ZION
Mikhal Weiner

By the waters of the East River we knelt and wept and
prayed to you, Zion,
although your promises had long since gone
down the river,
sails unfurled
anchors weighed
your eyes trained on constellations
shining guidance through the night.

And from the corners of our eyes
briny tears dripped on the mud
catching on the brownish weeds
coalescing with the flood.

And the salt flowed onward with the stream
joining the common tides of grief
that glue together the continents –
dirt to dirt brings no relief.

—

By the waters of the East River we lay down and wept
and prayed to you, Zion,
although you'd left us in your wake
watching ripples t
urn to waves
the wind was rough and even though
rain was leaking from cracks in the clouds
not a one of us was able to get clean

So we held one another in tired arms
the blood still sticky on our skin
the stench of bile and war and fear
filling our nostrils from within

And the towers we'd built to raise us up,
monuments to truths we thought would last
now came tumbling back to dust
beams of steel now turned to rust

302

—

Here is a truth

the heavens will always spit us out
and the river flows on to the sea
and the sea is swallowed by the ocean
and only the ocean is truly free.

so now we lay in the bed we've made
of mud and silt that paint our cheeks that are
streaked with tears of realization as we
squint at a heaven thick with smoke that
rises up from ancient fires
burnt up trees and funeral pyres handmade
endings.

And it may be we've missed our chance to
bask in the light of a merciful sun
all our thieving and plunder be done,
swords to tools that turn the soil
that breathes with life, that ebbs and flows and grows and
rests, like fingers folded neatly on chests
that rise and fall
that rise and fall.

By the waters of the Mississippi
By the waters of the Colorado
By the waters of the East River
we lay down and wept
for you,
Zion.

POETS TO READ DURING A PANDEMIC
Marjorie Hanft

Yeats   for the love of   flapping herons   & for more
weeping than the world   can understand   even
at this time   & Sexton for believing   there will come a time
when it's okay for kids   to pick gum   off the sidewalk
again   & Derek Walcott   even though   you could never
ever be   that stranger   who has loved yourself   your whole life
& because   at the beginning   of a reading   he once said to his
audience   *when you give a reading   basically   you wish that*
nobody was there   so will you please leave   & Jean Valentine
because   if someone you know   visits you in a dream
you almost always   have the urge   to tell them about it.

SPRING TRAIL PRAYER POEM
Marjorie Hanft

Heading off on a trail   that begins alongside   a field of cows. Do they go straight
on their way?   Do they sing?   & what do I carry today   or any day   an ark
on my back?   I think I'd rather be   a kokopelli   than a member of the tribe
of Kahat   at least when the moon wanes   carrying a flute   dancing   off
trail   wearing a mask   a few feathers   on my head   especially when
teenagers show up   congregating   which   they absolutely   are not supposed
to be doing right now   so that I hop away into a ravine   where a skink   or a toad
hides   spying fiddlehead fern fronds   jack-in-the pulpit   fading spring beauties   wake
robin   a hundred shooting stars (dodecatheon)   first dogwood blooms   & all else
that is ephemeral   &/or   holy   each & every spring   (oblivious to the plight
of humans).   May the box turtles   bless us and keep us   (dodging all mower blades)
& mayapples   deal graciously with us. May the phlox rings   puccoons   violets   Virginia
bluebells   & swamp buttercups   bestow favor on us   & grant us peace.

ON BREATHING
Alicia Jo Rabins

I'm OK during the day, but at night I get scared,
Which makes it hard to breathe, which is a symptom
Of the pandemic, which is what scares me.
Well played, anxiety, my old friend. You've always
Warned me something like this might happen.
You're a gift from my ancestors who survived plagues,
And worse. They wove you into my DNA to warn me,
So that I too might survive. Now that it's happening,
Anxiety, I don't need you anymore. I need
The ones who gave you to me. Hear me, ancestors
Who lived through danger times: I'm ready for you now.
All these years I've carried your worries in my bones.
Now I need your love, your thousand-year view.
Tell me it's going to be OK. Remind me you made it
Through, and we will too. Teach me to breathe.

READING EXODUS IN A TIME OF PLAGUE
Alicia Jo Rabins

I used to study the holy texts
Night and day
Certain there was some
Wisdom inside those words
Which would make me live
Fully for the first time

Now I immerse myself
In the news
With the same solemn
Devotion I once gave
The rabbis I have become
Acolyte of epidemiologists

I used to whisper evening prayers
Now I recite statistics
And watch the curves
The angel of death
Draws in the air
With his wing

Which color is the line
For my city,
Which for yours?
Which of us is Pharaoh,
Which Noah?

When we leave
This narrow place
And walk out into
The glaring desert beyond,
Will we recognize each other
In that light?

THINGS I'VE HEARD AND SAID THIS WEEK
Alicia Jo Rabins

Please mute yourself and listen
Please unmute yourself and speak
Let's take a moment to breathe
Let's take turns saying our names
Would you like to hold up your volcano?
Would you like to draw an elephant?

I'm so sorry I thought it was yesterday
I'm so sorry I thought it was tomorrow
How are we doing? Are we OK?
Everybody doing OK?
Here is an amulet to print
And hang above your door

Here an old story about a young woman
Who saved her grandfather by singing
Here is my living room my bedroom
My porch my basement my kitchen
Here are the windows across the street
And the faces behind those windows

When we venture out
We give each other
A wide berth
Like ships in rocky waters
Humbled by the sea
We wave to each other

Through windows and screens
We sing and raise a glass
Simultaneous but not together
Oh my friends my beloved strangers
I never knew our closeness
Until it was gone

COVID-19: THE TWILIGHT ZONE
Rivka Hecht

The space between being & becoming;
between white noise & the sound of silence;
between black & white;
between sunset & starstruck;
between hard & soft;
between wet & dry;
between desert & forest;
between inside & outside;
between the threshold & the Home;
between alone & together - בי‎דוד & יחוד;
between isolation & meditation - בי‎דוד & התבודדות;
between the Hebrew letters ח & ה;
between leavened & unleavened bread - חמץ & מצה;
between caterpillar & butterfly;
between human & animal;
between the darkest part of night & when the new day begins;
between land & sea;
between finite & infinite;
between what once was & what is to come;
between our old & new worlds;
between sleeping & waking;
between what is real and what is imagined;
between the mundane & the divine;
between heaven & earth;
between corona & coronation;
A transformation; a bridging of the gap; a space of nothing to become
everything in time - transcendent of all היינו כחולמים - for we were like
dreamers.

LOST AND FOUND
Esti Rosen Snukal

I've lost some little bits of me along the way.
And found some new parts to mend the gaps.
I've picked up some much needed clarity, stitched over patches of lost
sanity
And quilted a new mindfulness.
I've collected stories and bound them into mental albums;
Picture books of heroes and angels.
And loved ones.
I've lost time
And found a new calendar
I've embraced my most
extroverted-introverted self.
I've crawled into my cave
Curled up
And cried.
I've laughed too
And cuddled
And found that movie marathons with your 12 year- old can steady your
heart.
I've inhaled books like pure oxygen
Drank their stories from a tall cool glass
Baked too many cookies to count
And enjoyed every single, therapeutic bite.
I've found my lost self in the perfumed gardens that bloom wild and free
On my daily walks
Where the neon flowers, fragrant and sweet remind me
to literally
stop
and smell the roses.
I've zoom yoga-d in my pj's
In my bedroom
Next to the mountain of laundry taunting me.
I have found salvation
from the healing balm of truest friendships and sisterhoods
And fallen over and over again
into the safety net of my other half
I've gone on coffee dates with my sister
Through the gift of modern technology

Both of us together
But miles apart
I've discovered that TikTok with your 15 year -old is the new age Golden
Ticket.
And re-discovered how much unconditional love and free therapy
a dog can give.
I've sent my kids back to school.
And walked a new tightrope of panic and ambivalence
I have ached to hold my new baby niece
Inhale her new baby scent
And wrap my arms around my parents and my father in law
And not let go.
I've lost some sense of security
Reclaimed it.
Then lost it again,
I know it is waiting for me
On the ink- kissed pages of ancient text
And in the multitude of daily miracles.
I have seen the faint flutter of hope
From bell curves, graphs and charts
The same hope that surfs on a sunbeam through my bedroom window
Sent up from the prayer groups that gather daily below
Right behind my blooming mango tree
Where the park swings sway in the soft summer breeze
Dreaming of the familiar song that is childhood
and aching for the touch of tiny fingerprints.
I am masked in uncertainty and in my faith
I am both
Lost and found.
I am ever so grateful.

A SKIFF DOCKED AT THE PIER
Rabbi Paula Mack Drill

A skiff docked at the pier,
I am
tied up, hawser with a splice
anchoring bit to bollard,
battened down, unable to set sail,
rocking gently on the swells,
bow pointed to the sea.

Just there, in the bay,
in the turbulent winds of a hurricane,
tugboat, ferry, trawler, tall ship.
They are
pitching, rolling, breaking apart,
tossed and turned, capsizing.

I observe it all
I do not look away.
Under the same azure sky,
lit by the same sun,
in the same bay,
I am leeward and
they are in the storm.

PANDEMIC POETRY
Rebecca Minkus-Lieberman

Being married to a superhero

They told us to
separate. To make
The basement his home or
Better, another house or
Rented room, alone
Between shifts
Of triaging illness
And comforting
Desperate strangers.

They said keep six feet
Apart and never share
A meal or let your hands
Glance on the same object
at once.

Who are these experts on our shared isolation
Who pretend to know what will lead us to healing and health
What are their qualifications when they tell us
To turn away from the most tender balm we know
                    What do they know about these waves of absent love

But what if
we wear masks
What if
we keep our faces turned
Away from each other
But give our limbs permission
to reach out
And touch To caress the fear
His chest cupping my back
as I imagine
the look of his face

Pandemic love
A nod to duty and a step towards risk
Mournful aloneness

Safety
In an empty bed

Tiferet

Tender branches of the maple
Silhouetted on slate grey sky
Spring leaf buds dotting the limbs.

Eyes drawn upwards
To a small sparrow
Perched with perfect grace
On a slender bough
Balanced in proud fragility
Enthroned atop immensity
Enrobed in wind.

Beauty is its courage
To lift its wings
Flutter out
to that trembling edge
The arm that kisses the sky
Lifting its beak skyward
Singing songs
of a new morning.

Quarantine Mothering

Gutted
Scooped and seeded
like a cantaloupe
Sliced for breakfast
I offer myself a container

For their melancholy
Soaking up their grief

Sadness springs unbidden
When they turn a corner
Meets them in the bathtub beneath the bubbles, at the
Stove flipping pancakes, dragging
the garbage to the curb

In dirty slippers

This grief needs holding
Clears space around itself
Sits coiled on the chest
Until the next
Persistent pocket of light
Dims its darkness
Loosens its fingers
For a few
minutes
        Or maybe more

We feed ourselves sugar and sunlight and bunny rabbits and frivolous dance
routines and baked
bread to beat back the black-
ness

Can we ritualize this sorrow
to soften it?
Kriya
A tearing of something
outside the heart
to dull its sharpness

Their grief
Asks for accompaniment
Demands shared air
And so we sit nestled on the bed
And soak
each others' skin
In tears

Netzach #1

At night I scroll
Looking for elders.
I am searching for 70, at least
To counsel me through this.
For wise wizened ones
Who have seen it all and will

Tell me we will endure
And come out
Some other
side.

Stories of war and pain and
Tenacious survival
Temper the loss
Stories that hold our sadness
Alongside generations of sorrow
Black and white photos
Silent home movies
Stories
That sit me
down and rub my back
And pull out the history books and
Photo albums and say gently
This is nothing *chamudi.*
Stories of internment and illness
Isolation and emergence
uncoil the compression and
Loosen its weight
Soothe like a cup
Of chamomile tea.

Netzach #2

And yet the nightly family dinners
Are a *mechayeh,* meaning
They give us life.
Activities cancelled and
Meetings postponed we
Have nowhere to be but
Here around this weathered dining table
with each other.
The day's debrief, shared frustrations and a question:
        What endures?
Blank stares and eyes rolled and then
Clarifying:
        Endures when? Through this pandemic?
        Forever?
        But how can we know?

In this contracted time,
bared and essentialized
Between bites of guacamole
They wonder aloud.
Soccer. My love for soccer.
My need for friends. Face-to-face. Not
Through a screen.
Impermanence (that from a sixteen year old, which I mentally note for
later conversation).
Mystery and
Creativity. Energy to generate life.
These endure.
Maybe
And so we finish our fish tacos and clear our plates
Into the cluttered sink and bring out
The s'mores pie for
dessert.

TO BE A HERO
Genevieve Greinetz

Morning talks with God are the song i sing
til doves coo post noon. There's nothing
else to alert the end of shacharit, beginning
of mincha. Since

leaving Jerusalem
on a last flight late March, the pines
are the friends i bless with, i sing
my songs alone.

I'd wanted
to be a hero. To learn to walk
the San Francisco streets like a chaplain
in a covid unit. I'd wanted

to teach you to love your
self. To save you from a flinch
of unneeded pain. To uplift your
loneliness and save

you from it's white horizon. To tell you
its meaningful and move my lips with words like
love and *care* and *you can* to make my
self believe

in anything. Bleak reverie, the doves sing me
to tea time. Afternoon gazing at wind. I'd wanted
to slip a hand inside your chest, hold
your heart less alone. To tell you

i've got you. To lean into me. Dusk crows
call the pines and me to maariv. Still,
we watch sky mix itself into a home
for stars. I make a phone call

every day. To save a friend
from loneliness, to save myself from a bleak Spring
breathing in my healthy lungs. Distance is love, we say
together in the grey mist of alone.

OUT OF AN ABUNDANCE OF CAUTION
Rabbi Joseph B. Meszler

Out of an abundance of caution, I'm staying home.

Out of an abundance of caution, I'm washing my hands for at least 20 seconds, sometimes singing the ABCs, sometimes singing the itsy-bitsy spider, and sometimes saying a prayer.

Out of an abundance of caution, I am telling people how much I love them every day, sometimes multiple times a day. I can get annoying.

Out of an abundance of caution, I am waving frantically to the stranger across the street while I am out for my walk, making eye-contact, smiling and saying hello.

Out of an abundance of caution, I am not using the expression "social distancing." Physical distancing, yes. Social distancing, no way.

Out of an abundance of caution, I have subscribed to a joke a day.

Out of abundance of caution, I am looking out for people who might be stressed and hungry for food and love and giving more than I have before.

Out of an abundance of caution I am paying attention more than ever to the words of my prayers.

Out of an abundance of caution, I have faith that love and kindness are contagious, too.

Out of an abundance of caution, I am telling you I am here for you, I care about us, I need you, and I want everyone to know we are all in this together.

EVERY EXODUS LEADS TO ANOTHER
Matthue Roth

I am trying to tell my daughter
about Sinai. Every Jew together,
young and old and yet unborn,
and she says, But won't they get
corona?

In her short life it's one more rule
of a world she's still figuring
out. Snow falls. Flowers sprout
up. Great-grandparents die. We
quarantine.

So many things I wish I could
unlearn for her. The fighting in
Israel. The fighting in this house.
I want her to see the magic in the
world. I want to hide her from it
all.

God created the universe in perfect
order. God seeped us in chaos and
gave us creativity, the ability to
not believe, the option that we
can.

We had no choice. God held a
mountain above our heads. We married
too young, not knowing each other, not
knowing how far we'd grow apart.

People are stepping onto streets,
risking infection to reclaim this
world. It's dumb. It's too early. We
need to. It's this or sixty thousand
suicides, says a friend
who follows these things.

It's true, they could get corona,
I tell my daughter. But if
they wear masks, they have
the whole desert to spread
out in.

On Passover we're commanded
to imagine ourselves leaving Egypt.
When getting the Torah, we don't have
to.

We were there. The mountain
over my head, real as rocks, ready to
crumble, ready to end it all. The disease
so close, ready to crawl onto my skin, to
change everything. This roof over our
heads. These walls protecting
us.

Maybe it did change everything.
Maybe all we have to do is step out
and see.

POEMS FOR WHEN THE WORLD IS MASKED
Rabbi Menachem Creditor

from an inside place

Oh, that moment
when sunlight intensifies
and I rush to open my window
to just let it in

Oh, cover me!
suffuse my being
pervade my cells!
please!

But then,
through the open window,
comes a rush of very cold air
accompanying the blessed light

So, for now
I'll just sit here
and enjoy the light
from my warm
inside place.

Welcome Feelings

Deep, powerful feelings can be reawakened.
Even when the world is masked.

It can be a song.
Or the wind.
Or pairs of eyes on a screen, all facing out.

And, if tears then flow,
welcome them with a re-opened heart.

with my guitar

i play so they won't leave
maybe the right chord
maybe if i could finally learn that D minor
they'd stay
we'd be together again

over and over and over
every morning
i dig deeper and deeper
and try and try and try
but every morning
they leave
me
here
alone
with my guitar

Everywhere

Those faces
on the screen are real:
real people,
real faces.

God's Eyes, everywhere.
God's Heart, everywhere.

For my Friend on the Screen

as I sit here
in my bedroom
which has become my office
and also Sinai
and that coffee shop on Shattuck

distance is an illusion
so is time

these tears are a gift
of coming home.

(Another one poured out...)

attuned hearts
need not speak
to know

There is no such thing
as alone

your face this morning: a poem

i've never seen so clearly
how truly precious is every other
i mean i've known and i've taught
but now, with a shining sweet friend
on my screen, singing out
to me to you to the One

sitting still
feeling still
breath steadied
letting the light of a new day in

these tears purify my eyes
to see better
to feel
to hope again

i feel the fire in me
lit by the warmth of contact
birthed by the light
of your sweet face
dear friend

your soul
my friend
is luminous
and you share it
with purity

324

Tears

Oh, for the world.
Oh, for our children.

cover me, hold me, God.
but don't wipe my tears.
they have to follow their course.

for these

tears here, tears there
death here, death there
words everywhere
broken hearts everywhere

not enough, never enough
to stop the tears

for these do we cry
and there is no comfort
to revive our souls

until the tears
have no cause to flow
i will send my broken heart
everywhere

WE HANG BY A THREAD
Rabbi Karen Silberman

Maybe we've always known how fragile life is,
How tenuous the connection,
Just a breath, or no breath.
We hang by a thread.

But from where does the thread hang?

Maybe we've always known what truly matters can't be bought.
That meaning doesn't come from things,
Even when scarcity makes us want to believe it can,
We know what really endures.

Does living 'without' offer an opportunity to appreciate more of what
ultimately matters?

Maybe we've always known we will never know
Why bad things happen to good people,
Even when they did everything right.
We believe in Something beyond ourselves,

We have to.

The Breath of Life,
Who holds the thread.
Who values love over all.
Who makes uncertainty enough.

THE CHOICE
Rabbi Meir Bargeron

After all of this is done
(if it is ever all done),

after we throw our doors open and
run, run
purposely and joyously into the
embrace of
all our beloveds;

after we cast aside our masks to
breath, breath
in the Divine Essence of
each and every
human Creation we encounter
in the supermarket,
on the sidewalk,
in the small and the large spaces
of our lives;

May we take a moment (or a lifetime)
to consider deeply
a choice that
the Universe,
the Holy Blessed One has
placed before us.

Will we draw more closely to one another,
to heal our collective brokenness,
to seek justice,
to ensure that our collective wellbeing
is built upon the wellbeing of
each and every
human Creation?

Or

Will we forget our fear,
the masks,

the field hospitals,
the empty schools,
the nurses wearing garbage bags,
the refrigerated trucks full of bodies
(the sacred, empty vessels of beloveds),
the doors closed tight to
separate us;

And return to the regularly scheduled program
of individual interest and collective failure?

Will we have the courage to learn and
to change,
to accept the responsibility we have to
each and every
human Creation,
made in God's Image?

WHAT IS IT LIKE?
Rabbi Elyssa Joy Austerklein

It is not like the 40 days and 40 nights
on the mountain
when Moses laid up with God
and returned shining, luminous,
painful to see.

It is like the unwieldy weeds
that have sprouted gaily
around the trees
in my yard.
The muddy feet and entryway
that can't forget the daily tromps
outside But nowhere else.

Each room in the house becomes
a microcosm of some emotion
A place to reside
in the invention
of somewhere new.

Growth does not atrophy
but instead expands
in the constant confrontation
with new realities and surprising responses.

What is the science of connection?

Our love continues to flourish in this bubble of time. But the world
refuses it.

I find meaning in my own face. I find God resting there with me, when
I search in my eyes and my prayers run deep as heaven and earth
collide right in my house.

It is not like the 40 days and 40 nights on the mountain when Moses laid up with God but it is a revelation of blessing. The way that gratitude can seep into your veins and you cannot contain the joy of Being. God was, God is, God will be - and I am a part of that everlasting in life and in death and in life.

OPENING UP
Daniel Sherman

I'm walking Tux on Givat Titora, in Modiin,
under an almost-full moon.
The air is cool but pleasant, and from the top of the hill,
and I can see over Modiin,
past Maccabim, to Bayt Sira and Bayt Liqya and Safa and Mevo Horon.

Continuing east past them and other villages--Palestinian and Israeli--the
foothills continue to rise towards Jerusalem.
A bit to the north are lights from the suburbs of Ramallah.
The minarets in all of the Palestinian villages
are lit up festively for Ramadan.

Around me on Titora, teenagers are gathered here and there in small
groups--most wearing masks against Corona, but not all.
There is a feeling not just of the weekend starting but of a relaxed
opening up. Despite the fact that we just had rain (unusual for this time
of year), it is as if one can taste the coming summer.

Someone close by gently strums a guitar.

331

THRESHOLD OF GRIEF

Karen Erlichman

Threshold of grief
you summon me
again and again
to the altar
You call my name
beckoning
pulling me
toward the Holy of Holies
Sometimes I resist
and turn away
Other times I come looking
for You
when my soul is so heavy
and I need to be
made whole

BLESSED BE OUR PORCH
Aurora Mendelsohn

My husband used to be the first to snag the newspaper to devour with his breakfast.
Now the papers huddle in piles by the door, thin and shunned.

In the mailbox is a handwritten letter from a friend.

Bored children lie in wait for cardboard packages
and pounce with glee.

The doorbell rings.
We wait.
We retrieve our restaurant food from the porch.
As we scurry back inside we glimpse the back of the driver walking away.

Blessed be what arrives.
Blessed be the deliverers.

At dusk my middle daughter plays guitar while we sing with our neighbors.
Each of us from our own porch.

Dear friends sit on plastic chairs on the ground below.
A submerged yearning rises.
Their words float up.
We catch them and hold them close.

On the porch my youngest child climbs the rails.
She curls up on a cushion in the sun.

Blessed be this liminal refuge,
outside, but safe.

For its first hundred years other families sat on this porch.
We have known it for twelve years and have never seen a bird's nest here.
Now in the quiet, a robin builds.
Blessed be his hope.

From this threshold I cast my incantations to those who prepare to exit:

Wear a mask!
Change your shoes!
Fear others!

My oldest daughter sets off for her weekly trip to the supermarket
With a detailed list and anxious eyes.

I take a deep breath as I come back from a walk,
before slowly, carefully opening the front door.

Blessed be our going
and blessed be our returning
In health
And in peace.
Now and always.

Blessed be this shelter of peace.
Blessed be our porch.

18
Ariel Creditor

Dear God,

I shouldn't be here right now.
I should be banging on drums,
singing in my holy place.

Instead I am in my house,
arguing with my siblings
on my birthday.

I'm an adult now.
What the hell am I supposed to do?

I'm sitting on my bed in America
crying about my bed in Israel,
where I should be.

The world is at a standstill.
And I am standing still,
waiting to be ready for the world to move.

PANDEMIC POETRY 5780
Rabbi Margaret Frisch Klein

#1:
It came to pass at midnight

The moon is full tonight
Just like it was years ago
Years ago my people,
Our people
Were hunkered down
Inside
Waiting, Watching, Trembling
Lamb's blood on the door
Ready to flee at a moment's notice.

Tonight
The moon is full
After the hail
After the lightening
After the rain
It peaks through the billowing clouds
Against the night sky.
Ominous.

Our people
Are hunkered down
Inside
Waiting, Watching, Trembling
Seder plate on the table
Computer tuned to Zoom
Or not.

There are questions we could ask tonight.

How is this year different from all other years?

What will it be like
To exit
To cross the sea
Maybe just across the retaining pond I can see from my deck
To the other side?

How will we celebrate
Being free again?
Filled with joy
Joy tinged with sorrow
For we have lost
While we have gained new understandings?

Will it be with a timbrel as Miriam sang
Filled with relief and joy?
Those women knew to take their timbrels
There would be a time to celebrate

Will it be with a wine cup
As we spill out a drop of wine
One for each plague
Or one for each death?

How many drops of wine?
God chastened the angels...
How can you celebrate when My Creatures are dying?

We may be
Filled with relief and joy
Filled with the knowledge

When will we be allowed
To leave Egypt
To exit from our narrow spaces
From the safety of our homes,
Our protective ark?

When will it be safe
To go to the grocery store or the synagogue
To go to school or work
To go to the beach or the movies
Or even to a funeral?

To hug
When will we be allowed
To hug?

337

Tonight
We   hear
Echoes of another time.
The moon is full tonight.

Some year,
We will tell our children
What happened to us,
When we went forth
Out of the narrow places
And nothing was the same again.
Passover 5780, April 11, 2020

#2:
Bluing Up, In Memory of My Father

Did you notice?
The bright blue skies.
The sky seems bluer.
More intense
Less full of smog
We have gotten so use to the smog;
We don't even notice it is there now.

I remember this blue.
It was in the days after 9/11.
No airplanes in the sky.
Just an intensely blue sky.

I remember this blue.
When we first moved
From Chicagoland to Michigan
My father would comment:

"Do you see?," he said
"Do you see? You can see my shadow.
There is no smog."

We would be out in a primeval forest
Identifying wildflowers
Or in the backyard
Planting cucumbers for his beloved pickles

Or at the Fulton Street Market
Buying dill.

My father was a biologist
A geneticist
An atheist
One of the first ecologists
An organizer, with others
Of the first Earth Day
50 years ago.

It was like a picnic
That 4th grade girl thought.
We stood.
We danced.
We lay in the grass.
We collected litter.

And he argued.
On behalf of the earth.
With everyone.

My 4th grade teacher
And the Weekly Reader
Over a 4th grade article about the ozone.
The grocery store
Over aerosol deodorant.
DuPont
Over Agent Orange.

Proudly he called our house
Dandelion Acres.

How embarrassed I was.

Yet, he was right.
He sounded a clarion call.
A shofar if you will.

He would be embarrassed
By the shofar
Unable to reconcile

What he could see in his microscope
With the story of Creation
Unable to reconcile the Holocaust
With his understanding of God.

I never won that argument.

Yet, he was right.
We needed to protect the earth.
We need to protect the environment.

Can I find the compassion?
To forgive my embarrassment?
To forgive my father?

I must. This is his legacy.
He cared about the earth
Passionately.

Like Honi
As my father planted for me
So must I plant for my children and grandchildren

May this time of quarantine
One he worried may one day come,
Be a time of healing.
The scars.
Our relationships.
The earth.
Our world.

Did you notice?
The sky seems bluer.
It's bluing up.
I can see my shadow.
Even in Chicagoland.

Earth Day, 5780

#3:
Grocery Shopping On Earth Day in a Pandemic

Raspberries
I just wanted raspberries
I didn't need them
But for days I craved them
Thought they would bring me comfort
As a raspberry lime rickey.
And milk.
We were out of milk.
So I went.
Early.
Before they run out.
Just the essentials.
Mask on.
An avocado.
Pricey but I miss them.
Tulips.
I can survive
Surrounded by beauty.

Tomatoes.
Wait, what about the Immokee Tomato Workers?
I have supported them for years.
Where do these come from?
Who picked these?
Why all that packaging?
No, no tomatoes for me today.

What about asparagus?
No, not quite the right season yet.
Still from Chile or maybe Mexico.
No, no asparagus for me today.

What about ground beef?
No, it takes 14 pounds of grain for every pound of beef.
But they have it. Limit two packs.
No, no ground beef for me today.

What about Kerurig coffee cups.
Fair trade, Guatemalan coffee.

Are you kidding me?
Think of the waste! This is Earth Day, for God's sake.
No, no coffee for me today.

Raspberries.
What about the raspberries?
That's what I came for.
They are out. Fresh and frozen.
Who bought all the raspberries?
What is happening to our supply chain?
No, no raspberries for me today.

They had toilet paper though.

Did you buy anything?
Milk and bananas.
And potato chips.
A big bag,
Because it has a smaller carbon footprint.
Those are for stress eating.
After the trip to the grocery store.
For raspberries.

PRAYERS

.

SOUL AND BREATH: A PRAYER

Elana Stein Hain

Though it is necessary, it is really painful to have religious institutions, gatherings, and rituals taken away, just when so many of us are feeling vulnerable and are seeking something more transcendent than COVID-19. This tefillah is my attempt to reach for that transcendence. Putting pen to paper, inspired by Tanakh (Bible) and Hazal (our sages) has helped me connect to what I am praying for during these uncertain days. I hope it can do the same for others. May all of our individual and collective prayers be answered.

"Soul and Breath"   "נשמה ורוח"

Our God, the souls and breaths that you
have placed within is are pure
You created them, You fashioned them,   א-לוהינו, נשמות ונשימות שנתת בנו
You breathed them into us and You   טהורות הן
preserve them within us,   אתה בראתן אתה יצרתן אתה נפחתן
And for each and every breath   בנו ואתה משמרן בקרבינו,
we must praise You,   ועל כל נשימה ונשימה חייבים אנחנו
As is written, "Every *soul* (*neshamah*)   לקלס לך
shall praise God,"   כדכתיב,כל הנשמה תהלל י-ה,,[1] כל
"Every *breath* (*neshimah*) shall praise God.   הנשימה תהלל י-ה.[2]

Lord of souls and breaths,
We seek out Your face, and Your spirit
to hover over the deep   אדון הנשמות והנשימות,
that has opened up   מבקשים אנו את פניך ואת רוחך לרחף
To breathe into us once again   על פני התהום שנפתח
the breath of life   להפיח בנו עוד נשמת חיים
For we are in great travail –   כי בצרה גדולה אנחנו כֹּל אֲשֶׁר נִשְׁמַת
all who bear   רוּחַ חַיִּים בְּאַפָּיו ובאפיה
the breath of life   ואנחנו לא נדע מה נעשה
And we do not know what to do.

                                                       תן בכל צוותי הרפואה ומנהיגי תבל
Instill within all medical teams   רוּחַ חָכְמָה
and world leaders a spirit of wisdom   להבין ולהשכיל ללמוד וללמד ולעשות
To understand, to discern to learn,   ורוּחַ עֵצָה וּגְבוּרָה להחליף את כוחם
to teach and to do   ותן בנו רוּחַ דַּעַת לשמור על

A spirit of counsel and might
to renew their strength.
And instill within all of us a spirit
of knowledge to protect ourselves
And the fear of God to care for our fellow –
the weary, the exhausted and infirm
And to honor our elders.

נְפָשׁוֹתֵינוּ וְיִרְאַת ה' [3] לְטַפֵּל בְּזוֹלַת,
בַּעֲיֵפִים וּבִיגֵעִים וּבַנֶּחֱשָׁלִים,
וּלְהַדֵּר פְּנֵי זְקֵנֵינוּ.

Bless us with a spirit of forbearance for
we have not enough strength against
this great multitude that comes against us.
And fulfill through us that which is written:
"Thus said God the Lord, Who created
the heavens and stretched them forth,
Who spread forth the other
and that which comes out of it,
Who gives breath to the people upon it
and spirit to those who walk therein.
I, the Lord have called you
in righteousness and have taken hold
of your hand and protected you…"

בָּרֵךְ אוֹתָנוּ עִם אֶרֶךְ רוּחַ כִּי אֵין בָּנוּ כֹּחַ
לִפְנֵי הֶהָמוֹן הָרַב הַזֶּה הַבָּא עָלֵינוּ [4]
וְקַיֵּים בָּנוּ מַה שֶּׁכָּתוּב:
'' כֹּה-אָמַר הָאֵ-ל ה' בּוֹרֵא הַשָּׁמַיִם
וְנוֹטֵיהֶם רֹקַע הָאָרֶץ וְצֶאֱצָאֶיהָ נֹתֵן
נְשָׁמָה לָעָם עָלֶיהָ וְרוּחַ לַהֹלְכִים בָּהּ אֲנִי
ה' קְרָאתִיךָ בְצֶדֶק, וְאַחְזֵק בְּיָדְךָ וְאֶצָּרְךָ
[5] ''…

---

[1] Tehillim (Psalms) 150:6
[2] Bereshit (Genesis) Rabbah 14:9
[3] Isaiah 11:2
[4] II Chronicles 20:12
[5] Isaiah 42:5-6

(This prayer originally appeared in the Times of Israel
March 18, 2020)

ONE-BY-ONE: A PRAYER
AS THE COVID DEATH TOLL MOUNTS

Alden Solovy

God of consolation,
Surely you count in heaven,
Just as we count here on earth,
In shock and in sorrow,
The souls sent back to You,
One-by-one,
The dead from the COVID pandemic,
As the ones become tens,
The tens become hundreds,
The hundreds become thousands,
The thousands become ten-thousands
And then hundred-thousands,
Each soul, a heartbreak,
Each soul, a life denied.

God of wisdom,
Surely in the halls of divine justice
You are assembling the courts,
Calling witnesses to testify,
To proclaim
The compassion of some
And the callousness of others
As we've struggled to cope.
The souls taken too soon,
Whose funerals were lonely,
Who didn't need to die,
Who died alone,
Will tell their stories
When You judge
Our triumphs
And our failures
In these hours of need.

God of healing,
Put an end to this pandemic,
And all illness and disease.
Bless those who stand in service to humanity.

Bless those who grieve.
Bless the dead,
So that their souls are bound up in the bond of life eternal.
And grant those still afflicted
With disease or trauma
A completed and lasting healing,
One-by-one,
Until suffering ceases,
And we can stop counting the dead,
In heaven
And on earth.

(This essay originally appeared on tobendlight.com
May 27, 2020.)

ZOOMING IN
Shira Gura

Because of You, I'm zooming in.

Seeing faces I haven't seen in a long, long while.
Because of You, I'm zooming in.
Laughing, and playing, and remembering just how to smile.

But, it's not about zooming in.
It's about zooming out.
And finding You again.

Because of You I'm zooming in
With friends far away and even those that live close by.
Because of You I'm zooming in
Slowing down and taking one day at a time.

But, it's not about zooming in.
It's about zooming out.
And finding You again.

Feeling connected to everything, all around the earth.
Seeing Your hand in everything, keeping the faith.

Because of You, I'm zooming in
Enjoying the gifts I often forget I have.
Because of You, I'm zooming in
Loving the people I think I forgot how to love.

But, it's not about zooming in.
It's about zooming out.
And finding You again.

Feeling connected to everything, all around the earth.
Seeing Your hand in everything, keeping the faith.

10 WEEKS INTO SHELTERING IN PLACE
Rabbi Sarah Freidson

God of Truth
What the hell, God?

Are You crying, too? Do You see Your beloved children dying? Do You see our fear? I'm scared
of the virus
of the hate and mistrust
of the tearing apart of my stability.
The ground shakes beneath my feet. I want to lead, God, but where?

I'm in the wilderness and so far from home -- the one we left and the one we will build.

Did Your heart break, too, when the precious seven-year-old asked if I wasn't feeling good because of the coronavirus? When she asked if I was going to die?
Mine did. A crack, razor thin.
I promised I wouldn't.
Don't make me a liar, God of Truth.

What remains
The walls have fallen down, and what remains is pure, so pure. Pretense gone, values remain. My clothes don't matter, my soul does.
A reminder -- each life, each soul, each breath is precious.
We are so beautifully vulnerable and brave, Your children. Things change; we adapt.

The sun still shines, and yesterday I saw a butterfly.
The earth is green again, and I strive to feed my neighbors.
A community without a building remains a community.

My relationships deepen -- thank you.
My exercise becomes more consistent -- thank you.
The four of us are becoming a family -- thank you.
We play every day -- thank you.
For a roof and nourishing food -- thank you.
For growing children -- thank you.
For my health -- thank you.
For their health -- thank you.

349

For technology to stay in touch -- thank you.
For wisdom and creativity -- thank you.
For resilience and flexibility -- thank you.
For eight glorious hours of sleep every. single. night -- thank you.
For laughter and books -- thank you.
For the growth that will come -- thank you.
For the privilege of serving You, O Holy One, thank You.

Forgive Me
Can You forgive me, God, Source of Everything, for all I took for granted?
The bus that whisked the girls off to school; the dinners out because we didn't feel like cooking.
Handshakes, hugs, and group singing.
Birthday parties and Bar Mitzvah celebrations, and the sorrow that rippled through the crowd assembled at a funeral.
The seemingly endless possibilities nestled in the library shelves.

Can You forgive me for not appreciating every
small, precious, mundane moment?
Of working alone in a dedicated office.
Of the rush of energy and joy in teaching;
those invisible exchanges of knowledge and self.
Of the small talk with shopkeepers,
and schmoozing at Kiddush.

So many miracles, I never saw, let alone expressed my gratitude for.
And now
Each breath is worthy of praise
Each connection pierces loneliness.

I am so grateful for this messy house and this shedding dog and this imperfect family and the gift of each and every blessed day.

PSALMS 22 & 49

as interpreted by Brielle Paige Rassler

Psalm 22

For the enduring strength of Morning's Promise
A song for my Beloved

My God, My God
For what purpose is this feeling of distance?
Why must Your Salvationing Power feel so far
When the words of my roaring need are so near?

My God
I call to You by day
And there is no answer to be found
I call to You by night
And Still, the Sound of Silence roars on

And You
You, my God, are Holy above all else
Enthroned by the praises of all GodWrestlers

You, God of our ancestors
We put our Full Faith in You
And You God us to safety

We cried to You
And You rescued us
We trusted You
And we were not ashamed

In my selfish and small-mindedness
I am but a worm
Shamed by my humanity
Humiliating myself out of communion with Oneness Consciousness

People see me and laugh
Unleashing hatred in action and word

Revealing the essence of HaVaYaH
Hope for Deliverance lives on

351

You save us, my God
Because You truly want to

For it is You who Breathed me to life
From the safety of my mother's womb
You who she trusted
To guide me to her breast

I was sent to You, my God
From her womb to Yours
You, Divine Mother of all

Please, my God
Don't go
I need You now more than ever
Please, be close
You are my only hope

I am surrounded by wild beasts
Besieged by armies of shame

Mouths open wide
Ready to pounce
And tear me limb from limb

I am dispersed
A containerless puddle with nothing to grasp hold of
My bones – disjointed and my heart –
She melts like hot wax
Burning from the inside out

My strength has dried up
My tongue unable to move
I am done, spent
Laid to rest by the dust of the dead

Engulfed completely
Heartless wolves
My hands and feet light the way
To armies of evil noise
Marching circles 'round my soul

Counting my bones
I have nothing left
Still, they look on
Preying on my pain

Until, at last, the shirt on my back is theirs too
I watch, naked
As the dice of destiny rolls

And You, my God
I know You are not far off
I know You will hurry to my help
It is only a matter of time

Save my soul from the sword
Come quick, while my heart still beats to Your Oneness

Save me by Your Divine Light
Answer me by Your Great Rays of Reason

Save me, my God
So I can share the Song of Your Salvationing
And sing the Story of Your Saving

We Hallel You Yah
All who are willing to be WOWed
We honor the One
We, the sprouting seeds of GodWrestling

Because, my God
You do not hate the seeker
You cannot detest the poor
You will not hide from any of Your children
You Hear, always, the call of our cry

My praise flows
From You and to You
I join the Kahal of Ravs
Fulfilling the Promise of Your Peace
Fulfilling the Promise of Your WOWing

Suffering ceases to be

353

We are satisfied by our song
All whose seeking brings them to Life
Our hearts beat into Forever

We remember – and we return
To the One
All beings and non-beings
Every thing and non-thing
One Creation
Praising
The One Creator

Because, my God
You are the Finder of the Path
The Writer of the Play
Arranging all according to the Cast List of the Divine

We bow before You
Nourished by our Praise
Enlivened by the Earth that sustains us
We outlive the forces that seek to sink our souls

Thank you God
The seed of Your serving sings the Story of Your Saving
Generation after generation

Coming to tell of Your Righteousness
To those born
Of Morning's Promise

Psalm 49

A song – to guide the children through their winter time

Listen! Everyone!
All peoples in all places
Your children – and mine
Rich – and poor
Come together – and hear what I have to say

I will speak the wisdom of my lips

And the insights of my heart

I will listen too
As the story plays out
The opening – already underway
The sweet melody of Life's Mystery: Act One
And... Action!

For what is my WOWing
In these days of "evil"
Tripping over trials
Surrounded by unpleasantries

I hear the boastful bellowings of the arrogant ones
Those who rely on their own power
On the greatness of their own abundance

But their money cannot buy Salvation – it cannot buy Freedom
God's currency cannot be measured in dollars and cents

There is no price for your preciousness
Your soul's redemption is relegated to the Mystery alone

One may think they can live forever
Outsmarting the sight of death's certificate

Even though they see death befalling the wise ones
Even though they see the fools falling too
Leaving behind everything that they once called "theirs"

From within their own homes
One may think they can see forever
Generation after generation
Dwelling in this place that bears their name

But this is not true
At the end of the day
We lie silent
No better or worse than any of God's creatures

This is the path of the foolish
Always trying to catch up

Always trying – always wanting

They follow blindly
Into the pit of unanswerable questions
Lower and lower
They descend to their destiny

The honest and upright
They awaken to the morning
While the arrogant continue to decay down below

Thank You God
Only You can save my soul from the pit of unanswerable questions
Only You can take me into Your Holy Holding

So, my friends
Do not be WOWed by the wealthy
The ones whose honor comes only from paper, plaster, and plastic
None of that matters at the end of the day
None of that "honor" can follow them to the grave

They may seem blessed in this life
But True blessing comes from improving your Self
Material possessions may last a generation
But is it worth it – at the expense of Eternity's Light?

Our True preciousness is beheld only by the One
This is the lesson we are here to learn

Oh wait – you still don't get it, do you?
I am so sorry, my friend
Maybe next time?
End Scene.

A SILENT PSALM
Elke Weiss

A song of Elke, in the middle of COVID-19 Quarantine and Depression, for that what speaks in silence.

The walls are my prison and my refuge. They keep me safe from the plague outside but trap me with the doubts and fears of my own mind. They are a sheltering place to me and all the terrible thoughts in my mind. Robbed of distractions, I lay down in bed and did not want to get up. I could no longer find the dawn worthy of notice.

When I walk through the valley of the shadows of self-hatred, the fear inside me was raw and evil. It told me I would never reach the other side, I would remain forever a prisoner of this inky black darkness that had taken over my mind.

So many friends all tried to be with me. Their words and their love comforted me, and their silence testified to their trust in me. Still I felt empty.

I refreshed my soul in nature. I walked silent and masked through empty gardens, carrying the mental weight that threatened to smash me. I walked through the shadows in my own mind, whispering.

Vibrant tulips dying mocked me. "I am not worthy of love. No one will bring me flowers."

Empty parks depressed me. "My friends don't trust me. No one cares about me."

Large buildings dwarfed me. "I'm a failure. I'll never achieve anything."

The East River's shine made my own life seem so drab. "I'll never be happy again."

So where would my salvation arrive?

It is then I remembered, that greatness isn't found in great and strong winds of financial success, or earthquakes of dramatic stories. Greatness was not found in the smoldering fires of torrid romances.

Greatness was found in the small still voice inside me, the one voice I had stopped listening to. I closed my eyes and let myself touch the spark of light inside me, that I had been so sure had been snuffed out in my isolation. To my joy, it was there.

When your heart breaks, you are more than a fallen tree, you are also as a seed that is finally ready to sprout

And the old tree will nourish the new tree that grows. The roots will nourish, the branches will spread.

The small, still voice that gave me the silence I needed to see the cruel, crazy, beautiful world around me for the first time.

It was then I could finally remember where my salvation would come. It would come from the strength I had inside me, the love and wisdom my friends had given me, and the hope that even if I couldn't see the dawn, it would be there. It would be in self-care and medical help and forgiving myself. It would be in me.

It was I alone who had to find the green pastures and find the power inside to comfort me. In the end, I was the only one who could release myself from this prison of my own mind. Somehow, I would do it.

So now, when the night seems endless, I have this psalm to remind me not to fall into despair. I can look up and find the faint and faraway constellations of love that only appear only in the dark, and marvel at their majesty. I will let them guide me when I am lost and adrift until I find the pathway that leads me out of the mental and physical walls that create my valley of shadows, and into the next part of my life.

What I will find on the other side, I do not know. But that small still voice inside me tells me, be strong and face it head-on.

DESPAIR PRAYER
Rabbi Menachem Creditor

Dear One,
It feels like too much
to name this place I'm in "the depths"
but it's also, all of it,
just too much.

I know, I know,
we're supposed to wake
in the morning
with gratitude,
like a lion.
But that's not how I feel,
not this morning.

So, Holy One,
how can I ask for help
with a heart that isn't quite inflated today?
How do I find the words
when my mind feels a bit less sharp?

I just need time for myself,
time for my work,
time with my children,
time with others,
hugging...

The cells of my body, the facets of my soul
need more alonetogether time.
We all do.

The leaves of the trees outside my window
are rustling in the wind.
A neighbor just walked by.
That is the whole world:
wind and people.

Sharing this with you,
my Creator, helps.
Thank You.
Amen.

VACCINATE US
Rabbi Jen Gubitz

As our world suffers,
sickened by this virus - we pray:

Inoculate our hearts with fortitude
       to dismantle systemic racism
Inject our souls with compassion to love
       and then to love harder
Mitigate our structures of power
       against abuse, exploitation and violence.
Protect our siblings, among us and beyond,
       beloved humans who lay bleeding in our streets

Strengthen those wearied by oppression,
       with renewed energy, tenacity, hope and rest.

Fortify our hearts to listen deeply and amplify the voices
       of Black people
       of Brown people
       of Indigenous people everywhere

Immunize us, O Source of Healing,
Immunize us against this viral historic hate,
Course through our veins courage and conviction
       to reckon with our implicit bias
       to apologize for our role in the pain
       to fight to end this oppression
Vaccinate us, vaccinate us, O Source of Healing
       with the sacred power of love.

PRAYER BEFORE TURNING ON THE NEWS
Hila Ratzabi

I sit before the TV screen
with remote control in hand.
I want it to stay this way.
This dark, quiet room
without a world in it.
This nothing, this sweet
nothing. The fire truck
toy on the shelf beneath the TV,
look how it saves
no one. In this room
there is nothing
burning. Dear God, it is
possible. You are the one
with wings. Shelter us.
Let something have been fixed today:
The deal among the nations signed,
the guns, all of them, taken away,
a woman believed,
a man contrite. A border
covered in dust. God,
I need to know what happened
to those who tried to cross.
What happened after the storm
and earthquake and fire.
I can't be everywhere at once,
but you can. How can I convince you
we are worthy of miracles?
How much longer can I delay
the inevitable knowing,
the daily ritual of witness?
At least bear it with me,
dear God. Come sit
on the couch, put your feet up,
I'm making tea. Tell me
how this will end.
Tell me if there is a chance.
Or maybe we can bargain for peace?
Trade for redemption?

Give me something,
anything, before I let
the messengers into my room.
I will not look away.
Promise me
you won't either.

(This poem was first published in Narrative Magazine
Spring 2020. narrativemagazine.com)

RETURNING FROM THE COVID-19 PANDEMIC
USING IMMERSION TO PREPARE FOR OUR NEW NORMAL
Rabbi Hannah Estrin

During COVID-19 many of us ceased marking time. One day looked much the same as the one before and the one that would come after. Time moved forward, but there came with it a numbness. We were unable to attend family events in person. Birthdays and holidays were celebrated via zoom. Funerals, memorials, *shiva* and *yahrzeits* were attended in person by only the immediate family. And that was on the communal level. Our personal plans were, at best, put on hold and, at worst, eliminated completely. While we may not have been touched directly by COVID-19, we have all been affected. Many of us grieve for those things changed and lost.

As we move forward, we will become more aware of the individuality of our days. Hopefully our numbness will begin to lift, and our wounds will begin to heal. The grief that we have felt will begin to let go and we will enter the long-term period of healing. We will begin to unpack the trauma that the virus and the shutdown of the world has caused.

COVID-19 continues to have a significant impact on our lives. But we are resilient, and we will recover even as we create a new normal. Historically, we have seen water as a creator of significant changes in the world and life. Creator of a new normal. From the story of creation, to the birth of a child and eventually the washing of a body following death, water surrounds us our entire lives. It is the powerful flash flood, the gentle lapping wave, the all-encompassing embrace of submersion. Water is in our life force and is a symbol of renewal for many people around the world. We can harness the power and beauty of water to intentionally create our path forward.

In Judaism, water is often associated with the *mikvah*, or ritual bath. The *mikvah* can be any source of water which is considered to be 'living water.' Water naturally obtained - via rain, river, lakes and oceans. Water which can support life. Although the use of the *mikvah* has changed overtime its purpose has not. It has always marked time and prepared us to enter moments of sacredness. The *mikvah* precedes the sacred entrance to marriage, conception, Judaism and holidays. Today, the *mikvah* is also used to mark the distinction between, or separation from, difficulties of the past and the move toward healing.

As one who believes that water and the use of *mikvah* are powerful and embracing forces in life, I offer this *mikvah* ceremony for those who are ready to mark their transition toward a post COVID-19 new normal. A marking of the end, a marking of the beginning of the end. Through it I honor the emotional, physical and financial tumult we have experienced. I honor our personal struggles and strengths and the many people who supported us during this time. Finally, I offer this ceremony as an acknowledgement that we are entering a new phase that will hold both joy and hope as well as sadness. We have been forever changed, individually and communally. But we are strong and resilient. A visit to the *mikvah* or local 'living source' of water can be a powerful step in that process.

Post COVID-19 Mikvah Ceremony

On your way to the Mikva

Take some time to identify and name some of the most difficult parts of the COVID-19 time period and the necessary physical and social isolation that accompanied it. How did you react? What did you learn? What are the good things you discovered that you hope to maintain?

It may also be helpful to name those things which are in the future. How will you rejoin the community in person? Will it be hard to touch and be touched?

At the Mikvah

לַכֹּל זְמָן וְעֵת לְכָל־חֵפֶץ תַּחַת הַשָּׁמָיִם:
A season is set for everything, a time for every experience under heaven:
- Kohelet

Everything has a time -
A time for staying home and a time for physical distancing.
A time for masks and gloves and protections.
A time for buildings, parks and beaches to be closed.
There is a time for life to happen on-line. And a time to remain apart.

This does not mean that we have returned to life as it was. We cannot. The world has changed, and we have changed with it. Immersing in the

365

waters of life is a way to mark the sacredness of time. A way to move forward. A step toward rejoining the physical community.

I want to name and honor my reactions during this difficult time.

To know that my reactions, though different from those around me, were OK.

To recognize that my trauma and grief are real and honest. That each of us is different.

To honor the challenges I have experienced and those I may continue to have.

By honoring all that has been, I choose to let go and move forward. To acknowledge anew my trust in God, and God's control. With that, I pray to be open to my return to life as it will be and all the opportunities it will present.

If there are others who are joining you for your immersion:

There have been times when each of you has been a blessing to me during this time of difficulty. For your place in my life, for your loving kindness and support, I thank you and offer you my love.

Entering the Mikvah/Beach/

Recite at the mikveh steps:
As I step toward these waters of healing and preparation, I recognize the period where my life was turned upside down by outside forces. Where some days were easier than others but through it all I underwent a transition from who I was to who I will become. As I prepare to step into the healing waters of the mikvah I choose also to let go. I allow it to envelope me in a way that only the waters of God can envelope. To cradle and hold me as I prepare to step back into life. I remind myself that though people have been physically distant, I am always loved, held, and protected. That I am strong and I will be OK.

Enter the Mikvah

Enter the mikvah and immerse yourself completely. Allow the waters to surround you, to penetrate your skin, your heart and your soul. You have made the decision to step into the sacred space of life-giving water. Feel the water on each part of your body and be open to any thoughts and feelings that might surface. Step into the love and acceptance that only you can give yourself. Take your time.

When you are ready, surface and recite out loud or internally:

בָּרוּךְ אַתָּה אֲדֹנָי אֱלֹהֵינוּ מֶלֶךְ הָעוֹלָם אֲשֶׁר קִדְּשָׁנוּ בְּמִצְוֹתָיו וְצִוָּנוּ עַל הַטְבְלָה
Barukh atah Adonay Eloheynu melekh ha-olam, asher kidshanu b'mitzvotav v'tzivanu al ha-t'vilah.
Blessed are you, Eternal God, ruler of the universe, who sanctifies us through *mitzvot* and has enjoined us concerning immersion.

Once again immerse yourself completely in the waters, take your time. When you are ready, surface and recite out loud or internally:

בָּרוּךְ אַתָּה אֲדֹנָי אֱלֹהֵינוּ מֶלֶךְ הָעוֹלָם, שֶׁהֶחֱיָנוּ וְקִיְּמָנוּ וְהִגִּיעָנוּ לַזְּמָן הַזֶּה
Barukh atah Adonay, Eloheynu melekh ha-olam, shehekheyanu, v'kiy'manu, v'higianu, la-z'man ha-zeh.
Blessed is the Eternal, the God of all creation, who has blessed me with life, sustained me, and enabled me to reach this moment.

Immerse yourself a third and final time, take your time. When you are ready, surface. Take a moment to be with yourself, to meditate or to recite/read something that is meaningful to you.

As you exit the mikvah:

Adonai, my God who heals the brokenhearted and restores the body, I stand here before you. My heart has been broken and my pain is profound. I look to you for healing and strength as I return to the world we build it together. I know not what tomorrow will bring, but place my trust and my life in your hands. Together. You and I together with community and the world. May my days be filled with preserving the past and creating the future filled with your guidance, love, tolerance, peace and humility. Amen.

(A version of this ritual appeared on both RitualWell and RabbinicalAssembly.org.)

A MUSSAR PRACTICE IN THE PANDEMIC
Sara Kupor

Grateful

Open all my senses
To the one hundred blessings
Coursing through me
With each breath.

Purposeful and not so purposeful busyness drops away.

Multiple distractions of 21st-century American life dissipate.

My life has slowed down. I am emotionally able to embrace the *abundance* with which I am blessed and which I receive daily, hourly, moment by moment.

I now allow myself to do what is natural; i.e., what is in my nature, which is to focus on what is most essential… *being fully present.*

Recognition of the preciousness of everything in that essential category arises.

Certainty of being deeply connected to each person, plant, and rock in our orbit arises.

Deep *compassion* for each person, plant, and rock arises.

This is the truth that washes over me when only what I deem essential has been uppermost in my life for the twenty-four or forty-eight hours.

I am noticing that these feelings are identical to those that bubble up near the end of Shabbat or on day two of a really good camping trip.

My senses are heightened.

Life has been *simplified.* I am living both intentionally and intensely.
And I am freed to be able to respond genuinely to those in my immediate orbit.

368

Living in the context of the virus has a comparable effect to living with profound loss and grief. In the early months after the death of my husband almost five years ago, I felt that my heart was "broken open." This openness promoted honest and full encounters with everyone I met. The vulnerability we are all now experiencing is similar in that it creates a fertile ground for this same intimacy.

I am more able to *generously* respond to the invitation for personal sharing.

Tikkun

Fix my middot.
Balance me,
So I can mitzvah connect
To You, Adam, and Adamah.

מי שבירך
ג'וש ארונסון

מי שבירך אבותינו ואמותינו הוא יברך אותנו בזמנים קשים ולא נוחים אלו,
בזכות נחשון בן עמינדב שנכנס לים סוף באי נוחות, והמים עד מותניו, עד
שנפתח הים והוציא הקב'ה את עמו מאפלה.
מי שהוציאנו מאפלה, הוא ברחמיו ישוב ויוציא אותנו יחד מאפלה.
מי ייתן ובזכות משה ובני ישראל, מרים ובנות ישראל, נשיר את השירה הזאת
לה' כי גמל עלי.
ובזכות אהרון הכהן יבוא שלום על כל יושבי תבל.
שירפאו במהרה כל חולי תבל וביחד נצא לחירות בשלווה ובשוויון.
במהרה ונאמר אמן

A BLESSING FOR THESE TIMES
Josh Aronson

May the God who blessed our fathers and mothers bless us in these
difficult, uncomfortable times.

In the merit of Nachshon son of Aminadav who entered the Sea in
discomfort, with the waters rising up to his waist, until the sea split and
God brought the nation out of darkness.

May the One who brought us out from Darkness in Mercy
return and take us out together from darkness.

May God, in the merits of Moses and the sons of Israelites,
Miriam and the daughters of Israelites,
sing together the song
"for God was good in God's kindness "

And in the merit of Aaron the priest
may God bring peace on all earth,
so all earth will be cured fast
and together we go out in freedom,
tranquility and equality very soon.

Let us say:
Amen

PRAYER FOR HEALERS
Rabbi Ayelet S. Cohen

May the One who blessed our ancestors
Bless all those who put themselves at risk to care for the sick
Physicians and nurses and orderlies
Technicians and home health aides
EMTs and pharmacists
Hospital social workers and respiratory therapists

(Please include other frontline healthcare workers.
And bless especially _____)

Who navigate the unfolding dangers of the world each day,
To tend to those they have sworn to help.
Bless them in their coming home and bless them in their going out.
Ease their fear. Sustain them.
Source of all breath, healer of all beings,
Protect them and restore their hope.
Strengthen them, that they may bring strength;
Keep them in health, that they may bring healing.
Help them know again a time when they can breathe without fear.
Bless the sacred work of their hands.
May this plague pass from among us, speedily and in our days.

WITH AWE, TRUST, AND GRATITUDE: A PRAYER FOR HEALTHCARE WORKERS ON THE FRONT LINES OF COVID-19

Rabbi Seth Haaz

While most of us close ourselves off in quarantine through these troubling times, you open yourselves to those who are suffering. You may prefer to be at home, safe with your families, but you have answered the call to save our lives – at significant risk to your own.

While the rest of us conduct business through Zoom, Google Hangouts, Facebook Live, or GoToMeeting, no technology can replace intimate, face-to-face medical care. And, it is precisely the face-to-face aspect of your care that puts you at risk. We speak of you as doctors, nurses, respiratory therapists, EMTs, and healthcare workers, but we must also recognize that you are sons and daughters, brothers and sisters, husbands and wives, beloved partners, parents, and grandparents. You have people at home who love you and depend on you. But we depend on you as well, and, in this unprecedented, tragic time, you have chosen us over your own peace, comfort, and health.

We will owe you our lives and the lives of our loved ones. Yet, we know that with abundant need and scarce resources you will have to make devastating choices that will break your heart and crush your soul. We will support you in those decisions and forgive your shortcomings. Many lives you will not save, but many more you will. We have gratitude for your compassion, and we place our trust in the moral compass that guides your hearts and the skill that guides your hands.

May the One who blessed our ancestors, Abraham, Isaac, Jacob, Sarah, Rebecca, Rachel, and Leah, bless you for honoring God and caring for God's Creation. May God protect and save you from COVID-19 and send blessing and success to the work of your hands along with all others who are doing their part to ease suffering and save lives. May God bless you every time you rise up from your bed, walk out of your home, and go to work, and may you return to your loved ones each and every day in full health. Amen.

PRAYER FOR NURSES
Rabbi Deborah Waxman

God, Source of Life,
we discern your presence
through our actions here on earth.

We know you as Healer
through the care and attention
of the healers we encounter.

Compassionate One, be near to nurses
in this time of pandemic as they put their lives at risk.

Rock and Protector, help them be safe in their holy work.
Guide us and our elected leaders
to provide the resources they need.

Creator and Sustainer, strengthen nurses so that they may persist in the
face of fatigue. Help them find courage to persevere through fear and
despair. Shine light for them at dark moments.

Refuge and Comforter, protect their families and let them return home
and receive tender care themselves.

God of Renewal, accompany nurses and us through this time of
challenge. Grant us a fraction of their courage and tenacity so that we
may emerge from this crisis to create a world that is safe and just and
equitable.

(This prayer first appeared on Ritualwell.org.)

A 20 SECOND PRAYER WHILE WASHING YOUR HANDS
Rabbi Joseph B. Meszler

As I take up my hands
to wash them and
reassure my heart,
I pray for healing and wholeness
for the whole world.
I remember that every life
is unique and of infinite value:
from those living
on the most remote part of the globe
to those in our cities
to our neighbors and family members.
Let me use my hands for good
to help bring love
and compassion to others.
"Let us lift up
our hearts and hands
to the Eternal." (Lam 3:41)

A PRIESTESS'S PRAYER UNDER QUARANTINE
Rachel Kann

Let me be not deceived,
let me remember this
moment holds sweetness
enfolded in its deep grievousness.

Let me be a vessel for
the healing this planet
so deeply needs.

Use me
as a source of soothing
for everyone suffering
under every destructive
regime's undoing.

Use me
as a sukkat shalom,
as shelter from
the tumbling detritus
of crumbling empires,

as comfort
for those terrified
of this
natural catastrophe.

Let me awaken
the sleepers

and weave lullabies
for the sleepless.

Let me tend with
utmost tenderness.

Help me find the calm inside
so that I may grant it
expansiveness.

From within this cocoon,
use me to reveal
the mercy of retreat.

Use me as a tool
to teach
of Mother Gaia's
tremendous gentleness,

of her unfathomably vast patience
with this human race —

what unimaginable grace
she shows us.

What merciful tolerance
she bestows upon us:

to serve us
three-day-pay-or-quit papers,
rather than a
well-deserved
immediate eviction notice.

Remind me that I was born
for this moment.

Let this be the turning point,
we so desperately need,

let me be
empathy,

let me mourn
each soul's last gasp
of breath,

let me be compassion,
let me
radiate graciousness,

please,
hear this simple petition,
please
use me to priestess
the emerging world
Into existence.

A PRAYER IN THE TIME OF CORONAVIRUS
Rabbi Denise L. Eger

Holy Blessed Breath of Life, be our help in this time of Coronavirus. Ease our fear. Holy One, ease our pain. Ease our anxieties. Ease our sense of dread. Help us face the unknown with patience and hope.

We pray for the doctors and nurses, respiratory therapists and caretakers who are your agents of healing and comfort. Inspire the scientists and researchers to find a cure and treatments.

We pray for family, friends and neighbors; for community, for country and all who inhabit the Earth, your children.

Be our help in this time of uncertainty Holy One. Ground us in our faith. Ground us in the circle of Your love. Ground us in the wisdom of science - your gift to humanity.

Ground us in the knowledge that these days of isolation will pass and we will once again be in each other's physical presence, once again embrace each other, kiss each other, love each other with our full bodies.

Be our help Eternal Holy One. Draw close to us and help us to draw nearer to You even as we must distance ourselves from one another to preserve life and well-being.

.ברוך אתה יי אלהינו מלך העולם אשר קרבנו לעבודתו
Baruch Atah Adonai Eloheinu Melech HaOlam Asher Kervanu L'avodato.

Praised are You who draws us near to Your service.

THE JOY OF REUNION: SHECHECHIYANU
Nechama Liss-Levinson, Ph.D.

It has been a while since I have seen my children or grandchildren. Longer than I would like. It has also been a long time since I have seen some of my dear friends in person. Weeks, or when I actually count the days, I notice it is months. I miss them all.

I dream about seeing them again, even though we won't be able to physically embrace. The time of quarantine and even sheltering at home is finally beginning to shift. Small numbers of people will soon be able to get together in outdoor venues with appropriate social distancing.
I desire a ritual, and fortunately, Judaism has one all ready for me, just waiting to be dusted off.

The Talmud (Brachot 58b) states that one should recite the blessing of "Shehechiyanu" upon meeting a dear friend or relative who one hasn't seen for at least a month. This friend should be someone you are especially close to, who brings you great happiness, someone who makes your heart sing.

Each of us knows in our soul who these people are.

And although this custom hasn't been widely followed in recent years, the Age of Covid calls out for celebrating the Joy of Reunion. When we are finally able to see those we love, we can acknowledge the joy of this reunion. We can each say to one another, either separately or in unison:

> *Baruch Ata Adonai, Elohaynu Melech HaOlam,*
> *Shehechiyanu, V'Keyamanu,*
> *V'Higiyanu L'Zman HaZeh.*

> *Blessed are You, God, Source of All Being,*
> *who has kept us alive, sustained us*
> *and brought us to this very moment.*

The Talmud goes on to state that the blessing "Mechayeh HaMayteem" (who revives the dead) should be recited when you meet someone you love whom you haven't seen for twelve months. Some say this is only if you haven't been in contact for the year and you don't know if they are still alive. However, during this time of Covid, it would seem appropriate to say the blessing of MeChayeh HaMayteem when first seeing someone

379

you love who has recovered from the corona virus. Someone who has been snatched back away from the Angel of Death.

Baruch Ata Adonai, Elohaynu Melech HaOlam, Mechayeh HaMayteem.

Blessed are You, God, Source of All Being, who revives the dead.

The Joy of Reunion can also include a one sentence acknowledgement of the special happiness that this other person brings to you. "Your kindness and your smile light up my life."

And then, let the joy fully enter your body and your soul.

A PRAYER WHILE STANDING ON AN AMERICAN FOOD LINE
Rabbi Menachem Creditor

Source of Sustenance,
help us remember
this line is not like other lines.

Yes, the shock of lining up for food
today, here, now,
is real. And...

there is food
at the end of this line,
enough food for all.

HaZan et haKol, Nourisher of All,
may the fear we feel,
the anxiety reality provokes,
have its moment. And...

May we be patient with those ahead
and behind us in line.

May we treat with respect
those who tend to us
who pick and package
and restock and bag the food
we need. And...

May we be grateful
we'll have enough.

May we do what we can
to ensure others will also have enough.

May we remember
this is only a line.

Amen.

Contributors

Rabbi Alan Abrams is a spiritual care educator who lives in Jerusalem with his wife Rabbi Minna Bromberg and their two children, Bernice and Matar Nissim. He is the founder and director of HavLi and the HaKen Institute, spiritual care education and research centers based in Jerusalem. Alan received a PhD in May 2019 from NYU for his dissertation on the theology of pastoral care.

Sally Abrams is a wife, mother, Nanny to a rapidly growing number of grandchildren, Jewish communal professional, writer, speaker, and advocate for Israel and Jewish life. Cooking for loved ones brings her happiness.

Miriam Aronin is a writer and editor living in Chicago with her husband and daughter. She is the author of "Molly's Monday," a children's story that appeared in Honeycake Magazine, and various nonfiction and educational works for children and teachers.

Josh Aronson. I'm 33 years old, on the Autism spectrum, an immigrant from Manchester England, a journalist for Maariv newspaper, and for Shavim. I'm also the disabilities coordinator for the Israeli Reform Movement (I grew up in an ultra orthodox family of 14 siblings). I also work in the communications department of Keren hayesod- UIA. I freelanced in the past in Shiver production's on a cooperation between BBC and ITV. Besides finding time to volunteer in management of Meretz Jerusalem and as such an activist in the party. An Israeli success story and proving that people with disabilities can conquer the world.

Rabbi Dr. Bradley Shavit Artson (www.bradartson.com) holds the Abner and Roslyn Goldstine Dean's Chair, Ziegler School of Rabbinic Studies, is Vice President of American Jewish University, and dean of the Zacharias Frankel College in Potsdam, Germany, ordaining Conservative rabbis for Europe.

Rabbi Elyssa Joy Austerklein (www.elyssjoyauster.com) is rabbi of Beth El Congregation, Akron, Ohio. Rabbi Austerklein is a trained mikveh guide, has led Hallel with Women of the Wall in Jerusalem, and was a "rabbi on the road" for the Institute of Southern Jewish Life. Rabbi Elyssa is a Rabbis Without Borders Fellow and was named one of America's 33 most inspiring rabbis of 2015 by The Forward. She is an artist, tallit maker, certified yoga teacher and devoted wife to Hazzan Matt and loving mother to Georgie.

As part of Metro Chicago Hillel, Rav **Ezra Balser** and his wife Laura run Base Loop out of their home in the West Loop neighborhood of Chicago. He was ordained at the Hebrew College Rabbinical School.

Rabbi Meir Bargeron was ordained in 2020 from Hebrew Union College-Jewish Institute of Religion in Los Angeles. He entered the rabbinate following a career in clinical social work and non-profit administration, and serves as the rabbi of Congregation Achduth Vesholom in Fort Wayne, Indiana.

Shira Pasternak Be'eri is a Jerusalem-based editor and translator. She is married to Leonard (aka Eliezer) and is the proud mom of three boys, two of whom are soldiers in the IDF. Born and raised in New York, she has been living in Israel since 1982. And yes, she is Velvel Pasternak's daughter.

Rivka Begun is a writer and photographer based in Zurich, Switzerland. She has been published in Format Papier, Naturally Curly and Slippage Lit. Rivka is currently quarantining with her suegros in Mexico City while working on her Jewish magical realism novel. You can find her on twitter at @BegunRiv or through her website at rikareviva.com.

Rabbi Marci N. Bellows is rabbi of Congregation Beth Shalom Rodfe Zedek in Chester, Connecticut.

Rabbi Todd Berman is the Associate Director at Yeshivat Eretz HaTzvi. In addition, he has held numerous posts in education from the high school level through adult education. He founded the Jewish Learning Initiative (JLI) at Brandeis University and served as rabbinic advisory to the Orthodox community there for several years. Previously, he was a RaM at Midreshet Lindenbaum where he also served as the Rav of the dormitory.

Yossie Bloch is an American-born rabbi who has taught at Yeshivat Har Etzion and Yeshivat HaKotel, and led a congregation in Canada. He lives in Israel with his family, and works as an editor and translator. He has written a series of children's books about famous sites and historical figures in the Holy Land.

Rabbi Robyn Fryer Bodzin, MSW is part of the Spiritual Leadership Team at Beth Tzedec Congregation in Toronto, where she leads the Centre for Spiritual Well-Being. She spent more than 20 years living in the United States, working for the Jewish community in a plethora of leadership positions.

Rabbi Daniel Bouskila is the director of the Sephardic Educational Center and the rabbi of the Westwood Village Synagogue.

Cantor Vera Broekhuysen is the spiritual leader of Temple Emanu-El of Haverhill, MA, where she has served as Cantor since June of 2016. She was ordained by Hebrew College in June of 2016, when she also earned her Masters Degree in Jewish Education.

Lela Casey is the daughter of an Israeli Sabra and an American cowboy. She grew up deep in the woods of Pennsylvania in a home full of international travelers and vagabonds. This unusual childhood enriched her with a lifetime of stories that she shares on the sites she edits and writes for: Hevria and The Wisdom Daily.

Rachel Chabin is an aspiring Jewish communal leader based in Washington Heights, New York. She graduated with a degree in Spanish Literature from Stony Brook University in 2019, and recently completed a year fellowship at Yeshivat Hadar. Rachel currently works as a transcriptionist and live captioner for several Jewish educational organizations across the United States.

385

Rabbi Ayelet S. Cohen is Senior Director of the New Israel Fund's New York/Tri-State Region. Previously, she was Director of The Center for Jewish Living and The David H. Sonabend Center for Israel at The Jewish Community Center in Manhattan. She served for 10 years at Congregation Beit Simchat Torah, the world's largest LGBT synagogue serving people of all sexual orientations and gender identities. Passionately committed to progressive and feminist Judaism, she is an activist and an advocate for full inclusion and celebration of LGBT Jews in the Jewish world, and an advocate for LGBT civil rights. Rabbi Cohen has been profiled in the New York Times, was named one of the "Heeb 100," Heeb Magazine's "hundred people you need to know about," and was honored at the 2005 Ma'yan Seder as a leading young Jewish feminist activist. She is a member of the Rabbinical Assembly and the New York Board of Rabbis.

Rabbi Tamara Cohen is Vice President, Chief of Program Strategy, of Moving Traditions and oversees the development of new programmatic initiatives including the Rosh Hodesh Reboot and Moving Traditions' online program for trans, non-binary, and gender questioning Jewish teens, in addition to being a lead trainer and coordinator for Moving Traditions' National Training Conferences. Prior to Moving Traditions, Tamara worked as a spiritual leader and as an educator in Jewish community and higher education settings, with a focus on Jewish feminist, LGBT, and multicultural issues. A published writer and liturgist, Tamara holds a rabbinical degree from the Reconstructionist Rabbinical College, an M.A. in Women's History from Sarah Lawrence College, and a BA summa cum laude from Barnard College. Tamara lives in Philadelphia with her partner and two children.

Rabbi Elliot Cosgrove is the rabbi of the Park Avenue Synagogue in Manhattan.

Ariel Creditor is graduating from The Leffell School this year.

Rabbi Menachem Creditor serves as the Pearl and Ira Meyer Scholar in Residence at UJA-Federation New York and was the founder of Rabbis Against Gun Violence. A frequent speaker in communities and campuses around the United States and Israel with over 1 million views of his online videos and essays, he was named by Newsweek as one of the fifty most influential rabbis in America. His 21 books and 6 albums of original music include the global Jewish anthem "Olam Chesed Yibaneh" and the anthology "None Shall Make Them Afraid." He has been involved in the leadership of American Jewish World Service, AIPAC, the Rabbinical Assembly, and the One America Movement, an organization dedicated to bringing together Americans of different faiths and opinions. He and his wife Neshama Carlebach live in New York, where they are raising their five children.

Rachel Sharansky Danziger is a Jerusalem-born writer and speaker who's in love with her city's vibrant human scene. She writes about Judaism, parenting and life in Israel for the Times of Israel and Kveller, and explores storytelling in the bible as a teacher and on 929.

Rabbi Paula Mack Drill is one of three rabbis of the Orangetown Jewish Center, Orangeburg, New York. A social worker who returned to Jewish Theological Seminary after twelve years in the field, she was ordained in May 2004. Paula's passions are making Torah accessible for all, creating inclusive communities, and advocacy on behalf of vulnerable people.

Ruth Ebenstein is an award-winning American-Israeli writer, historian, public speaker and peace/health activist who loves to laugh a lot and heartily. She is the author of the forthcoming memoir, Bosom Buddies: How Breast Cancer Fostered an Unexpected Friendship Across the Israeli-Palestinian Divide. Ruth has also penned a children's book entitled All of this Country is Called Jerusalem. Find her online at RuthEbenstein.com, on Facebook at Laugh Through Breast Cancer – Ruth Ebenstein, and on twitter @ruthebenstein.

Rabbi Denise L Eger is the founding Rabbi of Congregation Kol Ami in West Hollywood CA. She is the editor of Mishkan Ga'avah: Where Pride Dwells a Celebration of LGBTQ Life and a Ritual (Ccarpress,2020).

Dr. Arnold M. Eisen was the seventh chancellor of The Jewish Theological Seminary. Before coming to JTS, he served on the faculties of Stanford, Tel Aviv, and Columbia universities. Dr. Eisen sits on the advisory boards of the Tanenbaum Center, the Covenant Foundation, and the Taube Foundation for Jewish Life and Culture.

Jake Epstein is an intern at The Times of Israel. A native of the Greater Boston Area, he recently graduated from Lehigh University with a BA in journalism and international relations.

Estelle Erasmus is an award-winning journalist, essayist and writing coach. She writes for The New York Times, The Week, Parents Magazine and more about parenting, health, psychology and publishing. She is also a adjunct instructor at New York University, an editor at Narratively and hosts the podcast ASJA Direct: Inside Intel on Getting Published and Paid Well.

Karen Lee Erlichman, D.Min, LCSW provides psychotherapy, spiritual direction, So(U)L coaching and mentoring in San Francisco, employing a mind-body-spirit approach to healing. She is also a longtime community faculty member at University of California-San Francisco in the Department of OB/GYN and Reproductive Sciences. Karen has been in practice for over thirty years and currently serves as senior consultant for Ethics of Care and Resource Development with The Dinner Party, whose mission is to build community for young adults in their 20s and 30s who have experienced the loss of a loved one. Her writing has been published widely in numerous journals, blogs and anthologies, including Presence: An International Journal of Spiritual Direction, Tikkun, Feminist Studies in Religion and in the interfaith anthology Spiritual Guidance Across Religions.

Rabbi Hannah Estrin (rabbihannahestrin.com) is a licensed Israel Tour Guide, combines a background in Judaic and Rabbinic Studies, informal education pedagogy and a love of Israel to share the amazing land and history of Israel with visitors from around the world both in Israel and abroad.

Lisa Farber is the mother of two teenagers and works in Jewish Education in Melbourne. She is passionate about community, Jewish continuity and the power of words to transform the way we think.

Ittay Flescher is an Educator and Journalist in Jerusalem. In his many years as a high school teacher, he realized that the questions we ask are often more important than the answers we give in creating a world that is more just and equal for all. Twitter: @ittay78

Mark S. Freedman is the former CEO of the Jewish Federation of Nashville and Middle Tennessee (2011-2018) and the Jewish Federation of San Antonio (1995-2008.) He is currently an Independent Consultant residing in Parkland, Florida.

Rabbi Sarah Freidson is the rabbi of Temple Beth Shalom in Mahopac, NY.

When **Joyce Miriam Friedman** isn't isolating at home during COVID-19, she is an avid pianist, singer and fiddle player. She has been a hospital clown for twenty years with the Hearts and Noses Hospital Clown Troupe in the Boston area. Joyce has written and performed several one-woman shows that have both universal and personal themes. In addition, she has written several children's picture books. You can find her at joycefriedman.com. During this pandemic, Joyce has taken on the practice of writing one poem a day reflecting this unusual and challenging time. She lives in Newton MA with her husband of forty years and her grown daughters and grandsons nearby.

Sari Friedman's writing has been nominated for Pushcarts and appears in Beloit Fiction Journal, Woven Tale Press, So It Goes, Blue Lake Review, Satirist, Daily Freier, Ilanot Review, Manhattan Poetry Review, San Francisco Chronicle, Times of Israel, Huffpost Canada and in several anthologies and other publications. She has received an "Exceptional Talent" grant from the Israeli Ministry of Culture, and is currently finishing my first novel which is about a woman who remembers her past-life 4,000 years ago in the Land of Canaan.

Rabbi Shoshana Meira Friedman serves as the Director of Professional Development at Hebrew College in Newton, MA, where she mentors clergy students and teaches about leadership, Torah, and social change. Her blog Beloved on the Earth: Honest Reflections from a Beautiful and Unsafe World is available at rabbishoshana.com. She lives with her son, Abraham, and husband Yotam in Roslindale, MA.

Abrielle Fuerst is CEO of Wandering Fighter. She holds a third-degree black belt in Taekwondo with belts in kung fu, kuk sool won, and hapkido, and experience in krav maga, judo, karate and Brazilian jiu jitsu. She began teaching at sixteen, running martial arts courses for kids and self-defense seminars for corporations nationwide.

Rabbi Aaron Gaber is the spiritual leader of Congregation Brothers of Israel in Newtown, PA.

Rabbi Lisa B. Gelber serves as spiritual leader of Congregation Habonim Community in New York City. Co-editor of A Journey Towards Freedom: a Haggadah for survivors of domestic violence, Rabbi Gelber has lectured nationwide about domestic violence in the Jewish Community, and served on the Board of FaithTrust Institute (formerly Center for the Prevention of Sexual and Domestic Violence). A long distance runner, long time fundraiser for the Leukemia and Lymphoma Society through their Team in Training program, and trained spiritual director with certification from the Yedidya Center, Rabbi Gelber uses running as spiritual practice and believes in the power of contemplative practice to strengthen community and family relationships. Parent to an elementary school aged daughter, Rabbi Gelber's journey to parenthood is featured in the Emmy nominated documentary ALL OF THE ABOVE: Single, Clergy, Mother.

Akiva Gersh is the editor of the book "Becoming Israeli" (www.becomingisraeli.com), a compilation of blogs and essays that speak of the inspiring and the sometimes wacky and crazy experience of making aliyah. Akiva himself made aliyah in 2004 with his wife Tamar and they live in Pardes Hanna with their four kids. He teaches Jewish history at the Alexander Muss High School in Israel in Hod HaSharon. He is also a musician and in 2010 formed Holy Land Spirit, an uplifting and spiritual musical experience for Christian groups visiting Israel.

Joey Glick is a rabbinical student at Hebrew College, originally from Pittsburgh, PA.

Aayisha Ruby Gold is an onscreen and award-winning stage actor specializing in the modern classics, as well as a theatrical director and teacher. She studied drama and film at Columbia College Chicago (BA '13) and is an alumna of Piven Theatre Workshop. Aayisha is a proud Jewish woman of color who continues to explore her complex family roots: one rooted in traditional Judaism and the other in Black liberation. She is also an advocate for women at the Cook County Jail and teaches theater therapy to child survivors of traumatic experiences. She met her beshert, Jacob Gold, in 2015. They married in 2019, the same year she became a proud mother of her beautiful son, Asher.

At time of writing, **Jacob Gold** teaches 9-12th grade STEM subjects for Chicago Public Schools while on hiatus from anthropology doctoral research in mainland Southeast Asia; he was also a news reporter and translator in that region from 2007-2012. He holds a BA in Anthropology from Princeton University ('06) as well as MA's from the University of Michigan ('12) and the University of Illinois-Chicago ('15). Also a Chicago native, Jacob has maintained a lifelong interest in Torah learning, as well as the diverse strands of Jewish histories and cultures through the lenses of oral tradition, text, and material archaeology. He met Aayisha in 2015. They married and became parents in 2019.

Rabbi Shefa Gold is a leader in ALEPH: the Alliance for Jewish Renewal and received her ordination both from the Reconstructionist Rabbinical College and from Rabbi Zalman Schachter-Shalomi (z"l). She is the director of C-DEEP, The Center for Devotional, Energy and Ecstatic Practice in Jemez Springs, New Mexico. She teaches workshops and retreats on the theory and art of Chanting, Devotional Healing, Spiritual Community-Building and Meditation. Rabbi Shefa composes and performs spiritual music, has produced ten albums, and her liturgies have been published in several new prayerbooks. She is the author of Torah Journeys: The Inner Path to the Promised Land and In the Fever of Love: An Illumination of The Song of Songs, both published by Ben Yehuda Press. Her latest book, published by Jewish Lights, is The Magic of Hebrew Chant: Healing the Spirit, Transforming the Mind, Deepening Love.

Anne Gordon is the deputy editor of Ops & Blogs at The Times of Israel. She is the co-host of the daily podcast, Talking Talmud, and a co-founder of Chochmat Nashim. A native of Boston, Anne is also a veteran educator, having taught Judaic Studies in the US and Israel for nearly 30 years.

Rabbi Jeremy Gordon (rabbionanarrowbridge.blogspot.com) is the rabbi of New London Synagogue and the author of Spiritual Vagabondry.

Laurie Gould is a writer who lives in the San Francisco Bay Area. She loves writing, and feels joy when others find her writing to be moving or meaningful to their lives. Laurie was inspired to write this piece in part by seeing scenes of people around the world singing alone, and together from their balconies, during this pandemic.

A student at Hebrew College Rabbinical School, **Genevieve Greinetz** holds an M.A. from Graduate Theological Union in Berkeley, CA. She is a certified yoga teacher and worked as an organic farmer, studied Chinese tea, is a published poet and founding editor of an up-and-coming inter-cultural journal.

Rabbi Jen Gubitz is a rabbi at Temple Israel of Boston and directs the Riverway Project, which connects 20s and 30s to Judaism and each other. A COVID pivot which required her to postpone her own wedding, Jen has teamed up with Rabbi Karen Perolman to host "With This Mask, I Thee Wed: Jewish Spiritual Tools for Wedding Postponement" to support couples in the same situation. Jen was ordained from Hebrew Union College-Jewish Institute of Religion and is a graduate of Indiana University's Borns Jewish Studies program.

Shira Gura is on a mission to create an emotionally healthy world. She is the creator of The unSTUCK Method, the author of the book Getting unSTUCK: Five Simple Steps to Emotional Well-Being (winner of the 2017 International Book Award in self-help), and host of the Getting Unstuck podcast.

Rabbi Nicole Guzik has served as a rabbi at Sinai Temple in Los Angeles for ten years, and four years prior as Sinai Temple's rabbinic intern. She is married to Rabbi Erez Sherman. Together they are the proud parents of daughter Annie and sons Zachary and Henry.

Rabbi Seth Haaz is the senior rabbi of Har Zion Temple in Penn Valley, PA.

Joel Haber (aka Fun Joel) lives in Jerusalem and works as a licensed tour guide. He also performs stand-up, and is working on a book about Jewish Food as a window onto Jewish Cultural History. He can be found at www.fjisrael.com and www.tasteofjew.com

Dr. Elana Stein Hain is scholar-in-residence and director of faculty at the Shalom Hartman Institute of North America, where she serves as a lead faculty member and oversees the content of lay and professional leadership programs.

Rabbi Joshua Hammerman is author, most recently, "Embracing Auschwitz: Forging a

Vibrant, Life-Affirming Judaism that Takes the Holocaust Seriously," and Mensch-Marks: Life Lessons of a Human Rabbi – Wisdom for Untethered Times (HCI Books). An award winning journalist, he has served Temple Beth El in Stamford, CT for over three decades.

Marjorie Hanft has a BA from Beloit College where she majored in literature and composition and MA from Brown University's graduate writing program. She also has an MA with a counseling emphasis from the University of Oklahoma. Since 2008, she has served as lay worship leader of the Mattoon (IL) Jewish Community, identified in 2012 as the smallest Reform Jewish congregation in North America. Following work in university counseling and community mental health, she taught psychology for 27 years at Eastern Illinois University. Her poems have appeared in First Literary Review-East, Calyx, and Mississippi Valley Review and translations of ancient Greek melic lyrics were published by Brown University.

Kelly Hartog was born in England, raised in Australia, made aliyah and then headed to America. It's why she has an accent with an identity crisis. She trod the boards at an early age before turning to journalism as a fall back career. She spent 12 years working as an editor at the Jerusalem Post while simultaneously founding and running Israel's only professional English language theatre company. After surviving an Al Qaeda suicide bombing while on assignment in Mombasa, Kenya, she moved to Los Angeles where she now lives with her Golden Retriever, Bronte (named after Charlotte, not Emily) and is the managing editor of the Jewish Journal of Greater Los Angeles.

Rivka Hecht has worked and studied in areas of Law, Medicine (conventional and alternative) and Education, in Australia, the USA and Israel. Her credentials include a Juris Doctor (JD) from the University of Melbourne, a BA in Liberal Arts with a major in Education, certifications in Laboratory Regulations and certifications in Traditional Oriental Medicine. Over the years, Riv has taught and led programs worldwide for both school aged kids and adults. She regularly researches, writes and lectures on areas of philosophy, health, women's issues, and other contemporary areas of interest. Riv believes in inspired leadership and entrepreneurial vision to create positive change in meaningful and lasting ways. In her free time, Riv loves to sing, interior decorate, photograph, travel, read, and experience the great outdoors, especially through horse-riding, long jump, and archery. Riv is currently living in Jerusalem, Israel and working at Ethnics - an Artists' Cooperative Gallery of handmade Israeli art where she divides her time between the business management & strategy, as well as being an integral part of the creative & design process. She is also a freelance writer/editor and manifests her entrepreneurial visions and creative ideas through her concept "Live with Riv" #livwriv aimed at inspiring, motivating, and sharing life's goodness with others. This includes a number of projects and initiatives, such as: The creation of her blog, Riv's Rivers (rivkablog.wordpress.com/) - a blog that combines the best of words, creativity, classic quotes and her scenic photography; and her previous Chai יה Tea House (facebook.com/chaiteahouse18) - a creative social venture for women to awaken their essential life core and shift the paradigms of their lives, through the essence of tea.

Shira Hecht-Koller is the Director of the Dr. Beth Samuels Summer High School Program at Drisha and Director of Education for 929 English. She teaches Talmud and Jewish identity to a wide variety of audiences, and writes and speaks on topics of education, creative living and family life. She was a Fellow at the Paideia Institute of Jewish Studies in Stockholm, where she continues to serve as a consultant. She holds a certificate in Experiential Jewish Education from M²: The Institute for Experiential Jewish Education, where she is adjunct faculty. She is a graduate of the Beruria Scholars program at Midreshet Lindenbaum and holds a JD from Cardozo School of Law. Prior to embarking on a career in Jewish Education, she was an associate in the Intellectual Property department at Debevoise & Plimpton, LLP. She is an avid tennis fan, amateur photographer and loves to hike and explore the world with her partner Aaron and children Dalya, Shachar, Amitai and Aiden.

Rivka Hellendall is a graduate student of English Literature and Jewish Studies at the University of Amsterdam and a freelance journalist for the Dutch Jewish Weekly news magazine. She enjoys great cappuccinos, reading, traveling to Israel, and creating community. Her Dutch Ashkenazi heritage allows her to relish the custom of having a dairy dessert only one hour after a meat meal.

Rabbi Lauren Grabelle Herrmann serves as the rabbi of SAJ-Judaism that Stands for All, the synagogue founded by Rabbi Mordecai Kaplan, in New York City. She is a graduate of the Reconstructionist Rabbinic College, an alumni of JOIN (The Jewish Organizing Initiative and Network) and was the founding rabbi of Kol Tzedek in Philadelphia. She is active in T'ruah, New Sanctuary Coalition, and Jews for Racial and Economic Justice.

Yael Hirsch-Biderman serves as Director of Human Resources for BINA: The Jewish Movement for Social Change. (www.bina.org.il)

Jordana Horn is a host of the podcast CALL YOUR MOTHER, and is a contributing editor at Kveller.com

Jonas Kadah was born in 1986 to a Swedish mother and an Israeli father. Jonas moved to Sweden in 1998 and has since then thrived both on a professional, educational and private level. Jonas is currently employed in a law enforcement agency but will soon embark on a larger educational mission in Criminology and Law at UC Berkeley. Jonas is married to a journalist since 2009 and they together have managed to raise two sons so far. Jonas lives close to the arctic circle in northern Sweden, which he enjoys since he appreciates the quietness, the nature and last but not least - a peaceful and equal society where everyone has the same rights and obligations. Jonas has no special belief more than trusting himself, but in times of hardship Jonas thinks that believing or being tasked with something makes life easier.

Rachel Kann is a poet and ceremonialist. She is currently matriculating toward Smicha (BzH 8/1/20) through Kohenet Hebrew Priestess Institute. She is the 2020 New England Jewish Poetry Festival's Featured Poet and a WORD: Bruce Geller Memorial Prize recipient for her latest poetry collection, How to Bless the New Moon, from Ben Yehuda Press. Her Realize Paradise ceremonies and services are intended to invoke sweetness.

Lawrence J. Kaplan is Professor of Rabbinics and Jewish Philosophy in the Department of

Jewish Studies of McGill University.

David Karpel is a writer for Hevria.com and teaches middle and high school History and English in Atlanta, where he lives with his wife, a third grade teacher, their daughter, and dog, and from where he regularly Zooms with his son. He also coaches wrestling, dances in his kitchen while cooking favorite dishes from his insatiable Juban pallette, and struggles to learn through every experience. He'll be fifty August 2020 and still feels like he's just beginning. @karpeldiem

Rabbi Avi Killip is VP of Strategy and Programs at the Hadar Institute. She was ordained from Hebrew College's pluralistic Rabbinical School in Boston and holds degrees from Brandeis University in Jewish Studies and Women & Gender Studies. She was a Wexner Graduate Fellow and is a current Schusterman Fellow.

Rabbi Margaret Frisch Klein is a rabbi living in Elgin, IL, just 30 miles west on Gulf Road from where she first celebrated Earth Day 50 years ago in Evanston. She is the rabbi of Congregation Kneseth Israel and blogs as the Energizer Rabbi, www.theenergizerrabbi.org. She is the author of two books, Climbing Towards Yom Kippur about the 13 Attributes of the Divine and Enduring Spirit about healing from sexual abuse and domestic violence. She was active in planning Earth Month activities in Elgin.

Miryam Kabakov is living her dream as the executive director of Eshel. She has a background in organizational development, social research, program evaluation, fundraising, and has a passion for community building. Kabakov is the editor of Keep Your Wives Away From Them: Orthodox Women, Unorthodox Desires (North Atlantic Books, May 2010) a collection of writings about the challenges and joys of LBT+ Orthodox Jews. Previously, she was the national program director of AVODAH: The Jewish Service Corps, Coordinator of LGBT programming at the JCC Manhattan, and the first social worker at Footsteps.

Rabbi Sharon Kleinbaum serves as spiritual leader of Congregation Beit Simchat Torah. For many years Rabbi Kleinbaum has been ranked by Newsweek among the 50 most influential rabbis in America.

Rabbi Claudio Kupchik is senior rabbi of Temple beth El of Cedahurst, NY.

Jessica Levine Kupferberg is a writer and former litigation attorney. She made aliyah from La Jolla, California with her family during Operation Protective Edge in July 2014 after driving across America. She blogs for the Times of Israel and her work has appeared in Kveller.com, The Jewish Journal, The Forward, Jweekly, aish.com and as part of Project 929 English.

Sara Kupor has an MA in Jewish Studies from Brandeis University and has taken post graduate classes at the Jewish Theological Seminary (New York), the University of Judaism (Los Angeles) and the Hebrew University (Jerusalem). She is the Shamash Resident at the JCC of the East Bay.

Rabbi Barry Leff is finishing a year-long assignment as interim senior rabbi of Herzl-Ner Tamid (Conservative) on Mercer Island (suburban Seattle), WA. After a 20-year career in high-tech as an entrepreneur and executive in Silicon Valley he went back to school and became a rabbi. He looks forward to dividing his time between his two homes, Las Cruces, New Mexico and Jerusalem. He's the proud father of five daughters. He's also a flight instructor: he likes to tell people he can get them closer to God one way or the other! He blogs at www.neshamah.net.

Rabbi Danielle Leshaw lives in Pittsburgh, PA with her family, and works for Hillel International.

Nechama Liss-Levinson, Ph.D. likes to help people. Her books for children all offer help on dealing with a difficult situation, like the death of a grandparent, or the death of a pet. Her own Grandma Blumie died when she was ten years old, and she has wanted to help kids learn coping strategies since that time. Recently, Nechama was awarded the Sydney Taylor Manuscript Award for her novel, "When the Hurricane Came," written after two amazing volunteer relief missions that she worked on after the devastation of Hurricane Katrina. "When the Hurricane Came" was also selected as a FINALIST for the National Jewish Book Awards for Children's and Young Adult Literature. When Nechama is not busy as a writer, she is a psychologist, as well as a wife, mother and grandma to three cutie pies.

William Liss-Levinson is vice president, chief strategy & operations officer of Castle Connolly Medical Ltd., a consumer health research, information, and publishing company. He holds a Ph.D. in education, is a member of the board of directors of the Jewish Book Council, and is Chair of the Board of Trustees of the Academy for Jewish Religion.

Dahlia Lithwick is a senior editor at Slate, and in that capacity, has been writing their "Supreme Court Dispatches" and "Jurisprudence" columns since 1999. Her work has appeared in the New York Times, Harper's, The New Yorker, The Washington Post, The New Republic, and Commentary, among other places. She is host of Amicus, Slate's award-winning biweekly podcast about the law and the Supreme Court. Lithwick earned her BA in English from Yale University and her JD degree from Stanford University. She is currently working on a new book, Lady Justice, for Penguin Press.

Since making aliyah in 2006, **Benji Lovitt** has performed stand-up comedy and educational programs for groups including Jewish Federations, Chabads, synagogues, Masa Israel Journey, and Birthright Israel. His perspectives on aliyah and Israeli society have been featured on Israeli TV and radio and in publications such as USA Today, Time Magazine, the BBC, and more. Benji has worked as a cross-cultural trainer with groups including the Ministry of Foreign Affairs and Masa Israel and is a popular presenter on the Limmud International circuit. During 2014's Operation Protective Edge, his humorous observations on the war led to his being called in Israel "the only reason to go on Facebook."

Leora Londy-Barash, currently a rabbinical student at the Hebrew Union College in Jerusalem, is Director of Community outreach for The Daniel Centers for Progressive

Judaism.

Rabbi David Lyon was ordained in 1990, at Hebrew Union College-Jewish Institute of Religion (HUC-JIR), in Cincinnati. Rabbi Lyon has served as Senior Rabbi of Congregation Beth Israel, in Houston, since 2004. Rabbi Lyon is a Vice-President of the Central Conference of American Rabbis (CCAR). He serves on the national board of the Jewish Community Legacy Project (JCLP). In Houston, Rabbi Lyon is a board member of the United Way of Greater Houston; board member of Interfaith Ministries; a member of ADL's Coalition for Mutual Respect; and a member of the advisory board of Holocaust Museum Houston. He is honored to be a Lifetime Honorary Board Member of the Institute for Spirituality and Health at the Texas Medical Center. Rabbi Lyon can be heard on iHeartRadio's KODA 99.1 FM, every Sunday at 6:45am, and on the podcast, "Heart to Heart with Rabbi David Lyon," which can be found at Sunny99.com. He is the author of "God of Me: Imagining God throughout Your Lifetime" (Jewish Lights 2011). Rabbi Lyon is married to Lisa; and they have four grown children, and one adorable grandson.

Rabbi Sarah Marion serves Congregation B'nai Israel in Bridgeport, CT. Originally from Westchester, New York, she completed her undergraduate degrees in Near Eastern and Judaic Studies and Women's and Gender Studies at Brandeis University, and received rabbinic ordination from Hebrew Union College-Jewish Institute of Religion. During her rabbinic studies, she also earned her M.A. in Religious Education. Though she is excited and energized by all areas of rabbinic work, Rabbi Marion has focused her rabbinate on organizing for a more just and equitable world, engaging with families of young children, and creating pathways for girls and women to grow into their fullest selves.

Akiva Mattenson currently resides in Chicago, where he studies philosophy and Jewish texts. He has previously studied at Yeshivat Ma'ale Gilboa, Yeshivat Chovevei Torah and Yeshivat Hadar.

Aurora Mendelsohn is a university administrator who writes about Judaism, ritual, feminism and parenting at the blog Rainbow Tallit Baby. She has written for the Forward, Jewschool, The Jewniverse, The Toronto Star, Lilith and Sh'ma.

Ruth Messinger was president of American Jewish World Service for 18 years and is currently the organization's first global ambassador. AJWS is the leading Jewish organization working to fight poverty and pursue justice in the developing world. Prior to AJWS, Messinger served as a City Council member in New York City and as Manhattan Borough President. A tireless advocate and social change visionary, Messinger mobilizes faith-based communities throughout the U.S. to promote human rights. She is also currently doing international human rights work for AIDS Free World and, in 2017, became the inaugural JTS Finkelstein Institute Social Justice Fellow.

Rabbi Joseph B. Meszler is the spiritual leader of Temple Sinai of Sharon, MA and the author of many books including Facing Illness Finding God (Jewish Lights).

Miriam Metzinger is a freelancer writer, actor, and playwright. She lives in Jerusalem and is a single mother to three sons.

Rebecca Minkus-Lieberman is the co-founder and executive director of Orot: Center for New Jewish Learning, a home for transformative Jewish learning and spiritual practice. Through her work at Orot, Rebecca seeks to open up the well of Jewish wisdom and to help others use its richness to bring wholeness and meaning to their lives. Over the past 20 years, she has taught in a variety of Jewish educational institutions and schools. Rebecca received a B.A. in Jewish Studies from Princeton University, a M.Ed. from DePaul University, and a M.A. from the Divinity School at the University of Chicago with a focus on Modern Jewish Thought and the philosophy of Franz Rosenzweig. Upon graduation from college, Rebecca spent time in community organizing on the west side of Chicago while also leading Jewish environmental backpacking trips. She currently lives in Skokie with her husband David and her three children where she enjoys running, writing poetry, cooking and practicing yoga.

Rabbi Avram Mlotek is director of spiritual life and co-founder of Base Hillel.

Rich Moline is a Jewish educator, non-profit executive, and volunteer leader living in Chicago.

Rabbi Jeffrey Myers serves the Tree of Life \Or L'Simcha Congregation.

Jaclyn Novatt lives in NY with her husband and two children. She loves leading services for grown-ups and Tot Shabbat programs for the little ones. In her other life, she is a biochemist and Assistant Dean at a College of Pharmacy.

Rabbi Avi S. Olitzky serves as spiritual leader of Beth El Synagogue in St. Louis Park, Minnesota.

Karen Paul is the principal of Catalyzing Philanthropy, a boutique fundraising and development consultancy. Karen was also Washington Director of New Israel Fund and Executive Director of the Tikkun Olam Women's Foundation, where she was dedicated to improving the lives of women and girls in the DC region and in Israel. Karen and her late husband, Jonathan Stern, received the Heschel Visionary Award from Jews United for Justice in 2016 for their dedication to telling the story of his illness with compassion and honesty. Currently, she is working on a book about her experience as a caretaker for a spouse with glioblastoma. She blogs regularly on her own site, "Life in the (Widow) Hood," and has had essays, short stories and poems published in the Washington Post, Lilith Magazine, S'hma, Guideposts, Seltzer, Modern Loss, Red Wheelbarrow Literary Magazine, Scribblers on the Roof, and Heartscapes anthology.

Rabbi Sonja K. Pilz, PhD, earned her doctorate from the department of Rabbinic Literature at Potsdam University in Germany and holds Rabbinic Ordination from Abraham Geiger College in Germany. Prior to joining the Central Conference of American Rabbis as Editor of the CCAR Press, she taught Worship, Liturgy, and Ritual at HUC-JIR in New York, the School of Jewish Theology at Potsdam University, and in many congregational settings. She has served as a rabbinic intern, adjunct rabbi, and cantorial soloist for congregations in Germany, Switzerland, Israel and the US. Not surprisingly, she loves to write poetry, midrashim, and prayers. Her work has been published in Liturgy, Worship, the CCAR Journal, and in a number if anthologies. She is the author of Food and Fear: Metaphors of Bodies and Spaces in the Stories of Destruction.

Laurie Pollack is a Philadelphia area computer programmer and poet. Her Hebrew name is Liora which means "Light. She lives with her partner of 26 years/legal spouse of 6 years, Mary and two cats. Laurie is involved in local activism around immigration issues and is currently exploring Jewish Reconstructionist, Reform, Renewal and secular humanist practices and communities to see where she fits in. She prefers questions to answers, gray areas over boxes, tries to tell the truth even when it is complicated, and believes that all human lives are sacred/of infinite value and so we must care for each other.

Rabbi Rachel Putterman was ordained by Hebrew College in June 2020. While in Rabbinical School, Rachel was a chaplain intern at Brigham and Women's Hospital. She also interned with the Center for Small Town Jewish Life, Boston College Hillel, and the Hadassah-Brandeis Institute. Rachel is the creator of All Genders Wrap, a series of tutorial videos featuring a diverse cast demonstrating how to wrap tefillin.

Alicia Jo Rabins is a poet, musician and Torah teacher based in Portland, Oregon. She holds a MFA in poetry from Warren Wilson College; her first book, Divinity School, was awarded the American Poetry Review/Honickman First Book Prize, and her second, Fruit Geode, was a finalist for the Jewish Book Award. She travels internationally performing original musical midrash about women in Torah with her songwriting project, Girls in Trouble.

Dr. Brielle Paige Rassler is a therapist, spiritual artist, and ALEPH Rabbinic/Hashpa'ah student from Fort Lauderdale, Florida. Brielle holds BA, MS, and PsyD degrees in Dance, Substance Abuse Studies, and Clinical Psychology. She is currently working with families who have lost loved ones to COVID-19 as the coordinator and lead therapist of the Penn Medicine PMC Grief Counseling Program. Brielle has released two albums of original music, authored a 260+ page reference guide to the Talmud, a treatment manual for religiously integrated treatment of Jewish women with Eating Disorders, and is currently working on an interpretive translation of the Book of Psalms, two of which she is honored to be sharing in this volume. Learn more at www.BriellePaigeRassler.com.

Rabbi Yael B. Ridberg serves as the spiritual leader of Congregation Dor Hadash in San Diego, California. In addition to her congregational responsibilities, Rabbi Ridberg serves on the Board of The San Diego Jewish Academy. She lives in La Jolla with her husband and four daughters.

Rebecca Rona-Tuttle is a professional writer, and social, environmental and political activist. In 2018 she was honored by the Los Angeles County Democratic Party as the Eleanor and Franklin Roosevelt Democrat of the Year for the 54th Assembly District. She founded the grassroots organization "Together," which promoted positive human relations and understanding among people of all backgrounds. She worked to end fracking in the Inglewood Oil Field, the largest urban oil field in the country. She has been the driving force behind the successful effort to convince Culver City to form its Equity and Human Relations Committee. Currently she serves as Director of Communications for South Los Angeles Health Projects. She is married to Rick Tuttle.

Matthue Roth co-created Hevria, an online creative community of faith, and is the author of Never Mind the Goldbergs and Rules of My Best Friend's Body. By day, he's a writer at Google. He lives in Brooklyn with his daughters and keeps a secret diary at matthue.com.

Rabbi Adrienne Rubin has been bringing meaning into people's lives at synagogues for over 30 years. She is the Interim Rabbi at Temple Beth Ahm Yisrael, a Conservative Synagogue in Springfield, NJ. Prior to this, she served as Cantorial Soloist at Temple Micah, an unaffiliated, egalitarian synagogue in Lawrenceville, NJ, for 24 years, as the High Holy Day Cantor for the University of Rhode Island for five years, and as a guest cantor and soloist for several synagogues in Massachusetts. Rabbi Rubin graduated from Princeton University in 1988 with a B.A. in Music Theory and Composition and she is a trained opera singer. She received S'micha from the Rabbinical Seminary International and is a member of the International Federation of Rabbis, Rabbinical Fellowship of America, the Women Cantors' Network, 18Doors (formerly Interfaith Family Network), Equally Wed and the Rainbow Wedding Network. Rabbi Rubin lives in Princeton, NJ, with her husband Doug and their son, Elian, who is a student at Oberlin.

Marilyn Russell. I was born and raised in New Jersey. 1960 was a busy decade. I received my Masters in Library Service from Rutgers University, experienced a life changing Summer in Kibbutz program at Kibbutz Amir in the Upper Galil, began a career as librarian at Newark Public Library, moved to Tel Aviv for a year, returned to my job in Newark, moved to New York and worked for New York Public Library and Queensborough Public Library. In 1969 I moved to Venice, California and lived briefly above the Israel Levin Center. My parents followed and lived the rest of their lives in Santa Monica. I married my husband in 1977, moved to Culver City and was a librarian with Los Angeles Public Library for 26 years. I had a formative experience as a member of Temple Beth Torah in Mar Vista, which later merged with Adat Shalom. I am currently a member of Mishkon Tephilo in Venice, California.

Rabbi Charles E. Savenor serves as the Director of Congregational Education at Park Avenue Synagogue in New York.

Rabbi Craig Scheff has been with the Orangetown Jewish Center since 1995. A former attorney, Rabbi Scheff received his rabbinic ordination from the Jewish Theological Seminary in 1998, where he currently serves as Adjunct Lecturer for Senior Seminar in Practical Rabbinics and as a mentor in the Rabbinical School's Resnick Fourth Year Internship Program. He and his wife Nancy both grew up in Rockland County, and are proud to have raised their four sons in our community. Beyond the synagogue, building community partnerships, supporting Israel, Camp Ramah, USY, coaching basketball, and mentoring future rabbis round out the ways he chooses to spend his time.

Rabbi Evan Schultz serves as Senior Rabbi of Congregation B'nai Israel in Bridgeport, Connecticut.

Timna Seligman is originally from London, but found her home in Jerusalem many dawns ago. She is the Curator of Ticho House, and usually writes about art rather than the sounds of the night.

Alexander "Jake" Shapiro works at the Shaharit Institute, an Israeli NGO working to create common cause amongst Israel's diverse populations. Jake previously served as a volunteer activist and researcher in the mixed Arab-Jewish city of Lod. Jake studied international relations and political science at the University of Maryland - College Park.

Daniel Sherman is a strategic and organizational consultant focusing on peace and development issues. He served as a general staff officer in the Israel Defense Forces where he worked on the peace process; developed social welfare programs for Jewish communities in central and eastern Europe with the Joint Distribution Committee; and was international relations director for an Israeli human rights organization. He lectures regularly in Israel and the United States and has spoken at Israel's National Defense College, Brown University's Watson Institute for International and Public Affairs, the Hebrew University of Jerusalem, Vassar College and the University of California, Irvine. He has also presented at conferences within Israel's Knesset.

Rabbi Karen Silberman is an avid writer and painter. She lives in Massachusetts with her husband, Don, and their puppy, Lucy.

Gila Silverman is a researcher and writer, working at the intersections of religion, spirituality, and health. She is a visiting scholar at the Arizona Center for Judaic Studies.

Born in Chicago, **Caren Singer** spent the wonder years in Fort Worth where her civil rights activism was born. At fifteen, she and her family moved to Los Angeles where four months later, she met her now husband and best friend Robert Wolin. After graduating from Fairfax High School and UCLA, she worked for Roger Corman as assistant director and production manager on films including Rock and Roll High School. Caren later sold ads and wrote articles for The Animal Press. She loves theatre, movies, music, and animals; has a house full of flowers and crystals; and enjoys dark chocolate, wine, vodka martinis, and good food. She is the language arts half of the teaching and test preparation business she and Robert have in Silver Lake where she is active in community affairs and lives happily with Robert and their two cats, Little Lulu and Baby Izzy.

Esti Rosen Snukal is a writer for the Jewish Link of New Jersey. She made Aliya with her husband and four sons on July 12, 2012 to Chashmonayim. Esti is also the adopted mom to a lone soldier from Highland Park NJ and an active volunteer at the Lone Soldier Center in Memory of Michael Levin.

Alden Solovy is the Liturgist-in-Residence at the Pardes Institute of Jewish Studies in Jerusalem. A liturgist, poet, and educator, his teaching spans from Hebrew Union College-Jewish Institute of Religion in Jerusalem to Limmud UK and synagogues throughout North America. He's the author of "This Grateful Heart: Psalms and Prayers for a New Day" and has written more than 750 pieces of new liturgy. His new book, "This Joyous Soul: A New Voice for Ancient Yearnings," was published in 2019. He made aliyah in 2012. Read his work at www.ToBendLight.com.

Rabbi Benjy Spiro is the West Coast Coordinator for Chesed Shel Emes; a non-profit founded over 40 years ago comprised of over 400 members nationwide, to help people and their families during their hardest moments with the burial process, as well as burying those with no one left for them or those lacking financial means.

Rabbi Abby Stein is a rabbi, educator, author, speaker, and activist, born and raised in a Hasidic family of rabbinic descent, now working to raise support and awareness for trans rights and those leaving Ultra-Orthodoxy. She co-founded Sacred Space, and her book, Becoming Eve, was published in November 2019.

Sarah Tuttle-Singer, author of Jerusalem Drawn and Quartered and the New Media Editor at Times of Israel. She was raised in Venice Beach, California on Yiddish lullabies and Civil Rights anthems. She now lives in Israel with her two kids where she climbs roofs, explores cisterns, opens secret doors and talks to strangers, and writes stories about people. Sarah also speaks before audiences left, right, and center through the Jewish Speakers Bureau, asking them to wrestle with important questions while celebrating their willingness to do so. She also loves whisky and tacos and chocolate chip cookies and old maps and foreign coins and discovering new ideas from different perspectives. Sarah is a work in progress.

Rabbi Danielle Upbin is the Associate Rabbi and Prayer Leader of Congregation Beth Shalom in Clearwater, FL. She is also the Community Educator for the Jewish Federation of Florida's Gulf Coast.

Rabbi Deborah Waxman is president of Reconstructing Judaism. She is creator and host of the podcast "Hashivenu: Jewish Teachings on Resilience."

Mikhal Weiner is a writer and musician, originally from Israel, currently working and living in Brooklyn with her wife and son. She is a regular contributor to local and international publications such as the Lilith Magazine, GO Magazine, the Philadelphia Jewish Exponent, and Entropy Magazine on topics ranging from op-eds to music and book reviews and profiles/interviews.

Rabbi Aaron Weininger serves as a rabbi of the Adath Jeshurun Congregation, where he has held the Berman Family Chair in Jewish Learning for eight years. He earned his BA in Anthropology and Jewish Near Eastern Studies at Washington University in St. Louis, and received ordination and an MA in Hebrew Letters from the Jewish Theological Seminary in 2012. In 2007 he became the first openly gay person admitted to rabbinical school in the Conservative movement, and he studied at JTS as a Schusterman Rabbinical Fellow. Trusting in the power of Jewish community to transform, Aaron believes in connecting the spark of each person to the warmth of relationships. He is entering his third year as co-chair of the Minnesota Rabbinical Association.

Elke Weiss is a New York-based lawyer, historian, and blogger of Israeli heritage. Having previously been privileged to use her legal education and Masters in Urban Affairs as an Israel Government Fellow working on Biodiversity policy, Elke still yearns for the

Jerusalem sunset. She is currently hard at work writing her first novel, and trying to earn the 4th rank in Krav Maga, the study of which inspired this poem.

Jamie Wendt is the author of the poetry collection Fruit of the Earth (2018) and winner of the 2019 National Federation of Press Women Book Award. Her poetry, essays, and book reviews have been published in various literary journals and anthologies, including Feminine Rising: Voices of Power and Invisibility, Lilith, Literary Mama, the Forward, Third Wednesday, and Saranac Review. She holds an MFA from the University of Nebraska Omaha. She teaches high school English and lives in Chicago with her husband and two children. Website: jamiewendt.wordpress.com

A native of Colorado who now makes her home in Brooklyn, New York, **Eden Wofsey** is a storyteller and longtime teacher of storytelling and chassidut as well as a practicing dentist. Having studied in both New York and Israel, she was first introduced to Chassidic storytelling at the Carlebach Shul in Manhattan and is a graduate of the Maggid program led by Yitzhak Buxbaum and Carole Forman. Recently, she has been leading Thursday Night Storytelling through the Park Slope Jewish Center, a project designed to facilitate the sharing of traditional Jewish wisdom stories and personal stories that may provide inspiration during the time of COVID-19.

Rabbi Shmuly Yanklowitz is the President & Dean of the Valley Beit Midrash (Jewish pluralistic adult learning & leadership), the Founder & President of Uri L'Tzedek (Orthodox Social Justice), the Founder and CEO of Shamayim (Jewish animal advocacy), the Founder and President of YATOM, (Jewish foster and adoption network), and the author of seventeen books on Jewish ethics.

Dr. Robin B. Zeiger is a certified Jungian analyst and free-lance writer. She works in private practice as a psychoanalyst and supervisor. She enjoys writing inspirational works amidst the beauty of her home in a small agricultural village in Central Israel.

Rabbi Morris Zimbalist is the Senior Rabbi of Congregation Beth Judea in Long Grove, IL.

David Zinberg lives in Teaneck, NJ with his wife and three sons and works in financial services.

Made in the USA
Monee, IL
23 June 2020